4-12-73

To Jesse "Charley" Prehn

With best wishes

Denton A. Cooley, MD

Cooley

HARPER'S
MAGAZINE
PRESS

Cooley

THE CAREER

OF A GREAT HEART SURGEON

Harry Minetree

HARPER'S MAGAZINE PRESS

Published in Association with Harper & Row, New York

Drawings on pages 274 through 286 by Herbert R. Smith, M.A., from *Surgical Treatment of Congenital Heart Disease* by Denton A. Cooley, M.D. and Grady L. Hallman, M.D., copyright © 1966 by Lea and Febiger. Drawings on pages 272 and 273 by Barry Baker.

FIRST EDITION

Designed by Sidney Feinberg

Library of Congress Cataloging in Publication Data

Minetree, Harry.
    Cooley: the career of a great heart surgeon.
    1. Cooley, Denton A 1920– 2. Heart—
Surgery. I. Title.
R154.C566M56 1973   617'.09'24 [B]   72–79716
ISBN 0–06–126382–6

For my mother and father.
For Judy and the children.
And in memory of Nona Gee.

Contents

Cooley

Introduction

The Zumbro is a venerable hotel for ambulatory patients and guests who come to Rochester, Minnesota, for their annual checkups at the Mayo Clinic. Across the dark wood frame over the entrance to the dining room is an inscription: WE KNOW YOUR OPERATION IS INTERESTING, BUT PLEASE DON'T DISCUSS IT IN HERE. Except for the following introductory paragraphs, which relate more to the subject of this book than to the medical history of its author, I intend to abide by the Zumbro management's good advice.

One bright morning in the spring of 1957, I entered a mobile x-ray unit on the Vanderbilt University campus, filled out a card, and, before the pretty attendant had a chance to instruct me, assumed the proper stance before the screen. Having undergone surgery seven years earlier for coarctation of the aorta (a narrowing of the first large artery out of the heart), I was an old hand at x-ray protocol. I was expert on the correct placement of blood pressure cuffs, too, and knew where and how to locate and puncture my best veins. Such a small, simple vanity prompted me to enter that x-ray unit. I was recently married,

1

father of a new baby boy, happy, and as far as anyone knew, healthy as a horse. If it had been raining that morning, or if the attendant hadn't been so innocently inviting, I probably would have passed on by. And that would have been a fatal mistake.

Two days later a notice arrived from the University Hospital —there was something wrong in my chest. I immediately assumed that the radiologist who read the x-ray film had discovered some scar tissue from the earlier operation and wanted to run a routine check. I reported to the hospital and told the chief of cardiovascular surgery about the coarctation at Mayo. "That might be the problem," he said. Then he picked up the phone and ordered a sophisticated series of examinations for me. When the other doctors and the technicians began exhibiting that familiar, hopeful concern, I knew for sure the matter was as serious as I had secretly prayed it would not be. We left the baby with my parents and flew to Rochester, Minnesota.

At Mayo they took more x rays and did a cardiac catheterization, then my wife and I met with the surgeon and his consultants. It proved to be a grim affair.

In 1950, an acceptable arterial graft had not yet been discovered. Consequently, after removing the constricted segment of my aorta, my surgeon had followed the current technique and sutured the loose ends of the artery together. But the tension had been too great. Over the years the artery had weakened and ballooned into a flaccid, thin-walled mass called an aneurysm. It was only a matter of time before this would rupture, causing a massive hemorrhage and instantaneous death.

My surgeon reminded me that I was no longer a child, that I must face the gloomy facts of my condition and react like a man. He recommended that I enter the hospital at five that afternoon—he would operate in the morning. And the prognosis was equally dismal. "This will be an extremely difficult operation," he said. The consultants, who under the circumstances more resembled judges, nodded agreement. "And the fact that your chest is full of scar tissue from the previous intervention won't help matters." Again the consultants nodded. My wife began to cry silently. "I'll do everything I can." The surgeon looked directly at me. "But I must tell you, it may not be enough. I'm sorry."

Back at the hotel room, my wife and I sat on the bed and discussed the situation. Alone, I might have given in and gone with everything. Instead, I reflected her courage so that she would sustain it and resolved to figure a way out.

Dr. Hugh Stephenson was chief of surgery at the University of Missouri Medical School. We were not close friends, but we had met once at a party and had gotten along well. I remembered a conversation on heart surgery we had had, how sincere and deeply interested he had seemed.

I phoned Dr. Stephenson in his office at the medical school and explained what my surgeon had just told me. He said he was sorry but assured me that I was in good hands.

"I know I'm in *good* hands, Dr. Stephenson, but I'd rather be in the *best* hands." I asked him to recommend a place I could go where the odds might be better.

He said Mayo was a fine clinic with an excellent staff.

"I appreciate that. I understand. But it stands to reason that Mayo, or any other clinic for that matter, can't be the best at everything."

He agreed and repeated that I was in good hands.

To release him from any ethical compunction he might have had, I said I was leaving. I would not be wheeled into an operating room when there was so little hope of coming out alive. "I'd rather go home and die on my feet."

A pause.

"Do you really mean that?" he asked.

"Yes." I suddenly discovered I did. "Yes . . . I do."

"All right. I'll get you an appointment with Dr. Denton Cooley in Houston."

Dr. Cooley was three hours late for our appointment and looked as if he had just stepped out of a band box. He held a stethoscope to my chest, to my back.

"I've been waiting for you for three hours."

"Shhh!" He listened to my chest again. "Now what did you say?"

"I said it's eight o'clock. You're three hours late."

His smile was edged with arrogance. "I did six open-hearts today. What did you do?"

"Well." He was tall and tan in a gray silk suit and two-tone shoes. "You sure don't look like it."

"Some folks relax playing golf. I like to operate on people's hearts. Okay?" He winked. He had me. I smiled.

"Now, you've got an aneurysm in there as big as a grapefruit and it's about ready to burst. But you're a big, strong boy and I'm the best surgeon in the world, so if this had to happen, we've got the best possible odds."

"Well . . ." I had never heard anything like this.

"There are people here from all over waiting for me to operate on them. You take your wife down to Galveston, swim and get some sun. When we can work you in, my secretary will phone." He left.

Four days later, Dr. Cooley removed the weakened portion of my aorta and replaced it with eight inches of Dacron tubing that had been knitted on a retooled necktie loom.

Under the circumstances it would seem that I could not write objectively about the man. I can only say that I have tried.

HARRY MINETREE

Glynn Dower
Bodmin, Cornwall, England

Part One

The implantation of an artificial heart in Houston, Texas, on April 4th was a step forward in medical history. Dr. Denton Cooley, Dr. Domingo Liotta and others kept a patient alive for 64 hours with a mechanical heart before he received a natural heart transplant. While the patient eventually died of complications following the second operation, the important fact is that the Houston doctors proved that an artificial heart can indeed replace a natural one in man.

WILLEM KOLFF, M.D.
inventor of the artificial kidney
(From *The Hospital Tribune,* July 14, 1969)

Chapter 1

The Implantation

ON March 5, 1969, Haskell Karp was admitted to St. Luke's Hospital in Houston, Texas. Ten years earlier, he had suffered a myocardial infarction, a deadly type of heart attack that kills a portion of the heart's muscle and reduces its efficiency. A second infarct occurred in December 1966, and Mr. Karp was subsequently hospitalized with incidents of irregular heartbeat, congestive heart failure (sluggish heart action which causes fluid to collect in the ankles and makes it impossible to lie flat without breathlessness and pain), and myocardial ischemia (a particularly painful condition caused by an insufficient blood supply to the heart muscle). Mr. Karp's heart was apparently an irrecoverable ruin.

To maintain his pulse, Karp was implanted with a calibrated device that stimulated the muscle with metronomic mini-shocks. By December 1968, the decomposition of his heart had so progressed that it was necessary to intensify his drug regimen and increase the rate of his pacemaker. He could not lie down without losing consciousness. On the least exertion he suffered severe pain accompanied by a shallow, ineffectual heartbeat of three times the normal rate, dizziness, and total exhaustion. Finally his doctors in Chicago referred him to Dr. Denton Cooley.

Dr. Robert Leachman and his staff of cardiologists at St. Luke's soon discovered that Mr. Karp had a complete heart block. The coronary vessels and those surrounding them were clogged to half their normal diameters with fatty deposits. Leachman couldn't tell for certain, but it appeared that as much as 50 percent of Karp's heart muscle was scar tissue. The doctors were amazed that the man was still alive. They advised a transplant, but there were no donors available.

"Whatever you can do," Mrs. Karp told Dr. Cooley. "My husband has already died a thousand times."

Gloved and gowned, Cooley's three assistants stand aside as Dr. Arthur Keats, chief of anesthesiology at Baylor, and the two orderlies help Mr. Karp from the gurney to the operating table. The shot he received in his room is now taking full effect. He blinks slowly, makes a brief appraisal of the distorted reflections in the chrome fittings on his right—the varicolored tanks of oxygen, cyclopropane, and nitrous oxide—then settles back.

"Breathe deeply now." Karp nods, and Dr. Keats fits the black inhalation mask over his nose and mouth. Ater four cool draws of nitrous oxide and oxygen, the patient's body goes limp.

Quickly then, needles from elevated bottles of Pentothal and glucose are slipped into the veins of the patient's arms and taped fast; two more in his wrists will record venous and arterial blood pressures. Leads from the electrocardiograph are fixed to his extremities. Electroencephalograph needles on yellow, red, and green wires are placed at two-inch intervals beneath his scalp; another in the left ear lobe. Heart action impulses from the cardiograph leads, brainwave impulses from the encephalograph needles, as well as the venous and arterial pressures, are collected in the polygraph—a dial-covered, transistorized mechanism to the right of the table. The patient's life signs are recorded on graph paper and simultaneously projected to a television screen across the room, so at any moment the surgeon has a comprehensive profile of the patient's condition.

To ground against countershocks and the Bovie electric needle used to cauterize bleeders, the circulator places a steel plate beneath the patient's buttocks. While a curved plastic breathing tube is being fitted over Karp's tongue and into his throat, Dr. Bloodwell passes a lubricated catheter through the penis to the bladder. A quick wash of diluted blood, and the accordion-like bag below the table begins to expand.

Watching through the glass above the scrub sink, Dr. Cooley rinses his hands and arms, then walks across the room to the instrument table where the scrub nurse hands him a sterile towel. With his entrance, the atmosphere in the room is immediately more relaxed.

"Everybody tooled up?" Cooley splays and inspects his fingers, looks at Euford Martin, the heart-lung technician. "You know the degree of difficulty for this operation, don't you?"

"No sir, tell us. Please," Martin replies.

"Dura mater," Cooley says. "Tough mother." Dr. Keats shakes his head. The scrub nurse rolls her eyes. "Somebody turn up the radio." His request comes perfectly timed at the peak of their laughter.

Some are amused, others appalled, but no one who visits Cooley's surgery leaves unimpressed with the invariable levity. Once, during the placement of a Dacron graft, a seventy-year-old man's aorta ruptured. Wrist-deep in blood and guided only by touch, Cooley sutured up the jagged tear before the patient bled to death. An unbelievable display of calm under pressure. "That ought to get you a chapter in the new Bible," the first assistant remarked. Cooley looked up. "If it does, see that I'm next to Ruth in Gomorrah."

A lady homesteader from Alaska flew down for a mitral valve replacement. Believing the patient to be fully anesthetized, Dr.

Keats nodded for Cooley to commence. But when the scalpel was touched to her chest, the patient's knees drew up and she let out a low moan. Cooley smoothed the small wound with his finger, sighed. "Better give this gal some more gas, Arthur. She's going to get up and walk back to Fairbanks."

He slips on the gown, grips into a pair of rubber gloves, and ties the wrap-around sash as he steps up to the table. According to the positions they have taken, Robert Bloodwell is first assistant, Bruno Messmer is second, and Domingo Liotta is third. There have been no formal assignments. "Bob," Cooley says, "switch with Dom, will you? This is sort of his operation."

The nurses exchange glances.

The heart-lung machine, like half a glass door rising from a low panel of rotary pumps, is primed with glucose. Though most surgeons use whole blood in their machines, Cooley discovered that this sugar-water solution works just as well. If he were limited to the use of whole blood primes, he would not be able to operate so often because of its scarcity. Moreover, with glucose he avoids the infections one risks with blood and in the bargain has made open-heart surgery acceptable to religious sects whose beliefs prohibit them from receiving transfusions.

Martin anchors the heart-lung lines to the edge of the table. The scrub nurse holds a small basin of Mercresin as Cooley, using long forceps, swabs the patient from neck to thighs. Then he and Liotta lay the draping: first a fold of towel like a codpiece between the legs, a sheet over the heavy wire loop at his head, more bordering his body until, except for a narrow rectangle of Mercresin-stained chest, Karp appears mummified.

Dr. Keats checks the dilation of the patient's pupils, the life signature on the lined paper feeding from the polygraph. He nods to Cooley.

"Okay, Gwynn," Cooley says.

The circulator, one of five people in the suite who know what is about to take place, hastily crosses herself and turns a switch.

The lights dim, then quickly recover their brightness. The stranger in the corridor looks at his watch. OR One is on emergency power.

Karp is scheduled for a wedge procedure, a radical operation in which dying and dead muscle is excised from the heart. Cooley has performed the operation on many occasions, but he has reason to believe that in this case the deterioration of the tissue is so extensive that the heart might be unable to recover. If this proves true, Cooley has planned an emergency backup that has never been performed on a human being. Besides the patient's life to consider, he knows the future of a vital phase of research is at stake here. Success would assure his team a place in medical history. Failure would mean death.

Holding the skin at the throat taut between his thumb and index finger, Cooley taps the scalpel for a firmer grip and begins a deep, vertical incision into a thin layer of yellow fat going red the length of the breastbone. Bloodwell clamps and ties off spurting bleeders, while Liotta sears the smaller ones with the Bovie. Messmer is exposing the femoral artery deep in the right thigh. When the breast wound is open and dry, the scrub nurse hands Cooley the bone saw. Wisps of blue smoke and moist dust rise. The electric buzzing weakens under the strain as Cooley bears down on the blade and splits the breastbone from bottom to top. He seals the marrow with beeswax and fits a heavy retractor along the raw edges of the rib cage. Inch by inch he cranks the chest open, revealing the slick, mottled surfaces of the lungs. The thoracic vacuum broken now, the patient is unable to take in breath. Keats rhythmically squeezes a black rubber bladder, forcing oxygen down the tracheal tube. Pressing the lungs aside, Cooley lifts the pink pericardial membrane and carefully scissors it open. There like a dark fist is the heart, its scarred, irregular bulk undulating sluggishly with each clinching beat. From unique experience, Cooley knows and respects the idiosyncrasies of this organ. The life of the patient is now literally in his hands.

The large cava vessels that bring unoxygenated blood to the heart are dissected free. As Liotta holds the first vein with tourniquets, Cooley closes half of its diameter with a curved vascular clamp and puts in a circular, purse-string suture line. He then makes an incision in the middle of the sutures and inserts a plastic catheter tube from the heart-lung machine; Liotta secures it by drawing the purse strings tight. In like manner, another catheter is placed in the second cava vein. For the return of oxygenated blood from the heart-lung machine, Cooley inserts a smaller tube in the femoral artery Messmer has prepared. The ease and economy with which Cooley performs these delicate connections has prompted Dr. Christiaan Barnard to remark that the first time he saw Cooley operate, even before the heart was actually opened, he knew he was watching the finest surgical technician in the world.

"Okay, Arthur. I think we're hooked up."

Dr. Keats turns a valve, and the line leading to the patient's left arm is flushed with heparin, an anticoagulant to insure against clotting in the machine.

"Ready, Euford?" Cooley quickly checks the catheters.

"All ready."

"Okay . . . hit it!"

The rotary pumps begin to turn. Cooley unclips the hemostats from the cava and femoral catheters, and blood, like a time-lapse film of an unfolding red flower, blossoms in the sugar-water prime of the heart-lung window. With a right-angle clamp, Cooley closes off the aorta. The heart strains momentarily . . . then quivers . . . then stops. The flow into the femoral artery changes from deep to brilliant red. And the oxygenation and circulation of the patient's blood is assumed by the machine.

Mr. Karp's heart is a mess—much worse than the diagnostic

reports indicated. Liotta looks at Cooley. Cooley is looking at the misshapen mass in his hands. "Son of a bitch," he mumbles and begins dividing away adhesions where the left ventricle, the main pumping chamber, has grown to the membrane surrounding it. Cutting through alternating levels of muscle and scar tissue, Cooley lays open the ventricle. The interior wall is covered with a white, oily deposit. The entire septum between the left and right ventricles and two-thirds of the left ventricle have degenerated to inelastic knots. Hardly any viable muscle remains.

Avoiding nerves and major vessels, Cooley guides his scalpel along the perimeters of wasted tissue. "Number three silk." But the scrub nurse, anticipating the suture he wants, has a needle holder with a sharp steel crescent at his fingertips. Cooley draws the remaining muscle to a trident close and, with a rapid, whipping motion, sutures the heart wound shut.

"Let's try a partial by-pass, Euford." Cooley clamps two of the catheters as Martin reduces the flow from the machine. The assistants stand clear of the table. Cooley presses two spatulalike paddles to the nerve centers of the stilled heart and steps on a foot switch that lets loose a jolting shock of electricity. Nothing. Again . . . no response. Again . . . every fiber of the patient's body contracts in a violent spasm; the heart shudders once in fibrillation, then goes slack.

"Try some potassium." Cooley's hands are steady, his voice calm. Only the flush across his forehead indicates his concern.

"I already have," comes Keats's reply.

"Then try some more, damn it."

"I already have, Denton."

With a firm, descending motion, Cooley begins to massage the limp heart. He watches the polygraph monitor . . . a straight line. Massaging more . . . nothing. Harder . . . still nothing. "Getting anything on that paper?" Keats shakes his head and squeezes a liter of pure oxygen into Karp's lungs.

Cooley begins a peculiar ritual which has raised the pulse of life in hundreds of apparently lifeless human hearts. Hands poised limp-wristed and ready over the gaping wound, he lowers his head and stares at the glistening fist of quiet muscle in Karp's chest. But for the muffled turning of the rotary pumps and the intermittent hiss of the breathing bladder, the room is quiet. With the index finger of his right hand, Cooley gently smoothes the submerged network of weary nerves which he has tried everything to awaken. It's no use. The heart won't be resuscitated. Karp's brain is alive, but heart-lung time is running out. One more hour on the machine and the delicate processes of his brain will go the way of his heart. The patient on the table would once have been declared dead.

"Let's go back on full by-pass, Euford."

"You are going to do it, then?" Liotta asks, but the question is more a remark of resignation.

"Unless you've got any better ideas." Cooley then turns to the circulator. "Tell Sam Calvin to bring that thing in here and get it warmed up."

The observation gallery is crowded. Elaine Revis, Cooley's secretary, and Henry Reinhard are there. Sam Calvin is wheeling his piano-shaped apparatus into the operating room. Only a few of the interns and residents crammed into Cooley's small office at the end of the gallery can actually see the open chest, and it is apparent from their conversation that they do not understand what is happening.

The heart-lung machine pumping at full tilt now, Cooley quickly divides away the aorta and pulmonary arteries and begins a clean cut through the upper chambers of the dead heart. The circulator shakes her head. Messmer, reading nothing in Liotta's eyes, shrugs.

"What the hell is Dr. Cooley doing?" asks a crew-cut intern in the gallery. "He's slashing the guy's heart out, and there's no donor, is there? Huh? Can anybody see back in Two? Is there a donor?"

"Pipe down," a resident says. "He knows what he's doing."

"Well, what is he doing?"

"How should I know. He's going to improvise . . . I guess."

"Improvise?" the intern persists.

"For Christ's sake, will you shut up and watch!"

Followed by an orderly with three large cylinders of carbon dioxide, Sam Calvin brings on his machine. The front is lined with pressure gauges and rheostat controls. He plugs it into a wall socket and two jeweled red lights blink on.

"Now, look at this thing," the intern says. "Just what in the hell is happening here?"

"How you doing, Sam?"

"Fine, Dr. Cooley," Calvin says in a soft drawl. "Looks good. Just need a little warm-up."

"Sounds like you're sending a sub into a basketball game!"

Martin's comment brings a few nervous chuckles. Cooley winks his approval, completes his cut, and removes Karp's heart.

The intern was right; there is no donor in Two or Three. Nor for that matter is there a victim of irreversible brain damage waiting to be transported here from any emergency room in the country.

Denton Cooley is a pragmatist who many feel masks a deep-seated sentimentality with his straightforward, at times tough-minded, approach to the business of healing hearts. Thus the rock music, the jokes and wisecracks that shatter tenseness and offset the disastrous mistakes often born of panic.

"Don't be fooled by what appears to be casual indifference," cautioned a long-time Cooley associate. "Nothing around here is without purpose—least of all Denton's role. His movements are choreographed, his remarks—even those god-awful jokes—

are studied. As an ex-athlete who never really left the playing fields, he thinks in terms of winning teams and rousing psychological ploys. His eye and mind are always on the doughnut, never on the philosophical significance of the hole. One of his rivals—and Denton considers every heart surgeon a rival—cancels the day's operating schedule when he loses a patient. When Denton loses a patient, he adds more cases. It's his way of avoiding the confusion and depression that comes with brooding on a situation that's beyond doing anything about."

The easy efficiency of this team around the table in OR One is a testament to Cooley's leadership. But now, with the heart lying flaccid and formless, indistinguishable from a piece of beef liver, in a basin on the Mayo tray, with no donor forthcoming and a patient whose tolerance to the blood-damaging drive of the heart-lung machine is steadily diminishing, an unfamiliar swirl of disorientation and wonder momentarily muddles the composure of them all. They have never been here before. The emergency measure Cooley planned as a backup to the wedge procedure, for years a prime object of medical research, begins now. The goal is obvious—to keep the patient alive. The technique has been tested in animals, but this is not a dog or a calf. The territory from here is uncharted; the envisioned results, a hope based on determined hope.

Everyone is aware of the elite surgical team, the policeman at the gallery entrance, and Sam Calvin with his odd machine; throughout the surgical suite, there are whispered guesses as to what it all means. But no one seems to notice a six-by-four-inch object wrapped in a towel on the instrument table.

Cooley holds out his hand. For the first time since the operation began, the scrub nurse is confused. She picks up a scalpel, puts it down, then reluctantly offers a pair of hemostats. Without looking up, Cooley drops them. "I'm sorry, Dr. Cooley," she sighs, "but I don't know what you want."

"That." He points to the object on the instrument table. She hands it to him. The interns and residents in the gallery exchange puzzled glances and strain for a better view.

Laying the towel aside, Cooley takes the white translucent form in his hand and hefts it, as though trying to determine its quality and weight.

"My God!" the astonished crew-cut intern cries. "My God! It's a mechanical heart!"

Constructed of plastic fixed to a Dacron net, the eight-ounce mechanical device approximates the shape of a natural, human heart. Below the attachment flanges are two separate ventricles containing diaphragm pumps.

"Let's have some scissors." Measuring a plastic ventricle against the portion of the patient's heart left intact, Cooley trims the flange and begins a suture line with 0–3 Dacron. He has done conventional transplants in thirty-seven minutes; though the implant technique for the mechanical heart is essentially the same, there is no tissue-to-tissue cohesiveness. Besides being too large, the ventricle is stiff and unwieldy. Time and again his needle slips off the tough fabric.

Exasperated, Cooley breaks the Dacron thread and tosses the needle holder to the scrub nurse. "Come on now. Give me something sharper. I couldn't patch a pair of overalls with this goddamn mess. And turn the radio down, Gwynn. Art?"

Keats checks the polygraph and the heart-lung log. "He looks all right. But we've been on the pump for eighty-seven minutes." Two hours is the heart-lung safety limit.

"Sam?"

"Just waiting on you, Doc."

Cooley gives Calvin a wilting stare. "Is that right?"

Whether the new needle is sharper or Cooley has adjusted to the awkward task, he is moving more quickly now and getting a better seal. Liotta experienced similar problems implanting test models of the device in calves. On three occasions, the connections weren't tight enough, and negative pressure in the ventricles sucked air through the stitching, causing emboli and death.

The left ventricle firmly in place, Cooley tailors the flange on the right one. Back to back, the two chambers fill the pericardial space, making the second attachment doubly difficult. Under and around, Cooley loops the thin needle along the juncture of plastic and living flesh. *"Dura mater* is right." He slips a series of one-hand knots down the silk. "This is like trying to ligate the Florida peninsula with a cobweb. What time is it, Art?"

"An hour and forty-three minutes."

The arterial extensions are made of the same Dacron knit that Cooley uses for vascular grafts, so the feel is familiar. He quickly sutures on the aorta and the pulmonary artery, then positions the device.

"Now, Sam, if you haven't worn the thing out waitin' on me."

Calvin hands the scrub nurse two small plastic tubes; Cooley fits these over the two nipplelike protrusions running parallel along the ventricles. Liotta secures the tubes and removes the draping from the patient's chest. The flesh between the ribs is deep red and dry; the bones, eyed with hardened, porous marrow, have gone white from being too long exposed to the air and operating lights.

"I should examine the console." Liotta comes around the foot of the table and, careful not to contaminate himself, reads the pressure and rate gauges on the machine. "It's good," he says and returns to his place opposite Cooley.

"Let's have the protamine now."

To counteract the anticoagulant administered early in the operation, Keats injects twenty cc's of protamine in the pump of the heart-lung machine.

"Partial by-pass, Euford." Cooley's voice is calm, but his eyes are quick, and again the flush across the forehead.

Two of the rotary pumps come to a halt.

"Okay, Sam." Cooley removes the clamps from the cava ves-

sels and the aorta. Calvin twists a rheostat control, and an ar-
row-shaped needle climbs the face of a dial. A pulsing stream
of carbon dioxide rushes through the tubing to the diaphragms.
Cooley jabs the aorta with a hypodermic needle, releasing a
whisper of air from the working ventricles. He hesitates, hands
poised, and puts on the same stare that failed to raise life in
Karp's natural heart. Then from right to left, the grafts, the stiff
flanges and pumping chambers one by one go dark, as a snake-
like circuit of blood draws through them and is thrust out into
the body.

"Six liters per minute," Calvin reports.

"All right here," Keats says.

Cooley draws a deep breath and wipes his fingers on the front
of his gown. "Turn up the radio, Gwynn. It looks like we're in
business."

A place in medical history was guaranteed—indeed, two
places. Haskell Karp received the world's first artificial heart.
Dr. Denton Cooley was about to become the subject of the most
extensive series of investigations and litigations the medical
profession has ever known.

Chapter 2

The Christmas Meeting

FOLLOWING morning rounds the Saturday before Christmas 1968, Cooley was seated in his basement office at St. Luke's Hospital, signing case reports and the letters he had dictated the day before. Beneath a spotlessly white clinic coat, he wore a blue oxford cloth shirt and a wide regimental tie his wife, Louise, had given him.

At 184 pounds, he weighed the same as he had as a senior at the University of Texas, the year he led the Longhorns to the Southwest Conference basketball championship. The tan left from a summer of waterskiing on those weekends he had been able to get away to his Rio Brazos ranch or his "shack" on the San Jacinto was supplemented now with the aid of a sunlamp —"for appearances," Cooley would explain. "Nobody wants to be operated on by a slovenly surgeon." He often chided his chief cardiologist for wearing a wrinkled suit coat over a pair of stained scrub pants.

Whether a letter closed with "Sincerely yours" or "With warmest personal regards," the signature was the same: "Denton A. Cooley, M.D." The world clock on his desk did not keep

proper time. Cooley looked at his watch—it was ten o'clock—
and leaned back in the leather chair. In one hour, Dr. Domingo
Liotta would arrive and together they would plan the development and first human application of an implantable, mechanical heart. Except for the two of them, no one knew about this
meeting, and it is doubtful that either of them could have envisioned its far-reaching consequences.

In December 1967, Dr. Christiaan Barnard had performed
the first heart transplant, and already, for whatever reasons—
ignorance, blasted hopes, or an incapacity to follow any event
very long past the initial headlines—the public was losing interest. Heart invalids unable to move without breathlessness and
pain continued to arrive at St. Luke's, but they were dying now
because no donors were available. As usual, the emergency
rooms around the country admitted a steady stream of accident
victims with dead brains; anencephalic "monster" infants without skulls or hope were being born daily. Their hearts might
have been suitable for transplantation. But now they were kept
breathing with chemicals and respirators until pneumonia or
some other complication took its inevitable toll. They were not
sent to St. Luke's, and the people waiting for hearts continued
to die. Perhaps there had been too much publicity. The public
had expected miracles, and when the transplanted patients began to die, disillusionment set in, and that disillusionment had
invaded the medical profession, where from the outset there
had been considerable dissension. The confusion underscored
the AMA's position that the public, being ignorant of medical
matters, is unable to evaluate them properly and, consequently,
should remain ignorant. Cooley did not agree.

Cooley was not a maverick. He was active in medical societies
and firmly believed in the need to maintain a close organization. In a highly exclusive specialty where the heart surgeon is
commonly imagined as an instrument-throwing, eccentric
genius, Cooley's reputation was that of a calm and affable tech-

nical wizard who, while some of his colleagues spent their energies on theorizing and histrionics, went about the business of perfecting and performing intricate operations. He had not been one to rock the boat. But in opposition to the current trend, Cooley continued to believe in cardiac transplantation as a palliative measure for patients who were otherwise untreatable, and on several occasions he had attacked the lay and professional dissenters for being short-sighted and overly cautious. He argued it was often the quality, not the quantity, of life that mattered; that the heart was a grand pump but not the seat of the soul. The sin was not "cannibalizing" a dead body but committing viable organs to a rotting grave rather than donating them for extending the life of another human being.

Over the past twenty years, Cooley had been decorated by kings and queens and heads of state, yet not until the spring of 1968, when he removed the heart from a fifteen-year-old girl and put it in the chest of a Phoenix accountant, were his achievements known outside the profession. Since then, he had done eighteen more transplants and had become internationally famous. After seventeen years of operating in the shadow of Baylor University's illustrious chief of surgery, Dr. Michael E. DeBakey, Cooley unabashedly enjoyed the limelight and took the criticism in stride. When the press and the public became disenchanted with Dr. Barnard for his off-camera antics, Cooley assumed the role of international spokesman for the cause of heart transplants. But something went wrong, or perhaps it was already too late. As a man who spent more time inside human hearts than he did in his own home (Cooley insisted on spending family vacations near hospitals equipped for open-heart surgery), he had perhaps assumed too much: the public would not bend to his pragmatic justifications of heart transplants. The matter reached heights of vitriol but inevitably lapsed into apathy—reactions which Cooley neither sympathizes with nor tolerates. The public relations staff at St. Luke's thought he was

answering too many questions too directly. Whatever the expla-
nations, despite his pleas, the donors weren't coming in. That
was one reason he had called the meeting with Liotta. There
were others.

Cooley missed the fanfare and excitement that had accompanied the transplants. Seldom, though, had he the time or
inclination to examine his motives. Since childhood Cooley had
been a compulsive worker, what he had called a "work addict."
When the action subsided and there wasn't enough important
business to keep him occupied, he suffered withdrawal symp-
toms. He became depressed. And since he was not given to
introspection, he drove himself at a brutal pace. It was one of
the reasons he had chosen heart surgery as a specialty: "The Big
Game," as he referred to it.

Determination and chance timing had provided him with the
opportunities to contribute to virtually every phase of modern
cardiac surgery, from the first blue-baby operation to the transplantation of the human heart. The drama of the transplants,
the controversy, the subtle though definite competition among
participating surgeons suited Cooley. Indeed, inspired him. For
despite his disarmingly laconic calmness, those who knew him
well were aware that his sense of competitiveness bordered on
the fanatic. Once, after dubbing a tee shot, he practiced his golf
swing for fifteen minutes in the reflection of a club-house picture window, then won the match. When it occurred to him
that his business advisers knew more than he did but not as
much as they should, he took a night course in Investment and
Real Estate at the University of Houston and soon gained a
reputation for being one of the shrewdest land speculators in
Harris County. ("I try to excel for the same reasons as anyone
else—I want the admiration of my peers. But then, I'm an
overachiever, so I suppose my motives might go a little deeper.
Anyway, beyond admiration, I suppose I want to be envied.")
But heart surgery was his life, and his routine seldom varied:

Cooley would learn a new operation from the surgeon who developed it, then return to Houston, where he refined and streamlined the technique, and soon, in volume and results, made the new procedure his.

When Christiaan Barnard performed the first heart transplant, Cooley predicted immediate failure. When the patient lived to get off the operating table, Cooley knew that success was imminent, that a human could live with a strange heart in his chest. He was envious of Barnard and disappointed with himself for not having had the courage and foresight to have attempted the operation first. Convinced that he was the finest surgeon in the world, he set out to master the operation. Within five months he had performed three transplants in one week, reducing the time required from four hours to a matter of minutes. But it was not enough.

Christmas, too, had compounded his usual restlessness. Elective operations—which, within limits, most of his were—were invariably postponed until after the holidays. Over the years Cooley had developed a surgical assembly line with three operating rooms going full tilt from early morning till often late evening. When the pace slackened, the order and balance of his healing machinery and his life were upset. The concurrent waste of money and time appalled him (he never squandered a suture or a sponge; he used half the number of instruments required by the average surgeon—and those until they were bent and scored beyond repair), but boredom was worse. He had worked hard to diversify his life, to develop a spectrum of interests that would sustain him through slack periods at the hospital. Finally, though, no amount of waterskiing or golf satisfied his drive or exhibited his skill and control under stress like operating in the recesses of the human heart. It was the logical focus of Cooley's effort—the point at which his pragmatism, pressed to the limits, came to grips with the metaphysical confusion he otherwise so studiously avoided.

Now the pace was slowing. Recognition had rendered Cooley less inclined to follow someone else's lead. A few weeks ago, after 204 days of renewed life, Everett Thomas, Cooley's first transplant, had died. Like Dr. Barnard's Phillip Blaiberg, Thomas had been Cooley's living justification for what he had done. Public apathy, patients dying for lack of donors, exasperation and boredom had convinced Cooley that it was once again time for someone to shake the medical world. And he was determined to do just that.

The door to the outer office opened. But it was only a secretary. Dr. Liotta was due in fifteen minutes. Cooley put the last report aside and opened a folder that contained the notes he had made in anticipation of this meeting. Liotta had become involved ten years ago.

In 1958, while doing postgraduate work in surgery at Lyons, France, Dr. Domingo Liotta became interested in developing an artificial heart. Having completed his studies at Lyons, Liotta returned to his native Argentina as adjunct professor of surgery at the National University of Córdoba and as chief of surgery at the Hospital Nuesta Señora del Valle. In 1960, with plastics furnished by the Fabrica Militar de Aviones—an airplane factory run by a group of immigrant German generals—Liotta and his brother Salvador constructed one of the world's first implantable heart pumps. With financial backing of the Córdoba Public Health Ministry and Señor Tomas Taliani, an Italian engineer retired from the directorship of the Archimedes Institute in Rome, Liotta carried out hundreds of experiments on calves and dogs. The third prototype of his plastic heart was so successful, Juan Martin Allende, dean of the university, suggested that Liotta present his work before the American Society for Artificial Organs. Dr. Willem Kolff, who built the first artificial kidney while an inmate in a Nazi concentration camp, extended an invitation to the young Argentinian to come to America. Following a meeting in Atlantic City where Liotta

presented a definitive paper on mechanical cardiac replacement, Kolff invited him to continue his research in conjunction
with Kolff's own artificial heart program at Cleveland Clinic. At
the time, there was slight federal or foundation interest in cardiac replacement and Kolff was short of funds. But the East
Cleveland Rotary Club agreed to underwrite Liotta's research,
and he accepted the invitation to set up a small laboratory at
Cleveland Clinic. Despite language problems and financial
hardship, Liotta soon began making remarkable progress.
When Dr. Michael DeBakey learned of Liotta's research, he
offered him the extensive laboratory facilities at Baylor College
of Medicine and a financial arrangement that Dr. Kolff was
unable to match.

So in July 1961, at the beginning of the most sensational
decade in the history of cardiac surgery, Domingo Liotta
brought his knowledge and his bag of plastic hearts to Houston
and organized the first cardiac device program at Baylor College of Medicine. On Dr. DeBakey's directions, Liotta reluctantly set aside his research on total heart replacement and
concentrated his efforts on developing a left ventricular by-pass
—an extracorporeal pump that lightened the load on the heart's
main pumping chamber. The device was promising enough to
bring Liotta a grant from the American Heart Association. His
sponsor on that grant, the man with whom he was to write and
publish fifteen papers on cardiac replacement, was Dr. Denton
Cooley. But in 1963, after Dr. E. Stanley Crawford had used the
by-pass in a human, Dr. DeBakey persuaded Liotta to abandon
his AHA grant in favor of a federally funded National Heart
Institute program. On accepting DeBakey's proposal, Liotta
was appointed assistant professor of surgery in DeBakey's department, and subsequent publications on the by-pass included
his name, after Dr. DeBakey's, as co-author. It was accepted
academic procedure.

As he waited for Liotta, Cooley recalled his early work with the left ventricular by-pass. He considered himself a clinical surgeon, an operator. He had never been deeply interested in laboratory research except when it immediately preceded human application. But the fact that he had worked closely with Liotta before DeBakey in some way justified the move he was about to make.

Despite medical convention gossip, until the transplants the Cooley-DeBakey rivalry had been more or less friendly and certainly mutually productive. For years they had been trying to outdo one another in surgery and the media. But with Cooley's entry into the transplant race, when the publicity focus shifted from DeBakey to him, the breach between the two men widened until their communication consisted of press releases.

DeBakey's reply, via *Medical World News,* to Cooley's first three transplants in May 1968 was a declaration that the artificial heart would prove to be the answer to cardiac replacement. To which, on August 3, Cooley replied through UPI that a permanent artificial heart was closer to science fiction than reality. Then on August 31, after Cooley had surpassed all competitors with nine transplants, DeBakey's team tried one. To complete the continuing turnabouts, in late September, again through UPI, Cooley announced that because donors were becoming scarce he intended to build an artificial heart "on another basis from Dr. DeBakey's." The statement was not as impulsive as it might have seemed. Cooley knew that DeBakey's interest was consistent with that of Dr. Ted Cooper, director of the National Heart Institute: they both believed a partial by-pass was more immediately feasible than a complete artificial heart. Consequently, Cooley, who had received no NHI money, set out to prove otherwise. His advantages, he knew, were persuasiveness, expertise, and nerve.

Following several surgical trials with the left ventricular by-pass beginning in 1966, Dr. DeBakey directed Dr. C. William

Hall, a Baylor researcher, and Dr. Liotta to refine the device, but little money was made available to them. Hall and Liotta were having considerable difficulty in realizing their scheduled experiments with the by-pass and toward the development of a true artificial heart. There was the directive, but no funds. In April 1968, Hall sold ten boarding test animals to raise money for the equipment he and Liotta needed. The result was another directive from Dr. DeBakey: no equipment, materials, or animals could be purchased or sold without his written permission. In August, Hall accepted a position at the Southwest Research Institute in San Antonio. He was to begin work there on January 1, 1969, when his resignation from Baylor would become effective. From August, then, Liotta worked in the lab without assistance. (Hall's actual exit from the program in August and his formal exit in January were to become significant factors in the testimony he later gave regarding the design and construction of the artificial heart.) Liotta, his research stymied, sent monthly memoranda to Dr. DeBakey requesting money, consultation, and permission to move ahead from the by-pass experiments to total heart replacement research. The memoranda went unanswered; Liotta did not understand why.

At eleven o'clock that Saturday morning before Christmas, Liotta arrived at Dr. Cooley's office. A man of medium height and heavy build, a round, soulful face, his black hair combed straight back to the contour of his head, Liotta spoke softly with a strong Spanish accent.

For a while they talked of Christmas and their children. Liotta in his quiet, deliberate way stared off now and again and punctuated his words with brief silences; his hands were folded in his lap. Cooley talked little and listened politely, but his interest in the subject soon failed and he made no effort to feign enthusiasm. He was aware of the prerogatives lent by his position and avoided social superfluities as he avoided wasted motion during an operation.

Cooley interrupted Liotta's revery and asked about the situation in the laboratory.

Liotta recognized the approach. He was bewildered and flattered. Everything was as it had been since August. He could get no materials to do anything, and he had begun to consider his work a disaster. No criticism, no encouragement. The laboratory was at a standstill. It was too frustrating. Liotta was determined to go on half-time in the lab and begin operating again.

Cooley asked what it was Liotta really wanted to do.

Aware that Cooley knew the answer, Liotta explained anyway. He wanted to work on the artificial heart. He wanted money to find fabrics that would not traumatize the blood. To have animals for testing. To have help and advice with the technique of implantation. And he needed consultant engineers.

Unusually persistent, Cooley asked if Liotta was working on an artificial heart now.

Liotta said he had the hearts he had brought with him to Baylor seven and a half years ago, but that he had not had time to work on developing them. Moreover, they were not his hearts any more than they were Baylor's. Nor did they belong to the Córdoba Public Health or Tomas Taliani or Dr. Kolff or the East Cleveland Rotary Club or the American Heart Association. He stressed that they did not belong to Dr. DeBakey or the National Heart Institute either.

Cooley was less casual than usual about the artificial heart. Their earlier discussions of the matter had been brief and general, but lately Cooley was being more specific and severe in his questions and recommendations. This was to have been a meeting concerned with Liotta's joining Cooley's clinical staff for a few months. But Cooley had something more in mind.

Liotta went on to explain that the Baylor-Rice program to develop an artificial heart was in a state of confusion. Liotta had not seen or heard from Dr. DeBakey in over three months. Liotta then brought copies of the unanswered memoranda from his briefcase and read them to Dr. Cooley.

Cooley was quiet for a while, then he asked Liotta how much he was willing to risk in order to have facilities to make an artificial heart that would work.

At this point Liotta realized what was happening and why he was there. He said that he was a scientist, that the artificial heart was his life's work, and that he was willing to risk what was necessary to achieve his goal.

Cooley was satisfied. He said before he could do anything he had to be sure that the artificial heart program at Baylor had broken down. While he still had some reservations about a mechanical device as a replacement for the human heart, he felt it was worth whatever the cost to develop one that would sustain a patient long enough so that a donor for a conventional transplant could be obtained. He asked if Liotta was interested.

That Cooley annually donated to the medical school in excess of half a million dollars permitted him no prerogatives for his personal projects, but he did have backing from his own foundation and the Texas Heart Institute, a multimillion-dollar organization he had founded in 1962. The basic obstacles to their collaboration lay elsewhere.

Since 1964 when he had left Cooley and the American Heart Association, Liotta had been paid from National Heart Institute grants. In effect, he was working for the federal government, and Dr. DeBakey, who secured the grants, controlled Liotta's activities. Accordingly, before any human trials could be performed using devices resulting from Liotta's research, he was obliged to get Dr. DeBakey's permission and the permission of a peer review committee appointed by Dr. DeBakey. These controls protected the patient from unwarranted experimentation; also they gave Dr. DeBakey legal authority to take credit for any invention made by a member of his staff under the terms of the grant. However, the personal pique was less important to Liotta than the frustration that arose from DeBakey's failure to respond to his requests and the restrictions which seemingly prohibited him from securing support elsewhere. But there was a loophole.

As a full professor at Baylor, Cooley had unlimited access to the school's research facilities, the sole stipulation being that costs of any experiments unrelated to formal college programs be billed to him. Liotta had the highest respect for Cooley as a man and as a surgeon. From their earlier association, he knew they would work well together, that Cooley would contribute ideas and, when the time was right, would not hesitate to put them into action. The laboratories were available. After trying to foresee all eventualities, Liotta decided not to resign from the federally funded program. Instead, he would do whatever Dr. DeBakey requested and spend the remainder of his time working with Cooley on the artificial heart.

"To do what you plan, we don't need to worry about a highly sophisticated device with an implantable power source. We only need to work together and refine what we have. I will work with you. More than anything it is what I want to do." Liotta drew a deep, satisfied breath. Though, for the trouble that was to follow, he came to regret not resigning from the NHI grant.

The most important consideration was, of course, Dr. De-Bakey. As chairman of the Department of Surgery, president of the college, and principal investigator on the government grant, his power was absolute. Moreover, given the rivalry between Cooley and DeBakey, particularly in the light of their recent break in communications, if he were informed of Cooley's and Liotta's intentions, Liotta and Cooley were afraid that DeBakey might interfere with their collaboration before it began. On the other hand, if they worked quietly without broadcasting the direction of their research, they might possibly be able to construct a workable heart without interference. At that point Cooley would tell DeBakey what he and Liotta had developed—that they had an artificial heart and intended to implant it in a human when the proper occasion arose. In all likelihood, DeBakey would discover them, but they agreed to take the chance.

Cooley smoothed back his hair and smiled, reflecting a measure of Liotta's unabashed enthusiasm. After the first of the year, he would be out of this slump and operating all day. But he could be in the lab in the evenings and on weekends. Liotta was pleased. He thought Dr. DeBakey would monitor his activities less if he did his clinical work at Methodist Hospital instead of St. Luke's. In the meantime, he would make a pump that would work.

Although he had no further appointments, out of habit Cooley glanced at his watch. He asked about the power source.

The artificial heart would be activated by carbon dioxide gas pulsed through tubes from a control console. Liotta explained that several versions of the apparatus were commercially available, and he would check to see what might be arranged. He thought he would prefer working with a local company, Texas Medical Instruments. This situation presented another problem.

William O'Bannon, the Texas Medical Instruments specialist in power consoles, in his capacity as professor of engineering at Rice was a participant in the Baylor-Rice program that was financed by the same federal grant which supported Liotta's research. He was also a large stockholder in the company. Cooley, who believed firmly in the activating force of profit, assured Liotta they would be able to work out an arrangement.

For thirty minutes, they listed in sequence their approach to their goal: an artificial heart implanted in a human chest.

Three of the five line buttons on Cooley's phone were lit. He had a standing offer to consult on any case anywhere if the patient would furnish a chartered jet and make a substantial contribution to the Texas Heart Institute. He picked up the phone. The conversation with Liotta was finished. The collaboration began.

Chapter 3

The Experiments

THAT following Saturday Dr. Cooley met with William O'Bannon in his office at Rice University. He explained the project with Dr. Liotta and told O'Bannon they were interested in working with Texas Medical Instruments on the construction of a power console that would be capable of reproducing human pulse characteristics in an artificial heart.

"We're aiming for an implantable device that will pump approximately six liters of blood per minute. Nothing too sophisticated. What we want is something that will keep a patient alive until we can find a human heart to transplant."

O'Bannon was reluctant. He was worried about a conflict with the Baylor-Rice program, but he and the other engineers present were excited. Cooley had ability, prestige, money, and a relatively free hand to execute his ideas. Then, too, not only was the Baylor-Rice program suffering from lack of organization; unknown to Cooley at the time, Texas Medical Instruments was in deep financial trouble. It was not difficult to envision an exclusive contract for manufacturing the equipment to power a device that would come to common use in the world's heart centers. Cooley exerted wide influence. The instruments and equipment he used were accepted as standards and brought large profits to their manufacturers.

The power unit that Cooley required would cost about twenty thousand dollars. He was prepared to write a check for the amount now or on delivery.

Three days after their meeting, Cooley received a phone call from O'Bannon, who had discussed the matter with Dr. David Hellums, chairman of the Department of Engineering at Rice. Hellums agreed that O'Bannon could work on the console in his spare time and thus avoid conflicting with the federal grant. To circumvent any criticism or accusations that might be forthcoming, O'Bannon decided to build the apparatus at home in his garage.

On January 1, 1969, Dr. C. William Hall's resignation from Baylor became effective.* On the thirtieth, Liotta began a series of implantations of the artificial heart in calves.

Dr. Domingo Liotta: "There were many problems. The first model was bulky and difficult to attach. There were air and blood leaks at the atrial flanges where the device was sutured to living tissue. I met regularly with Dr. Cooley in his office, and at nights after rounds and on most weekends he was in the lab with me, going over the details carefully, checking everything. He suggested a new design for the attachment surfaces and recommended that we separate the two ventricles to facilitate implantation. Then after they were in place, we could reconnect them with surface stitches. It worked very well.

"Another thing. No one anywhere had come up with a satisfactory valve system. After the first four calf experiments, at the end of February, Dr. Cooley brought over four of the new

---

*At the Baylor hearings in April 1969, Hall testified that the artificial heart implanted in Karp was identical to Dr. DeBakey's device and commented on the inconclusiveness of the calf experiments. The calf experiments began at least one month *after* Hall's departure from Baylor.

Wada-Cutter valves. He was the only surgeon in the country with a consignment of these valves and had been having good luck with them. Cooley changed the inflow-outflow position of the valves; the result was a 40 percent increase in the efficiency of the pump.

"The fifth calf implantation proved successful until one of the diaphragms ruptured, necessitating a redesign. But that's why they were testing: to find faults and correct them."

Dr. Cooley's participation—his contributions to the entire surgical technique, his interpretations of the postmortems— gave Liotta a new outlook, and together they began making progress. After testing sixty fabrics, they found a synthetic material that would accept bloodflow without forming clots and thus they had overcome what had remained a major problem in artificial heart research.

On March 5, 1969, Haskell Karp was admitted to St. Luke's Hospital. On minor exertion, Mr. Karp experienced acute pain and tachycardia. The cardiologists at St. Luke's discovered he was suffering a complete heart block and severe atherosclerosis of the coronary and collateral blood vessels. A large percentage of his heart was scarred and decomposed.

Dr. Ted Cooper, director of the National Heart Institute, visited Baylor in the middle of March. Though Dr. Larry Lamb, a faculty member, had lodged a complaint against Dr. DeBakey for withdrawing his grant money over a personal disagreement (Lamb had refused to design a monitoring system for DeBakey's operating room), Cooper's appearance was in the nature of a site visit, not a confrontation with DeBakey. DeBakey took him on a tour of Methodist Hospital, the Fondren-Brown Cardiovascular Research Center, and the Medical School.

Cooley and Liotta suspected that DeBakey was aware of their collaboration. Cooley's presence in the laboratory invariably caused a stir. He had not done any serious laboratory research since the termination of the AHA grant in 1964, so it was a reasonable assumption that those who saw him working with Liotta late at night had concluded that something significant was going on. The medical school was DeBakey's bailiwick, his "camp," and he would be the logical recipient of any speculative reports as to Cooley's movement outside St. Luke's and Texas Children's.

So Liotta was shocked but not surprised when he received a call from a technician in the laboratory: "Dr. DeBakey is here with Dr. Cooper and he has asked to see one of the latest pumps. He says he's not interested in the left ventricular bypass, he wants to see the total replacement pump."

Dr. DeBakey had not been in the laboratory for seven months, and all that time Liotta had no communication whatsoever from him. He must have had an informant. There was nothing to do but show him the device.

From the shelf of his office, Liotta took an artificial heart that had been tested in a calf. He looked at it, sighed, and walked slowly down the corridor to the laboratory where DeBakey and Cooper were waiting. Although the heart had been developed without him, indeed, perhaps, despite him, DeBakey proceeded to explain the device he had never seen. Then he told Liotta to carry on and left with Cooper for the Cardiovascular Research Center, where Dr. Ted Diethrich had been working on an organ preservation chamber.

That afternoon Cooper paid Cooley an informal visit. They met between operations in his five-by-five office at one end of the narrow glass gallery overlooking OR One. The small desk was cluttered with Phonograms, plastic heart valves, excised specimens, and letters from referring physicians, thankful families, critics, opportunists, and madmen. The difference between this minuscule cubicle and the least opulent of DeBakey's four offices was remarkable. As remarkable as a comparison between Cooley's cramped operating rooms and the elaborate, futuristic, eight-celled theater in which DeBakey and his associates worked. And Cooley used the differences to good advantage. Protocol demanded that dignitaries visit the chairman's surgery before calling here. They were always impressed to discover the the largest concentration of the world's heart surgery was performed in such modest quarters. The set was simple and unglamorous, a neutral background that contributed to a more brilliant spotlighting of Cooley, a head taller than any of his assistants, isolated as he worked at the table.

In fact, the operating rooms were quite adequate. And the office had been designed as a place removed from the doctors' dressing room where Cooley could change into his tailored scrub suits, avoid solicitous families, and monitor openings and closings as he directed his business interests over the phone. He had the big fancy office downstairs where it didn't interfere with his real work.

Since there was no room to sit, Cooley and Cooper stood at the gallery window and watched three assistants wire closed the breastbone of a child whose heart Cooley had just rebuilt. Cooper, a small man with dark curly hair, was an administrator-researcher who only occasionally operated. He expressed his admiration of the surgery, though it was implicit in his demeanor—a reaction Cooley had come to assume—that he was as much impressed by the man as by his work.

Because Cooper believed that Cooley had the greatest collection of cardiovascular information in the world, he felt it was his duty to see that Cooley got National Heart Institute backing.

Cooley, who had never applied for or received federal money, agreed with a pause and a smile that was between acknowledging his due and ingenuous appreciation. "Well," he said, "when the Texas Heart Institute is completed, we'll be on our way toward having the facilities to do more research and more comprehensive followups. As it is, St. Luke's and Texas Children's are general hospitals. One research area puts three patients out in the street." He smiled. "And these operating rooms . . . it's not exactly a space-age arrangement." This was Cooley's stock response to critics who claimed he spent too much time in surgery and not enough time in the lab.

Closed off by glass from the banter between nurses and assistants, the quick efficiency with which one patient was removed, the room disinfected, and another patient prepped was fascinating to observe.

"We do the best we can under the circumstances," Cooley said.

The circulating nurse signaled that they were ready in Two, and Cooley left for the scrub room.

The meeting with Cooper perhaps held promise; Cooley wasn't sure. After raising millions of dollars for the Texas Heart Institute, he had learned not to bank money out of hand, regardless of assurances. Moreover, he was not at all convinced that Washington was eager to back him. Years before, when he had realized that he would be denied any portion of Baylor-administered federal grants, Cooley, partly from principle and partly in an effort to gain the support of individuals who were opposed to government give-and-control methods, had spoken out against the stifling bureaucratic ineptitude imposed on medical science by agencies of the U.S. Public Health Service. He had come to be a champion of those who feared that federal intervention was a prelude to socialized medicine. Cooley's role as a leader of these laissez-faire forces had undesired effects. The truth was that while Cooley preferred private support for the THI (as long as stipulations weren't unreasonably confining) he would accept money for the THI from any source, be it Israel (he had been given a million dollars in Israeli war bonds) or Franco's Spain (where he had a support-and-exchange promotion working) or the United States Government (where DeBakey's influence was pervasive).

If the record counted, Cooley might justifiably be hopeful. He led everyone in transplants, and if progress in his recent research with Liotta continued at the present rate, he would soon have the lead in artificial hearts.

That weekend Cooley and Liotta met and reviewed the situation.

Dr. Domingo Liotta: "After DeBakey's visit to the laboratory, when I showed him the artificial heart, a close associate of his came by asking questions about Dr. Cooley's participation in our experiments. Then one of Dr. DeBakey's scrub nurses watched a calf operation. Dr. Messmer [a Cooley assistant] was here and so was Dr. Cooley. In the hall, a resident of DeBakey's asked me how Dr. Cooley and I were doing with the artificial heart experiments. Everyone knows everything at Baylor.

"At the time, our only conclusion was that Dr. DeBakey was happy to get help for a failing program. Even with their personal differences, I thought he might be glad that a man like Dr. Cooley had taken an active interest. . . . Anyhow, we decided to go ahead as we had been and let Dr. DeBakey make the first move.

"Dr. DeBakey . . . maybe he didn't know how far along we were. The seventh calf experiment went well enough to convince us that in an emergency situation the device was preferable to the heart-lung machine; we knew we could keep a dying patient alive long enough to find a human heart."

Chapter 4

The Preparations

Tuesday, *April 1, 1969*

Henry Reinhard, a prematurely graying man in his early thirties, was an administrative assistant at St. Luke's–Texas Children's Hospitals. He also managed the administrative business of the Texas Heart Institute and Cooley's transplant program. He had a wife and three children and, besides his position at the hospital, attended evening law school. Reinhard handled many of the direct confrontations and details with which Cooley had neither time nor interest to deal. The press had come to respect him as a difficult man to outflank.

Early that afternoon, Reinhard and Opal Benage, the nursing supervisor, were discussing new equipment for the intensive care units when they were called to meet with the chief administrator. Newell France closed the door, cut off the intercom, and told them that Dr. Cooley was prepared to implant an artificial heart as soon as the correct situation came up.

"The machine that powers the heart is coming in this afternoon. We're putting it in the basement, in the urodynamics lab. They want to continue testing it."

Recalling the labyrinth of logistics surrounding the conventional transplants he had been involved in, Reinhard winced in anticipation of the work ahead. Miss Benage looked at her watch.

"Dr. Cooley has a patient in the house," France continued. "He was referred here for the excision of decomposed heart muscle, a wedge procedure. But according to the diagnostic studies, there's a chance that he can't be salvaged. He wants Dr. Cooley to try it anyway. He's not interested in a transplant, but if the wedge procedure doesn't work, he's willing to go on this artificial heart until a donor can be found. Then, if it comes to that, they'll put a human heart in him."

Miss Benage asked where the artificial heart had come from. She looked at Reinhard, then back to Mr. France.

"The device," France said, "has been developed over the past few months by Dr. Cooley, Dr. Liotta, and a group of Rice engineers."

Reinhard recalled that Dr. Cooley mentioned this last September and again in January or February during a talk at the University of Houston. "He predicted that an artificial heart would probably be used within the year. I remember that, and I remember wondering what his sources of information were."

France outlined the situation: Mr. Karp's surgery was scheduled for April 4, Good Friday. If the mechanical heart was to be used, they must make immediate preparations. Because of the holiday weekend, it would be necessary to insure that all key personnel be available. But there should be a minimum of talk in order to avoid any premature leaks to the news media.

Miss Benage would alert the nurses on her staff. Reinhard would arrange for an additional security guard. Because of extra loads on the electrical circuits for the power unit and the additional monitoring equipment, it was decided that the emergency generator should run during the time the patient was on the artificial heart.

At seven thirty that evening, William O'Bannon turned his camper truck into the hospital drive. John Creighton, a hospital official, and two orderlies were waiting for him.

"Is this the equipment from Rice?" Creighton asked.

Somewhat irritated, O'Bannon replied, "It isn't an *official* Rice project. Some of the engineering faculty built it in their off-duty hours."

"So?" Creighton shrugged. "It's for the artificial heart, isn't it?"

O'Bannon just looked at him.

The console, roughly the size of a two-by-four drawer filing cabinet, was rolled into the urodynamics laboratory where Dr. Liotta, O'Bannon, and Hardy Bourland, another Rice engineer, examined the unit to see if it had been damaged during the move. They plugged it in and got no response. O'Bannon sighed and began turning dials, then Bourland noticed that the receptacle circuit was open. An electrician arrived to repair it, and the console began to function properly.

Wednesday, April 2

Early in the morning, Reinhard stopped by the urodynamics laboratory to find a white Silastic heart immersed in water in a stainless sink, "the control console clicking rhythmically with a sound that resembled an automatic milking machine. A blip of green light through the oscilloscope traced the rise and fall of pressures that were recorded on a slowly unfurling sheet of graph paper. Alone in that room with the heart, I felt strangely related to history and for the first time realized the momentousness of what was about to take place."

On the way back to his office, Reinhard met Manfred Gygli, the hospital photographer who had provided numerous transplant pictures for *Life* and *Der Stern* and was always on the lookout for a moonlight scoop. Gygli's office was next door to the urodynamics lab; if he hadn't noticed the machine, chances were no one had.

"Mr. Reinhard,"—Gygli looked both ways—"listen." For five minutes, Gygli tried to sell Reinhard a Porsche automobile which his wife Suzi insisted they must get rid of—a baby was on the way.

With Dr. Cooley's advice and the help of his law professors, Reinhard had drawn up some of the earliest consent forms for heart transplant donors and recipients. At Mr. France's suggestion, he agreed to postpone his other duties for the time being and devise a special document for the Karp case. Cooley's accomplishments were to the hospital's advantage, in which instances individual egos and the public were served. This advantage was one of the reasons he always received full cooperation.

Cooley did thirteen operations that day, bought twenty acres on the outskirts of Houston, and laid plans for a vacation in Italy. Now and then Liotta came into the operating room and said simply that things were going well. Cooley nodded and continued cutting and sewing.

Thursday, April 3

The console and the heart had been functioning perfectly for three days. Dr. Liotta asked that an extra supply of carbon dioxide be available. Mr. McDowell in Inhalation Therapy would have ten large cylinders ready.

Between operations, Cooley discussed the consent form with Reinhard. Consistent with his usual manner, Cooley concerned himself only with the matter at hand and gave no evidence of being excited at what might be impending. Each had drafted his own version of the document. On review and comparison, they decided upon a combination of the better points of the two. It was doublechecked for legal accuracy and then typed.

That afternoon, Cooley went over the form with Mr. and Mrs.

Karp. Mr. Karp said it was fine and signed it. Mrs. Karp questioned Cooley about whether he thought the wedge procedure
would be successful. Cooley explained that he did not know,
that there was no way of knowing. The artificial heart, he repeated, was as yet untried on a human being. He would use it
only as a last-ditch effort to keep her husband alive until a donor
could be found. For fear of unduly boosting her hopes, Cooley
did not tell Mrs. Karp that he was an authority on the operation.
It would then have been necessary to explain the unpredictabil-
ity of an injured heart, and Mrs. Karp seemed to prefer this sort
of speculation to facts.

"We'll do the best we can to save your husband's life."

He meant that. It was as far beyond an anatomical problem
as he ever wished to venture. As others had so often before, she
tried to detain him with ambiguous and unanswerable questions. He could only say, "I don't know. I'm sorry but I don't
know the answer." He had never to his satisfaction discovered
the exact stance to assume. How does one instill confidence in
one's ability and in the same breath admit ignorance? He tried
to be a good listener—occasionally, he was not.

Returning later to verify the signatures, Reinhard found Mr.
Karp waiting for his wife to come back from the snack bar. Mr.
Karp wasn't in the least hesitant about discussing his medical
history or his impending surgery. He said he recognized the
risks involved and that possibly he would not live through it. He
observed also that he had no future without surgery and so had
no regrets about his decision. Mr. Karp was full of praise for his
hometown cardiologist, Dr. Arthur Levine, whose judgment he
held in high regard. He expressed explicit confidence in Dr.
Cooley and said that after investigating the matter, he was
satisfied that no other surgeon in the world could help him if Dr.
Cooley could not. He seemed fully aware of all the ramifications
of his heart problems and all the options open to him.

Dr. Cooley had six cases scheduled for the next morning. Mr. Karp's operation was to be the last, at approximately noon.

Mr. France was worried about having a statement ready for the news media. He did not want to move prematurely, but he was concerned as ever over the possibility of leaks to the press, and he wanted to be prepared. Not only was it a matter of accurate news dissemination; if the artificial heart was used, the hospital would rely heavily on the right sort of coverage to bring in a donor.

France and Reinhard sat down in the administrative conference room and began to prepare a statement. Dr. Cooley would be in surgery until late that night and had a full morning schedule. They would compile a list of questions and leave them in his gallery office.

Cooley took a break at eight thirty that evening and went to the urodynamics lab where Liotta and O'Bannon were making final checks on the console. With Cooley were Barbara Lichty and Gwynn Baumgartner, the nurses who would assist in surgery the next morning.

Cooley showed Liotta the authorization signed by Mr. and Mrs. Karp and by Reinhard. Then he handed it to O'Bannon. O'Bannon read it carefully and said, "It's okay."

After Cooley left, O'Bannon became nervous. Liotta tried to calm him down but couldn't.

Dr. Domingo Liotta: "He is an engineer, not a medical person, and I could understand his feelings. He said he didn't sleep last night and wouldn't sleep tonight. He said he was afraid of what might happen to Karp. He was particularly concerned about Dr. DeBakey's criticism.

"Dr. Cooley told O'Bannon that perhaps it wouldn't be necessary to use the heart. But O'Bannon was not relieved. Cooley speculated that, 'Perhaps under fire O'Bannon had lost confidence in himself and in his work. But I don't know why—the console performed perfectly. Engineers, they don't see people die everyday. But then they don't see lives saved because of their efforts, either.' "

Liotta had faith in the artificial heart and in Dr. Cooley's ability to attach it. But after the implantation, O'Bannon would be the key man keeping the device functioning. What if when the moment came to turn on the console and activate the artificial heart O'Bannon panicked? A failure, Liotta told his wife, is acceptable. A fiasco would be inexcusable and ultimately disastrous to the future of the procedure.

April 4, Good Friday

Dr. Cooley arrived at the hospital early and for an hour sat alone in his gallery office. At 8:15 he called Reinhard and asked if he would meet with Dr. Liotta and review the list of questions that had been left on Cooley's desk.

Reinhard and Liotta had met in the gallery and were on question six when Cooley, having decided that he should be aware of the matter, joined them. He was wearing a scrub suit and a surgical cap. Blood from the last operation had leaked through his gown and spotted his trousers. He changed them as Liotta began reading from the first question.

1. What individuals are to be credited with the design and development of the device?

The intrathoracic pump was developed by Dr. Liotta and Dr. Cooley at Baylor. The control system was developed by off-duty engineers (Hardy Bourland and Bill O'Bannon) at Rice University in conjunction with Texas Medical Instruments and Mr. John Maness.

(Because of the pending grant application involving Rice University and Dr. DeBakey, it was important that the console not be represented as a Rice project. Dr. Cooley said he had just spoken with David Hellums, chairman of the Department of Engineering at Rice. Hellums refused to permit O'Bannon to be in the building during the operation. Liotta said he would phone John Maness at Texas Medical Instruments about the matter.)

2. *How long did it take to develop this particular model of the heart device?*

It was a product of years of research by investigators throughout the world, the result of accumulated knowledge as it was shared among the membership of such organizations as the American Society for Artificial Internal Organs. The particular model was constructed and tested over a four-month period by Dr. Cooley and Dr. Liotta.

3. *When did research on this particular device begin?*

This device is a refinement of a prototype first reported by Dr. Liotta while doing research in his native Argentina in 1959.

4. *What institution or company is credited with the development or construction of this equipment?*

The intrathoracic device was constructed at Baylor University College of Medicine; the control console was constructed by Texas Medical Instruments.

5. *Where was the intrathoracic device built?*

At Baylor, and the control console at Texas Medical Instruments.

6. *To what extent has this device been tested in animals?*

The present device was the result of years of testing many different designs and models.

7. *How long did it sustain life in an animal?*

The postoperative problems of maintaining an animal after implantation of the device are considerably more complex than in a human being. For this reason, one should be cautious about assigning too great a value to the length of animal survival. This particular device had sustained a calf for forty-seven hours, at the end of which time the device was functioning properly and the animal was sacrificed.

8. Where were the animal experiments carried out?
Baylor University College of Medicine.
9. Are pictures of the artificial heart available for general release?
Yes.
10. Is this artificial heart in any way similar to the left ventricular by-pass pump used by the DeBakey team a year or so ago?
This device was built on an entirely different concept.
11. How is the artificial heart attached to the patient?
This intrathoracic device is attached in the same manner in which a human donor heart would be attached. The pericardial sac and the chest are closed over the device in the same manner as a conventional transplant. The device is connected to the control console by two polyethylene tubes through which carbon dioxide is pulsed to supply pumping action.
12. Is the patient able to move about?
The patient will be restricted to bed, although he could possibly sit in a chair. The patient can move about in his bed in the same manner as any patient with a tube leading from his chest.
13. Are preoperative photographs of the patient available?
Yes.
14. Are postoperative photographs of the patient available?
They will be if, in fact, the procedure takes place.
15. Are you willing to participate in a press conference?
Yes.
16. What members of the development team are available to participate in a press conference?
Dr. Denton A. Cooley and Dr. Domingo S. Liotta.
17. What is the correct term for the artificial heart?
It is an orthotopic (in place of) cardiac prosthesis.
18. How long can this device sustain a patient awaiting a suitable human heart?

Since there is no precise precedent, the question cannot be answered at this time. The orthotopic cardiac prosthesis is made of Dacron fabric in Silastic. The control system is not unique. Similar systems are available commercially, but in order to expedite the program, Dr. Cooley chose to construct our own control system utilizing the talents and capabilities of engineers in the Houston area.

Though no one was satisfied that the statement was comprehensive, Cooley, Liotta, and Reinhard discussed the questions until they were certain each understood and was conversant in the facts pertaining to the development and construction of the artificial heart and the console. Cooley added that there should be no mistake about their financial support, even if the rest of this proved to be an idle exercise. The money came from the Texas Heart Institute and the Denton A. Cooley Foundation, supplemented with funds from American Heart Association chapters in Alice, Huntsville, and Weimar, Texas.

After forty-five minutes, the meeting was concluded. Cooley and Liotta returned to the operating room. Reinhard gathered his materials and went to verify Mrs. Karp's signature on the consent form.

Mr. Karp asked Reinhard to see that his cardiac catheterization x rays were returned to Dr. Levine, and he wanted Dr. Cooley to call Dr. Levine after the surgery. Karp seemed less alert than yesterday, but he attributed this to the medications he had received that morning. Mrs. Karp was distraught—near tears.

Reinhard then delivered the question-response list to Newell France, who in turn reviewed the press situation with Lois Hill, the fast-talking head of public relations. They agreed that wide press coverage would be helpful in finding a donor, if one was needed.

Without divulging that anything more unusual than a conventional transplant was impending, Reinhard called Charlie Smith of Top Hat Jets to be certain that a Lear and a pilot would be available over the holidays. The request was not extraordinary—Top Hat had transported sixteen Cooley donors in the past.

While France was briefing Lois Hill and Cooley's private secretary Elaine Revis, Miriam Kass, medical editor of the Houston *Post*, who had been conducting an interview across the street at M. D. Anderson Hospital, stopped by the public-relations office on a routine visit. There was an awkward silence.

Joachim Zwer from Baylor Medical Photography was checking his movie equipment in the corridor outside the operating suite. Manfred Gygli, who would run the movie camera, picked over a Japanese light meter he didn't trust. They both wore unironed green scrub suits and surgical caps that looked incongruous over their long hair. Dr. Liotta visited with them. Pleased with the extended testing of the artificial heart and the console, he talked and laughed, uncharacteristic of his more usual severity. After ten years of dedicated research, from a thirty-six-bed hospital in Argentina to the greatest cardiovascular center in the world, the product of his time and effort was ready, and the possibility that it would be needed was high. If Mr. Karp could live without need of the artificial heart, that was as it should be.

More than anyone else involved in the momentous situation, Liotta was the pure scientist. But even he realized that without Cooley's surgical brilliance and personal aggressiveness, Liotta's contribution would remain anonymous.

Liotta was thinking of the plastic heart and its power, while Cooley was expertly, automatically feeding layers of tissue onto a thin, crescent needle. The hospital housekeeper, Mr. Flourney, and two helpers wheeled by a bulky apparatus under a green sheet and left it unattended in a cul-de-sac beyond the coffee room. Security officer C. T. Smith stood at the door to the gallery. No one was to pass except Cooley fellows and residents and members of the hospital staff as identified by Ruth Sylvester, the operating room supervisor.

Chapter 5

The Search for a Donor

AT five o'clock in the afternoon of April 4, 1969, the artificial heart had been supporting Haskell Karp's circulation for thirty minutes. Because of the cumbersome monitoring equipment and the impending second-stage transplant, the operating room was converted into a recovery area.

Henry Reinhard, Bonnie Sue Woolridge, and Dr. Liston Beasley were observing from the gallery when Dr. Cooley looked up. "Henry, can you hear me?" He couldn't. Then Gwynn Baumgartner turned on the intercom. "I can't leave now," Cooley said. "Go down and tell Mrs. Karp what we've been doing up here. And get a press notice out so we can find a donor."

Downstairs, Elaine Revis telephoned Lois Hill in public relations to say that she had just witnessed the first human implantation of an artificial heart. Sensing that something important was about to take place, Miriam Kass, the Houston *Post* reporter, had remained at the hospital. She was standing unseen at the open door behind Elaine Revis.

Dr. Beasley went with Reinhard to the family room, where

together they told Mrs. Karp, her son Michael, and Rabbi Nathan Whitkin what had happened and what the plans were.

Mrs. Karp reacted with overwhelming grief. Beasley explained that Dr. Cooley would be down as soon as possible and told her that the hospital needed to get a press release out immediately so that a suitable donor might be found.

It was agreed to delay notification of the news media until the two other Karp sons could be located and informed. But after several long-distance calls, when it was evident that they could not be reached soon, Mrs. Karp said that the securing of a donor was more urgent and asked Reinhard to proceed with the news release. Arrangements were made to screen visitors and calls for Mrs. Karp, and she was advised to refer all reporters' inquiries, here and in Illinois, to the public relations department at the hospital.

Dr. Michael DeBakey had left his office at 4:30 P.M. to catch Delta Flight 916, departing from Hobby Field for Washington National. He was to meet the next morning with Dr. Ted Cooper at the National Heart Institute. The occasion was a group council discussion of myocardial infarction and the artificial heart—the condition which had disabled Mr. Karp, and the device which had just been implanted in his chest.

At five fifteen, Jerry Maley, who handled DeBakey's affairs as president of Baylor, received a phone call from Barbara Akery, DeBakey's executive secretary. A Baylor cardiovascular fellow told her Dr. Cooley had just put an artificial heart in a patient at St. Luke's. Maley was stunned and amused. While he had been billing Cooley's animals and equipment in the Baylor lab, he had had no reason or authority to question the nature of the experiments.

Jerry Maley: "I could of course foresee what Dr. DeBakey's reaction would be. And then the irony that he was on his way to an artificial-heart meeting. Barbara asked if I thought we should page Dr. DeBakey at the airport. I said I didn't see any need for it—he would find out soon enough."

Word had gotten out. Lois Hill, France, Creighton, and Miss Woolridge were busy trying to hold off the newsmen. All but three or four residents, who were determined to see the operation from beginning to end, had left the gallery. As the last sutures were placed, Dr. DeBakey's plane lifted off the runway.

Mr. Karp's color and his life signs were good. The atmosphere in OR One was busy but relaxed. Cooley watched as Liotta made adjustments in the console, which emitted a steady pneumatic rhythm.

Cooley was worried about what progress was being made toward finding a donor. Although he said nothing, there was another matter on his mind. Karp had been on the heart-lung machine for over two hours; a grave possibility existed that he had suffered blood trauma and neurological damage.

Cooley went up to his gallery office and phoned Dr. Adrian Kantrowitz and Dr. Willem Kolff, two pioneer researchers in the field of artificial cardiac replacement. The press would undoubtedly approach them for comments, and Cooley wanted them to know exactly what had taken place. Both Kantrowitz and Kolff recognized the event as a milestone and conveyed their congratulations to Cooley and Liotta. Kolff, who returned Cooley's call from Zion National Park, Utah, said, "I'm having some of my Navajo friends make special good luck charms for you and Dom. I'm afraid you're going to need them later."

As Mr. Karp had requested, Cooley phoned Dr. Arthur Levine. He then left word for Dr. Ted Cooper at the National Heart Institute headquarters in Bethesda, Maryland. Ten minutes later, Cooper returned the call. He was surprised and apparently pleased to hear of the operation. Cooper said this two-stage approach was an important step forward in the search for a permanent artificial heart. He requested that Cooley phone in a progress report before the artificial-heart-committee meeting in the morning.

Meanwhile, the press had gathered in the administrative suite. Two local newspapers, three television stations, the wire services, and a number of radio stations were represented.

Cooley and Liotta, avoiding newsmen, rushed across the west end of the corridor to Chaplain Jorjorian's office, where Mrs. Karp had been since shortly before the operation. Cooley told her OR One would be straightened up in an hour or so and she would be permitted to visit her husband then. When she looked up to Cooley and asked why the Lord had allowed Haskell to suffer so with heart disease, he said he didn't know, adding that everything looked good and they were hopeful of getting a donor in right away. Yet the grave fact was, Mr. Karp still had not regained consciousness, and Cooley was increasingly anxious as to whether he had suffered brain damage over the long heart-lung time.

Earlier in the month, Cooley had agreed to an interview with Channel 13, the Houston ABC affiliate. The program was a charity gridiron show where local celebrities allowed themselves to be satirically attacked. Unable to contact Cooley and remind him, Linda O'Donnell, one of his secretaries, had phoned the station and told them to stand by for a possible interview later in the day. So when word of the Karp operation leaked to the press, the crew that had been waiting for the gridiron interview with Cooley was dispatched to the hospital well in advance of the formal news release. Their premature appearance on the scene was to contribute to the various controversies precipitated by the implantation.

By the time Lois Hill was halfway through reading the formal release, the four telephone lines in the administrative offices were banked up with incoming calls. While no press conference had been planned, they would try to have Dr. Cooley available for a comment. Because of the telephone tie-up, the hospital was unable to inform all the media simultaneously; most of them picked up the story from the wire services, and there were hard feelings.

Cooley and Liotta arrived at the administrative conference room shortly after six o'clock. They explained the development of the artificial heart and the rationale behind a two-stage procedure. Dr. Cooley showed the group a model of the device, a smaller output pump than the one in Mr. Karp, and answered questions about its function. He insisted that he did not know how long it would keep Mr. Karp alive and stressed the urgency of finding a suitable donor.

"This thing wasn't designed for permanent replacement. We have taken a desperate measure to save a man's life. What's important now is finding a donor."

Photographs of the artificial heart were distributed by Lois Hill. At this point, Dr. Hallman (a Cooley associate) and Dr. Bloodwell entered and announced that Mr. Karp was awake and responding to verbal commands. Hallman had an x ray of the device in place. When Cooley held it up to the fluorescent ceiling lights, there were tears in his eyes. He knew that no matter what the qualifications, from here on the artificial heart must be considered a success.

On leaving, Cooley again stressed the importance of finding a donor. He emphasized that full responsibility and any blame for the day's events rested on him. On the other hand, any success was to be attributed to Dr. Liotta, "who conceived, nurtured, and brought to fruition the world's first . . .'orthotopic cardiac prosthesis.' "

The reporters laughed, Liotta blushed, and Cooley left to see the patient.

Sometime after eight o'clock, when he put on a scrub suit and went in to examine Karp, Dr. Ted Diethrich, a staff surgeon at Methodist Hospital, phoned Dr. DeBakey at the Manger Hay

Adams Hotel in Washington and told him what had happened. Whatever came out of the Baylor laboratories was subject to his review and supervision. The artificial heart, Dr. DeBakey declared, had been stolen from him.

After Mr. Karp awakened, Mrs. Karp and Michael were escorted to the gallery. He could not speak because of the endotracheal tube, but Mr. Karp was reasonably alert and his color was excellent. Mrs. Karp was relieved to see him looking so well. She thanked Dr. Cooley and said she was satisfied that he and his team were doing everything they could.

So far, the photographers Gygli and Zwer had done a good job of recording the day's events on film, but Dr. Liotta was eager to get some waveform monitor tracings synchronized with movie footage of the pulsing noises from the control console. While there was a hospital ruling that prohibited newsmen from entering the surgical suite, a conditional exception was made. Channel 11, the local CBS affiliate, offered St. Luke's a camera crew—they would donate the film and the services of the photographers. Pete Maroney and Bill George arrived and began shooting the sequence under Liotta's direction. Dr. Keats reported to Cooley that it was time to remove the endotracheal tube from Karp's mouth. That the cameras coincidentally recorded Karp's first words following the operation was to be presented as evidence that Dr. Cooley had summoned the television station for purposes of publicity and self-laudation. The film was developed at St. Luke's and remained there.

The main switchboard was loaded with calls from across the country. Because any one of them might have concerned news of a donor, none was ignored, whether paid or collect.

An eighty-year-old lady in an Eastern nursing home said that since she was crippled with arthritis and wasn't going anywhere anyway, she would be happy to give Mr. Karp her "splendid" heart, and they could put the artificial device in her. A man from Atlanta had booked passage on a flight to Houston and complained that his civil rights would be violated if the hospital did not have a team ready to take his heart when he blew his brains out in the St. Luke's parking lot. A woman from San Francisco presented a similar argument. Another would give her heart if Dr. Cooley would raise her husband from the dead. Reinhard put on two additional security guards.

Cooley quickly realized that the public had a gross misconception of what constituted an acceptable donor. Though the requirements had been painstakingly stated to the press—brain death, consent, etc.—people had somehow gotten the notion that he was soliciting human sacrifice on the order of blood donations. Reinhard contacted the wire services, but it was too late. Besides, there was no traceable error in the reporting. It was, they concluded, people. Such calls continued to pour in.

At nine thirty, Reinhard found Cooley in his gallery office, eating pineapple yogurt and watching the recovery room nurses attend to Mr. Karp.

"Calls have been swamping us regularly at twenty-five after and five before the hour," Reinhard said. "The radio and TV stations around the country want up-to-the-minute reports for their newscasts, and frankly, I don't know what to tell them."

"Tell them, *frankly,* we don't have a donor." Cooley was on the verge of anger. "You can tell them that. Say, if they're not aware of it, this is a holiday weekend and we know the country's emergency rooms are full of accident victims, anyone of whom could provide this man with a heart. Tell them we're frustrated and disappointed." Cooley dropped the empty yogurt carton in the wastebasket. "I don't know what to say any more than you do. I guess just repeat what we've already said."

Just then the phone rang. Unable to locate Reinhard, the switchboard operator had transferred the call to Cooley. A general practitioner in Cleveland, a community fifty miles from Houston, was calling about a thirty-one-year-old housewife who had suffered an embolism to the brain while giving birth to a stillborn child. Her EEG waves were flat, she did not respond to stimuli, and she was not able to breathe without mechanical assistance. The family had requested that she become a donor for Mr. Karp.

"There's your ten o'clock report." Cooley dialed the recovery room. "We've got a donor coming in. They'll be here in an hour."

Mr. Karp was immediately given immunosuppressive drugs in preparation for the transplant. Since these injections reduced his ability to ward off infection, Cooley ordered complete sterile procedure in attending him. They could only hope for a good tissue match.

The transplant team was scrubbed and waiting when the ambulance screamed up to the emergency entrance on the St. Luke's side. The routine examination of the donor in the recovery room was brief: the lady, whose body was permeated with amniotic fluid, had been dead for over thirty minutes.

Cooley was dejected, disappointed, and angry. He threw his cap and mask in the scrub-room wastebasket and strode off to his gallery office. Why would any physician bring in a dead body as a heart donor? But then he recalled that transplanters from Barnard on had been evasive about the exact times and natures of donors' deaths. Cooley had simply assumed that doctors and medical people everywhere knew the truth: surgeons did not wait for a donor's heart to stop. When everyone was satisfied that the brain was dead and the donor could only survive as a vegetable maintained by mechanical assists and chemicals, the still-beating heart was removed and transplanted into the recipient. It was a reality fraught with moral and ethical problems for the public and the lay press, but one which Cooley, after nineteen transplants, had answered to his own satisfaction.

A dead heart in a patient already stiffening from rigor mortis was useless. Had the attendants in the ambulance been unable to keep the woman's heart beating, or had they not known it would make a difference?

The immunosuppressive therapy on Mr. Karp was immediately discontinued. But the balance of his disease-fighting mechanism had already been upset, and for a time he would be susceptible to infection.

Mrs. Karp had checked out of the Surrey House Motel. Until better accommodations could be found in the hospital for Michael and her, they would stay in the family room. After her son was asleep, Mrs. Karp sat at the small desk there and began writing.

Reinhard left word at the switchboard that he was retiring to the leather couch in Dr. Martin's office. From all over the country on the Friday before Easter, only one donor had arrived— an unsuitable donor at that. The medical people just weren't responding. And after discussing the matter with the physician who had accompanied the dead lady, Reinhard knew why: there were undoubtedly doctors who had potential donors, but cowed by Cooley's professional status and fame, they were questioning their own judgment in calling him. It was more than indifference. For fear of criticism or seeming presumptuous, they were reluctant to take part in an event which unquestionably would affect the course of medicine.

Calls arrived from Paris, Berlin, Buenos Aires, Tokyo—but they were from newspapers and radio and television stations.

Cooley, Liotta, and a rotating group of fifty worked with Mr. Karp through the night. His vital signs remained good, although his hemoglobin was steadily decreasing and there were indications that his kidneys were not functioning properly.

Saturday, April 5

At 6:30 A.M., Dr. Cooley called Dr. Ted Cooper and gave the requested progress report on Mr. Karp. The probable effects of the immunosuppressive drugs worried Cooley, but Karp was comfortable and his condition was stable. Their main concern, as it had been since the implantation, was to find a donor and perform the second stage. Cooper seemed pleased and impressed; he would report the good news to his committee.

Mrs. Karp came to the gallery office with a plea she had written during the night. She was eager to discuss it with Dr. Cooley. He was tired. In the midst of so many problems, disappointments, and difficult decisions, he was not inclined to listen to an emotional tirade, no matter how well intentioned or effective it might prove to be. She, however, felt a personal appeal would bring a donor immediately and was eager to have her work released to the news media.

Dr. Cooley summoned Reinhard to discuss the matter with Mrs. Karp. When he arrived, Cooley slipped out of the gallery office to Dr. Martin's couch, which was still warm from Reinhard's brief sleep. Cooley had been awake for twenty-six hours.

Reinhard agreed with Mrs. Karp—her appeal should be given to the news people. Certainly it couldn't do any harm. At ten o'clock, the release went out.

Someone—somewhere—please hear my plea. A plea for a heart for my husband. I see him lying there, breathing and knowing that within his chest is a man-made implement where there should be a God-given heart. How long he can survive, one can only guess.

I cry without tears. I wait hopefully. Our children wait hopefully, and we pray.

The Lord giveth and the Lord taketh. But the Lord also gave us gifted men—such as Dr. Denton Cooley and Dr. Domingo Liotta, who are instrumental in prolonging life.

Maybe somewhere there is a gift for my husband. Please.

Later that morning at Lawrence General Hospital in Massachusetts, Mrs. Barbara Ewan sustained brain damage while undergoing electrical shock treatments for an emotional disorder.

Dr. Cooper's announcement and the progress report of the

Karp operation received wide approval from the members of the Artificial Heart Council. Perhaps this would prove to be the incentive Congress needed to appropriate more money for artificial heart programs around the country—they had been wanting to see some results. But then Cooley, someone observed, had received no federal assistance on his project.

Following the meeting, Dr. DeBakey met privately with Dr. Cooper. He said he had serious doubts as to the origin of the device Cooley had put in Mr. Karp; in fact, he was convinced that the artificial heart had been developed in his own laboratories with NHI grant money to which Cooley had no right. These were grave accusations. If DeBakey was correct, then Cooley was guilty of misconduct on a grand scale—he had, without sanction or authority, used federal money to his own ends.

Cooper was aware of the long-standing rivalry between Cooley and DeBakey and was reluctant to become involved, but before their conversation was concluded, DeBakey had persuaded Cooper to write a letter requesting the Baylor administration to investigate the matter for the National Heart Institute. Dr. DeBakey, of course, was the Baylor administration. He phoned Dr. Hebbel Hoff, associate dean for faculty and clinical affairs at Baylor, and told him to call an emergency meeting of the Baylor committee on research involving human beings.

The television stations in Houston picked up Mrs. Karp's appeal from the wire services and contacted St. Luke's with the suggestion that a personal television appearance by Mrs. Karp could be of great benefit in helping the hospital find a donor. Dr. Cooley agreed to take part.

By the time the lights and cameras were set up in the administrative conference room, Mrs. Karp was in control of herself. A producer said it would be more moving and effective if young Michael were to read it. No, definitely not. She had written the appeal and she would read it.

The preparations seemed overlong. Cooley asked to see what

she intended reading. The statement seemed too indirect and dramatic, but it was hers. If such an emotional approach would produce a donor, than his reservations were unimportant. Cooley did, however, make one alteration. In the next to last paragraph, Mrs. Karp had written, "But the Lord also gave us gifted men—such as Dr. Denton Cooley and Dr. Domingo Liotta, who are instrumental in prolonging life." Cooley marked through this, then returned the paper to Mrs. Karp, insisting with a sharp nod that the sentence be deleted.

Without knowing what had occurred, some of the newspapermen who witnessed the scene assumed that the plea had been written for Mrs. Karp and that she had been put up to delivering it. Thus, another future indictment was registered.

Following Mrs. Karp's appeal, Cooley spoke to the cameras.

"This device is not perfected to the degree that it can support human life for very long. It was an act of desperation. Yesterday, Mr. Karp was dead on the operating table. His only chance to live another hour was to have this artificial heart attached. I have done desperate things before on behalf of my patients, and I have never regretted it. If this is cause for censure or criticism, then I lay myself on the mercy of the court.

"I must say that I'm disappointed and also somewhat surprised and alarmed that we have had so little response to this plea, because I am confident there are qualified donors in this country right this moment. There is a premature discouragement about transplants, not only among the lay people, but also in the medical profession. They have tended to overlook the fact that there are outstanding results. Philip Blaiberg in South Africa. Fredi Everman of our hospital is alive almost nine months after his operation. They have ignored cases like these and concentrated on those who have lived only short periods of time. It's hard for me to be discouraged, because Fredi Everman was dead when we operated on him last year. We have patients in the hospital waiting for donors. Without transplants, they will die waiting."

The efficiency of the artificial heart had been temporarily diminished by constrictions in Mr. Karp's vascular system, and his kidney function had still not returned to normal. But there were no signs of irritation or infection. He was conversant, and his condition was officially listed as satisfactory. There was nothing to do but wait.

Cooley's energy and staying power were long since legend, so no one was surprised that, despite having slept no more than three or four hours in the past two days, he was alert and showed little sign of fatigue. But Reinhard was exhausted and felt he would be unable to coordinate a transplant if he did not soon get a few hours of uninterrupted rest. After conferring with Cooley, Reinhard dictated a list of instructions to supplement the usual transplant procedure:

"If a donor call should arrive and Dr. Cooley is out of his office, he can be contacted on his beeper [a small two-way radio Cooley wore on his belt]. Dr. Cooley will determine the feasibility of transferring the donor. Miss Opal Benage should then be notified to arrange for a nurse attendant, a medical kit, and supportive equipment for the patient en route.

"If the arrival of a donor is imminent, Dr. Arthur Beall at Methodist Hospital has requested the opportunity to use one of the lungs. Dr. Morgen, also of Methodist, needs kidneys for two patients who are awaiting transplants.

"The team leaving here to bring the donor back to Houston should carry consent forms. In the event that the next of kin is unable to accompany the donor, the forms must be executed prior to leaving the donor's hospital.

"An inquiry should be made as to the landing strip or airport nearest the hospital and whether or not a Lear Jet can land and take off there. If air-ambulance service is required, call Mr.

Charlie Smith, chief pilot of Top Hat Jet Service, located at
Wanda Hangar on the east corner of Hobby Field. Top Hat has
several aircraft but only one stretcher. If additional donors are
transported simultaneously, we can borrow a collapsible litter
from the V.A. Hospital.

"For alternative air-ambulance service, contact Aira Jet Corporation in Dallas or Air Transport Inc. In Houston, they have
a Cessna and a Beechcraft for shorter trips.

"For surface transportation of a donor in or near Houston, call
Mercy Corps. Otherwise, arrange for them to meet the air-
transported donor at Wanda Hangar.

"All bills should be sent to Henry Reinhard's office; St.
Luke's–Texas Children's and the Texas Heart Institute will assume responsibility for their payment."

At midnight, having received no response from Mrs. Karp's
appearance on television, Dr. Cooley went home and slept for
six hours.

Easter Sunday, April 6

There had been no donor calls during the night, and for the
first time since the implantation Cooley was becoming noticeably anxious. He had hoped to have a donor within twenty-four
hours. For an hour and a half, he phoned physicians, surgeons,
and medical centers around the country asking them to be alert
for donors. Most of the individuals were out of town or otherwise unavailable. The hospitals promised to help, but the situation did not look hopeful.

After hiding Easter eggs for his five daughters and seeing
them and their mother off to church, Cooley returned to the
hospital.

Latest x rays revealed a consolidation resembling pneumonia
in the lower lobe of Mr. Karp's right lung. His urine output was
dangerously low, and it was intermittently necessary to put him
on a respiratory assist. Mr. Karp's hemoglobin level had con-

tinued to fall, but he was conscious. The heart and console were maintaining an adequate blood supply. Although he was not receiving anticoagulants, there was no evidence of clotting in the artificial heart or in Karp's blood vessels.

Henry Reinhard, who had assumed the vigil after Cooley left at midnight, was removing the aluminum foil from the Easter dinner his wife had brought to the board room when Bonnie Sue Woolridge entered and asked if he could accept a call from Florida. It was Dr. John Renilla at Broward General Hospital in Fort Lauderdale.

A patient of Dr. Renilla's was bleeding profusely from a fibroid uterus. Though she had consented to surgery, as a Jehovah's witness she had refused a blood transfusion. Her hemoglobin was less than 25 percent normal. Without a transfusion, the surgeons had refused to operate. It was a stalemate. In the meantime, the woman was bleeding to death. Dr. Renilla explained that her husband, who was not a Jehovah's Witness, had said that since his wife was going to die anyway, she might as well become a donor for Mr. Karp.

The ethical problems in the proposal were myriad. Jehovah's Witnesses considered transplants a form of cannibalism and were violently opposed to them. They had, however, not spoken out against Cooley because he used sugar-water rather than blood primes in his heart-lung machines, and thus had come to be something of a savior to members of the sect who needed open-heart surgery and yet refused to accept blood.

Reinhard found Cooley in the basement cafeteria having lunch with his wife, his mother, Silvia Herring, and Robert Herring, president of the Texas Heart Institute.

"I don't think we'd better try it," Cooley said. "According to rumors from across the parking lot, we're going to have enough problems without alienating an entire religious denomination. Tell them thanks." Cooley turned to Herring. "It's odd, isn't it, when you consider how little cooperation we've had finding a donor in this country . . . and then news of the artificial heart waking up South Africa. Barnard did his fourth transplant this morning."

Cooley returned to his office and tried unsuccessfully to reach Dr. DeBakey. Unbeknown to Cooley, Dr. DeBakey's team in his absence had just transplanted a lung in Joseph A. Bunch, a San Angelo, Texas, service station manager. The announcement to the press was that Mr. Bunch was "the only living lung transplant."

At three o'clock in Lawrence, Massachusetts, after thirty hours of flat EEG waves, Mrs. Barbara Ewan's condition was declared irreversible. Her brain was dead; if the mechanical respirator was turned off, her heart would stop. The family, who had seen Mrs. Karp and Dr. Cooley on television the day before, asked Dr. Robert Lennon, a staff anesthesiologist at Lawrence General, to call Dr. Cooley. The requirements were satisfactory; total decerebration, good cardiac action, O positive blood, and consent of the next of kin. It was six thirty in Houston.

Chapter 6

The Second Stage

Following the instructions he had dictated the night before, Reinhard alerted Charlie Smith at Top Hat Jets, and, after checking with Miss Benage to be certain that the donor kit was ready, he phoned Landis Hudkins, a male, former Army nurse specialized in patient resuscitation. He requested that Carol Martincheck, the recovery room supervisor, accompany him. Hudkins and Mrs. Martincheck loaded the donor kit (which consisted of three metal tackle boxes of medications and equipment, a portable suction, a portable respirator, and five small "D" tanks of oxygen) into Reinhard's car, and he drove them to the airport.

The Lear Jet had already been cleared for a straight-line medical emergency flight and was warmed up and waiting on the taxi ramp at Wanda Hangar when they arrived. As the commercial liners from Hobby Field held their positions, Smith fired the jet down the runway and, neglecting the traffic pattern, found his compass heading for Lawrence, Massachusetts. On the way up to 45,000 feet, they caught a tailwind in the jet stream and for a while maintained a ground speed of about 850 miles per hour.

It was a beautiful, clear evening. The distant sky to their left was full of the northern lights. Winifred Wobbe, the copilot, switched on the speakers in the passenger compartment so Hudkins and Carol Martincheck could hear the checkpoint stations along their line of clearance call out course corrections and divert other aircraft in the vicinity.

At 8:45 P.M., Melvin Kirkman, the airport manager at Lawrence, received a call at home from the Federal Aviation Agency in Nashua, New Hampshire. He was given the approximate arrival of the Houston plane and was requested to have jet fuel available. Kirkman alerted Bill Seamans of Four Star Aircraft, the only establishment on the field that had jet fuel, and then left for the airport. At 11:00, Mrs. Joanne Palombi was monitoring the Nashua FAA station when Charlie Smith was given his final heading from just west of New York. The jet touched down twenty-five minutes later.

Three police cars and a Lawrence Fire Department ambulance, their red lights turning silently, waited on the dim runway apron. In the ambulance, Mrs. Barbara Ewan was being kept alive by a portable respirator. The jet approached the terminal and was met by Kirkman, who instructed Smith over his two-way car radio to follow the automobile to Four Star's ramp, where copilot Wobbe helped Bill Seamans balance the fuel load. There was only one pump.

Leaving Mrs. Martincheck in the plane to doublecheck the donor equipment, Hudkins met Dr. Robert Lennon, the referring physician, and Mrs. Ewan's three young daughters in the lounge. They had misunderstood the arrangements and were all packed for the return flight to Houston. Hudkins explained there would only be room for two passengers in addition to Mrs. Ewan. It was decided then that Mrs. Carol Burns, the one daughter of legal age, and Dr. Lennon would make the trip. Gail and Sharon would remain.

Before leaving the refueling area for the runway apron where the ambulance waited, Smith, on a routine check, traced a pressure change to an air vent in the fuselage that had accidentally filled with overflowing fuel. He quickly stopped the leak and drained the vents, avoiding certain catastrophe.

The breathing apparatuses were exchanged, and the jet with the donor aboard took off for Houston at 12:25 A.M.

Mrs. Ewan's condition was worse than Hudkins had anticipated. Her blood pressure was dangerously low, and phlegm and a discharge from her lungs were blocking the air passage in the endotracheal tube. Because of the pressurized cabin, it was impossible to control the medication by an ordinary gravity feed. Instead, Hudkins attached a three-way stopcock and syringe to the intravenous tube in Mrs. Ewan's arm, gauging the forced flow of glucose and Aramine as best he could. Aramine, a vasopressor drug, would raise the blood pressure to the vital organs by causing the smaller vessels in the extremities to constrict. Hudkins worked a foot pump on the suction as Carol Martincheck intermittently drew the phlegm from the breathing tube. Dr. Lennon attempted to assist them, but the conditions were too cramped and Hudkins asked him to sit down. Mrs. Burns looked out the window and asked questions about the aircraft and where they were. Not only had she never flown before, but this was her first trip out of Massachusetts. Dr. Lennon wrapped himself in a trenchcoat and went to sleep.

The speaker system had been a source of distraction, and shortly after leaving Lawrence, Carol Martincheck had asked Smith to switch it off, so neither she nor Hudkins knew where they were or what was happening when a quick series of mechanical rumblings from the lower fuselage was followed by a sudden and steady loss of altitude.

"What's happening, Charlie?" Hudkins called through the thick curtain that separated the cockpit from the passenger compartment.

"Nothing much," Smith said. "I'll let you know."

They had been ninety minutes out of Lawrence when a bank of red warning lights on the plane's control panel had begun to flash. From fluid loss, or whatever, the entire hydraulic system had gone out. The noises from under the plane had been Smith lowering the landing gear with the aid of a manual compressor. But the brakes and the flaps, which would have slowed the plane to a safe landing speed, were inoperable.

Smith now put out an emergency landing bulletin, alerting every airfield in the south-central United States. He then radioed ahead to Houston, where the call was relayed to Dr. Cooley at St. Luke's. Smith's plan was to attempt an emergency landing at Barksdale Air Force Base near Shreveport, Louisiana. Mrs. Ewan's blood pressure had dropped to sixty, and Hudkins and Carol Martincheck were too busy working with her to overhear the exchange with Dr. Cooley or to notice that the plane was now rapidly losing altitude.

Cooley's anxiety about Karp's worsening condition, as well as his eagerness to get Mrs. Ewan to Houston, was overwhelmed and altered by the danger facing those in the crippled jet. The copilot, Carol Martincheck and Hudkins, Charlie Smith, Dr. Lennon, and the daughter were as much his responsibility as Karp. Perhaps more so. To his mind, Mrs. Ewan was dead, unsalvageable; except for supplying organs so that others might live, she was as good as in the ground. Faced with the possible deaths of six people who played voluntary roles in the effort to save the life of one human being, Cooley wondered if Karp's life outweighed the risk to six others. Perhaps he should have allowed him to die on the operating table. Of what value was Karp's life compared to that of Carol Martincheck, a mother of three children? Cooley recalled a recent incident: an elderly man's heart had arrested. Carol was operating the controls of the electric defibrillator when a loose connection caused the charge intended for the patient's heart to reverse into her own body. She was knocked unconscious to the floor. On his knees, Cooley had worked over her until she revived. The memory was indelible, except he could not remember if the elderly patient had lived or died.

Smith knew that the landing gear on the plane was of light structure and could stand little more than the stress of a normal landing. Without the additional lift afforded by the flaps, he would have to come in fast. However, the higher the speed at which he touched down, the more runway necessary to stop the plane. The engine had no reverse thrust and the brakes were out, too. Compounding these dangers, Hudkins, who was sitting sideways on the floor at Mrs. Ewan's head, was unable to strap himself in and attend to the patient at the same time. She was on the verge of arresting, and against copilot Wobbe's advice, he refused to leave her. It was the same with Carol Martin-check, who was kneeling directly forward of the stretcher, which they had been unable to secure properly. With any violent impact, the metal frame would cut Carol in half. And she was pregnant with her fourth child.

Barksdale was a SAC base, closed to civilian aircraft. But the runway was 11,000 feet, the longest in the area, and Smith decided to risk the ire of the military rather than crash the jet on a shorter field.

The field lights were dim, marking only the outer boundaries. He lined up a straight-on approach and roared down, touching the eastern edge of the runway at nearly 200 miles per hour. At that speed, the surface was like corrugated iron, rumbling in the skin of the ship and vibrating the passengers to near numbness. In the quivering beam of his flashlight, Hudkins noticed they were more than halfway through the last small tank of oxygen. Carol Martincheck was trying to draw another syringe of Aramine. To Charlie Smith, helpless without any mechanical means to slow the plane, it seemed they would roll until they dropped off the edge of the earth. Less than fifty feet from the western limit of the runway, the jet coasted to a halt.

All the living were unhurt. But Hudkins, unable to raise Mrs. Ewan's blood pressure, was switching from Aramine to Levophed, a more powerful vasopressor. They must have more oxygen within the next five minutes.

Red lights and sirens approached rapidly from the rear. Smith, expecting firetrucks and ambulances, knocked open the forward hatch to request oxygen and discovered that the plane was surrounded by jeeps, manned 50-caliber machine guns, and troops with police dogs. Suddenly spotlights from either side blinded him.

"Identify yourself," a voice on a bullhorn sounded.

Smith shouted who he was, that this was an emergency landing on a medical emergency flight.

"Follow the jeep in front of you. Move the damn thing off the runway fast, and don't get out of the plane."

When the officer in charge saw the patient and was satisfied they were on a medical mission, he instructed one of his men to bring five full "D" tanks of oxygen from the ambulance to exchange with Hudkins. He said they had risked their lives interrupting a highly secret military exercise, but he did not elaborate further.

Fifteen minutes later, a second Lear jet arrived from Houston, Mrs. Ewan was transferred, and the journey continued.

At 4:30 A.M. they were met at Wanda Hangar by three Mercy Corps ambulances and the klieg lights and cameras of an NBC television crew. Despite the more powerful medication and an abundance of oxygen, Mrs. Ewan's lungs were congesting and her blood pressure had once again fallen off. She was moved to the ambulance. Mrs. Burns sat with the driver. Hudkins, Carol Martincheck, and Dr. Lennon rode in the back with the patient.

Following a near accident during ambulance transportation of an earlier donor, Hudkins had been told not to declare an all-out emergency unless it was absolutely necessary. But Mrs. Ewan's condition was sufficiently critical to warrant one last risk. Flanked by the other two ambulances, red lights flashing, they screamed down the freeway at ninety miles an hour. At the second five-minute interval when Hudkins checked Mrs. Ewan's blood pressure, there was nothing. He pressed her femoral and carotid arteries but could find no pulse. Her heart had stopped. Quickly Carol Martincheck straddled the stretcher and began giving external heart massage. Hudkins, holding the respirator and the suction, stood at an unsteady angle and worked the foot pump, while Dr. Lennon tried to find syringes of sodium bicarbonate and adrenaline.

"Hurry up," Hudkins yelled.

Dr. Lennon, who had been angry from the beginning of the flight when they had asked him to move away from the patient, gave Hudkins a cold glance and continued searching.

Just then, the ambulance reached an interchange and skidded into a sharp turn. Hudkins was thrown against Carol Martincheck. Her back was wrenched between the force of his body and the side of the ambulance. He struck his head on the window molding and lost his glasses. But they recovered quickly and resumed their positions. Dr. Lennon found the syringes. In less than a minute, they had Mrs. Ewan's heart beating again.

They entered the emergency room—Carol Martincheck holding the glucose and Levophed bottles, as Hudkins, walking quickly beside the stretcher, continued massaging Mrs. Ewan's heart. The attendants attached another respirator.

"Where is Dr. Cooley?" Dr. Lennon asked a nurse. "I want to see Dr. Cooley immediately."

"You'll *see* one of his residents," Hudkins said. "He's waiting for this transplant, which I'm satisfied is more important than whatever you have to say to him."

Standing in the doorway just past Dr. Lennon, his face strained with eagerness, stood Mr. Karp's son Michael.

"Get that kid out of here," Hudkins yelled, then mumbled "For Godsake, this isn't a meat market."

Three of Cooley's Texas Heart Institute fellows arrived and, with Landis and Carol Martincheck, took Mrs. Ewan to the third-floor recovery room. Cooley met them there. The relief and gratitude he felt were profound but brief. Everyone was quickly busy with preparations. And the familiar ambiguous feeling which occasioned each transplant the Cooley team performed came over the room: it was the sad hopefulness of losing one life to save another. No one spoke more than was necessary.

As soon as the tissue matching and neurological examination were completed, Karp was started on immunosuppressive drugs and Mrs. Ewan was moved to the table in OR Two. At 7:00 A.M. the replacement of the mechanical heart with the heart of a human donor began.

Dr. Grady Hallman moved his scalpel down Mrs. Ewan's chest and prepared for the removal of her heart.

Dr. Denton Cooley: "Mr. Karp's incisions had not yet healed, so opening him was a matter of clipping the wires that held his sternum together and then taking out the inside stitches. I suctioned off some thrombus material from around the device and cannulated the cava vessels and the femoral artery for the heart-lung machine. The attachment surfaces of the artificial heart had been designed in such a way that I had only to cut out the sutures to perform what amounted to a conventional transplant.

"We went on full by-pass and switched off the carbon dioxide from the console. Then I called to Grady that we were ready, and he brought over the donor heart from Two—it was in a steel basin covered with a damp surgical towel. I took out the artificial heart, a chamber at a time, and put it on the table. I then trimmed the donor heart and removed the old suture lines from Karp. After that, it was simply a matter of sewing the new heart in place. A continuous suture. End-to-end connections of the pulmonary artery and the aorta. I removed the aorta clamp, and the heart began to fibrillate. One countershock and it went into regular rhythm. We removed the cannulae and closed.

"Karp had been too long on the heart-lung machine during the first operation, then the premature immunosuppressive therapy when we thought we had a suitable donor coming from Cleveland, followed by more than sixty hours on the artificial heart and a transplant. He had been through a lot. From there, I only knew we had a chance."

That morning at eight thirty, Dr. DeBakey phoned Jerry Maley from his surgical suite at Methodist. Maley had been expecting the call.

DeBakey asked where Liotta was.

Maley said he wasn't sure but he thought Liotta was at St. Luke's.

DeBakey ordered Maley to remove everything from the laboratory where Liotta had been working. Plastics, molds, valves, grafts, files, pictures, notebooks—everything. He said to clean it out, to lock the laboratory and see to it that no one entered there—particularly Liotta and . . . Cooley. Then De-Bakey told Maley to get Liotta in his office as soon as possible. DeBakey hung up.

Less than an hour after the transplant, Mr. Karp regained consciousness. His urinary function was seriously depressed, and further x rays indicated that the localized area in his right lung had increased in density. The donor heart was working well. Dr. Cooley phoned the report to Dr. Ted Cooper, who was relieved that a donor had finally been found. He was favorably impressed that Karp had been kept alive by an artificial heart for so long. No one would have believed it possible.

Mrs. Karp and Michael met with Dr. Lennon and Mrs. Burns. She was distressed at the death of Mrs. Ewan but hopeful that her husband now had a chance to live. "We have died over and over again with my husband during the past few years. Just to know that he's alive because he wants to live makes me happy. The doctors in Chicago told me he would be an invalid the rest of his life, but I felt since I had him with me why take a chance on something else. He talked me into it. He wanted to live like a man, not lie there as a vegetable. It was his decision."

Jerry Maley: "While he was waiting for Dr. DeBakey to arrive, Dr. Liotta told me the story of how he and Dr. Cooley had gotten together to develop the artificial heart. He said no one in the lab was guilty of mistrust and that if there was going to be trouble, as there apparently was going to be, he would accept all responsibility. Whatever Dr. DeBakey wanted him to do was now all right. They had made the heart, and it had worked. That was most important to him. Then Dr. DeBakey appeared and they went into the office."

Tuesday, April 8

Thirty-two hours after the transplant, Mr. Karp's pressure dropped and his lungs began to fail. Eight surgeons, including Cooley, worked over him for thirty minutes, but to no avail. Cooley looked up to Reinhard, who was watching from the gallery, and slowly shook his head. Together they went to the family room to see Mrs. Karp.

She was broken and anguished. She wept, and wondered if she had done the right thing. Dr. Cooley reassured her that they had grabbed at the only hope there had been. Cooley was visibly moved by the situation. Among his colleagues he was known as a compassionate man, but with an amazing ability to shift gears and tear away from tragedy and the inaction it imposes.

When Cooley was satisfied that he had done all he could do to console Mrs. Karp, he left her with Rabbi Whitkin. In the corridor, Reinhard remarked that the fruits of their labors were arriving late; while Cooley and the others had been trying to resuscitate Mr. Karp, word was received that three donors were on the way. To Reinhard it was incredible. Cooley's entire countenance changed. "Let's get on it, Hank," he said enthusiastically. "Let's get something done!"

Meanwhile, committees were forming in Houston, Chicago, and Washington. One of the most publicized investigations in the history of American medicine was about to take place. Besides the prestige and reputation of Dr. Cooley, some traditional foundations of the profession were on the line: the validity of institutional protocol, the guidelines of research and federal control, and the moral-ethical obligations of a physician to his patient.

Part Two

Chapter 7

The Blalock Influence

Alfred Blalock was born in Culloden, Georgia, the son of a prosperous merchant, and, like Denton Cooley, was named after an uncle who was a bank president. He was a bright, ambitious young man, but his grades as an undergraduate at the University of Georgia suffered because of his involvement in extracurricular activities. Blalock had a reputation as a ladies' man and a party boy who played tournament-caliber tennis. Despite his unremarkable scholastic record at Georgia, through persuasion and presumption he managed to get admitted at the age of nineteen to Johns Hopkins Medical School in the fall of 1919.

At Hopkins, Blalock earned the bulk of his expenses by managing the student bookstore. True to his earlier form, he made average grades and passed what appeared to be an inordinate amount of time playing tennis and golf and dating socialites at nearby Goucher College. Because the coveted surgical internships at Hopkins were awarded on the basis of class standing, Blalock failed to get an appointment and instead accepted a less desirable position as house medical officer in urology.

Blalock was profoundly disappointed. Unable to overcome what he considered the disgrace of having missed a surgical residency, after three years of postgraduate work at Hopkins, he accepted a surgical professorship at Vanderbilt University Hospital in Nashville, Tennessee. Later he summarized his feeling at the time: "I thought I was finished, going down there to that school in the backwoods."

Though an average surgeon, Blalock was unusually diligent and perceptive, and he had an amazing ability to distinguish the important elements of a complex clinical problem. At Vanderbilt, he became principally interested in research.

After two years of intense laboratory work, Blalock contracted tuberculosis. While he was confined to a sanatorium, with the help of a former colleague, he published the first definitive paper on shock. His theories were to save countless lives during World War II.

On returning to Vanderbilt, Blalock became interested in the complexities of cardiac output. His method was to think through a problem, theorize some possible solutions, and then prove or disprove his conclusions in the dog lab. His closest associate was Vivien Thomas, a young Negro whom Blalock had trained in experimental laboratory procedures. As a research team, Blalock and Thomas were unbeatable. Among the many experiments they performed was one in which lobes were removed from the lungs of a dog in order to reduce the oxygen saturation of the blood flowing from the heart; then the blood was rerouted in order to counteract the condition they had created. Though they had nothing of the sort in mind at the time, this experiment laid the groundwork for the first blue-baby operation five years later.

Blalock was a prodigious worker, a Southern gentleman who was considerate to his subordinates and sympathetic with students. In contrast to him, Dr. Barney Brooks, the chief of surgery at Vanderbilt, was a severe, sarcastic man. Brooks continuously forbade Blalock to attempt innovative operations and rigidly controlled all of Blalock's activities.

In 1941, Blalock accepted the chairmanship of the Department of Surgery at Johns Hopkins. In a letter to Dr. Edward Churchill, Brooks admitted that he had wanted the position for himself and in a postscript added that Blalock was "too much disposed to outside activities and diplomacy." It was an interesting coincidence that Denton Cooley, who was to learn much of his social style from Dr. Blalock, would encounter just such an antagonist at a major turning point in his own career.

Over considerable opposition from the staff at Hopkins, Blalock revamped the surgical residency program. Mindful that he had once been denied a position in the program because of his low class standing, he began looking for well-rounded men who were capable of more than scholarly competition. It was no secret that Blalock hero-worshiped athletes.

It was a Saturday morning in the spring of 1944. Cooley, who had been at Hopkins only a few weeks,* was on his way to a morning lab, when he met Les Persky, a classmate. Because it was a beautiful day, they decided to skip lab in favor of a few sets of tennis on the Quadrangle courts. At eleven o'clock, Dr. Blalock and his entourage of assistants walked by the courts on their way to Harriet Lane Home, the children's hospital. Cooley was afraid Blalock had recognized him and that he would be in trouble for neglecting his studies, but since the group had

---

*After finishing his undergraduate degree, Cooley had entered The University of Texas College of Medicine at Galveston. Midway through his second year there a Texas Congressman had brought a charge of communism against Dr. Arnold Smith, dean of the medical school faculty. Professors and students were split in their allegiances and there were open physical conflicts. Eventually, the Texas Rangers, replete with sidearms and riot paraphernalia, were brought to the campus to maintain order.

Disputes among the faculty were fierce; there were resignations and recriminations. Total chaos seemed inevitable. Anticipating a loss of the school's academic accreditation, Cooley applied to Harvard, Johns Hopkins and Duke. Hopkins accepted him immediately, and Cooley decided to go to Baltimore.

moved on they continued their game. Twenty minutes later, Dr. Blalock returned without his assistants. He sat down on the grass directly opposite Cooley, screwed a cigarette into an ebony holder, and watched the match. Convinced now that he was in trouble, Cooley bore down, pretending not to notice his observer, and played the quickest and best tennis he was capable of. After taking three straight sets from Persky, Cooley was happy to give up the court to a group who had been waiting to play doubles. He had grabbed his press and a can of balls and rushed toward the residence hall, when he heard Dr. Blalock call to him in a soft, Southern drawl.

Rather than reprimand Cooley for his absence from the lab, Dr. Blalock complimented him on his serve, his strong backhand, and the over-all aggressiveness of his style. Cooley was flabbergasted. He looked for Persky, but Persky was gone. "I assume," Dr. Blalock said, "that a young man who plays such a powerful game of tennis is also adept at ping-pong."

Cooley said yes, and smiled. In fact, he considered himself much better at ping-pong than at tennis.

Blalock rose and brushed off his trousers. "In that case, I'd like to invite you to spend next weekend with my family and me down on Gibson Island." And Cooley, a junior medical student, agreed.

That weekend, as soon as they arrived at the cabin on Gibson Island and unloaded the station wagon, Dr. Blalock announced that he would be ready for "that game of ping-pong" after he had changed into his sneakers. "In the meantime," he said, "why don't you make us a couple of cool drinks?"

Dr. Blalock had a reputation as a bourbon drinker, so the type of whiskey was no problem, but there was, as Cooley explained to Mrs. Blalock, a small but significant dilemma: "I don't know exactly what to do," he said. "If I mix them too weak, he'll think I'm a sissy. If I mix them too strong, he'll think I'm a toper."

Mrs. Blalock assured Cooley that he could not mix a drink too strong for the professor and suggested that he fix whatever he wished for himself.

Blalock was waiting at the ping-pong table on the front porch. Cooley, a bit anxious, handed him his drink. Dr. Blalock tasted it, hesitated, then looked at Cooley's obviously less potent portion, and then tasted it more deeply again. "Excellent," he said, and they pinged for serve.

He tried hard, but Cooley could not decorously contain himself to Dr. Blalock's advantage. The weaknesses in Blalock's game were soon apparent and he knew the competitive drive that arose in him at such times would overpower his sense of diplomacy. He won the first three games with ease, but for a while in the fourth, Blalock gave him some trouble.

"Well." Blalock rattled the ice in his glass. "You're quite as good as I thought you would be. And now if you'll let *me* fix the next drinks, we'll resume our series."

Dr. Blalock returned from the kitchen with opaque amber drinks. He tipped his glass to Denton and took a long swallow. Denton followed suit, and the game soon changed dramatically in Blalock's favor.

During the rest of the weekend, between hard-fought confrontations at golf, swimming, diving, and more ping-pong, they discussed athletics and the present and future of surgery. For the first time in his life, Cooley had met a competitive spirit as deeply ingrained as his own. Dr. Blalock's curiosity and stamina were boundless. He questioned Cooley about every aspect of his life, from his childhood through college to the way he held a ping-pong paddle. Although he was more at ease with Dr. Blalock than he usually was with anyone else, Cooley felt that he was in the presence of greatness, and he knew then he had made the right move in transferring to Johns Hopkins. By the end of the weekend, Cooley was exhausted with conversation, whiskey, and contests, but in the course of it all, Blalock had become his hero, the man to emulate, and he strongly suspected that Blalock felt positive toward him as well.

That May, Denton Cooley was inducted into the service as a member of the Army Specialty Training Program. After three months, he was automatically raised in rank from buck private to private first class. He received a small salary and full tuition, which at Hopkins was $650 per semester compared with $25 per semester at Galveston.

In August 1944, he was graduated from Johns Hopkins, tied with Dick Kiefer for first in the class. He was commissioned a second lieutenant in the Army and immediately began an accelerated postgraduate program: nine months as an intern, nine months as an assistant resident, followed by nine months as a surgical specialist. If he was lucky, he would make it through without being interrupted by a call to active duty. If he developed into the sort of surgeon he knew he was capable of becoming, he would be named chief resident under Dr. Blalock, perhaps the most coveted position of its kind in the United States.

Three months into his internship, Dr. Denton Cooley became once again the recipient of the type of good fortune that was already becoming commonplace in his career. By sheer chance, he was on Dr. Blalock's service when one of the most significant surgical procedures involving the human heart took place.

Following a routine surgical conference at Johns Hopkins in 1943, Dr. Helen Taussig, a pediatric cardiologist, asked Dr. Blalock if he had any ideas regarding a surgical correction for pulmonary stenosis in children, a malfunction of the valve between the heart and the lungs that retards the amount of blood oxygenated in the lungs, causing the victim to be cyanotic, or "blue." Dr. Blalock replied that he and Vivien Thomas had performed some dog experiments in Nashville five years previous that might possibly hold the answer. Blalock and Thomas, who had accompanied him from Nashville, began immediately to rework their Vanderbilt experiments.

For fifteen months, Dr. Blalock and his team of specialists had been working with a child who was suffering from a complex, four-lesion heart condition known as tetralogy of Fallot. The girl had a severely enlarged heart, a hole between the main chambers of the heart, a mispositioned aorta (the main artery stemming from the heart), and pulmonary stenosis—the condition about which Dr. Taussig had questioned Dr. Blalock. On being fed, the child turned vivid blue, rolled her eyes, and lost consciousness. If no remedy was found, she would soon die. The heart-lung machine was ten years in the future and there was no way of attacking the hole between the chambers in her heart or the mispositioned aorta. The dog experiments, however, convinced Dr. Blalock that the pulmonary stenosis, the primary cause of the child's blueness and tendency to lose consciousness, could be alleviated by rerouting part of her arterial blood flow. Under the circumstances he felt obliged to try.

On November 29, 1944, students and professors crowded into the double-deck observation gallery above the eighth-floor operating room in Halstead Clinic. Because there was a danger of losing the child before the operation began, Dr. Merel Harmel decided not to use a strong anesthetic and put her slowly to sleep with a diluted mixture of ether and oxygen. Dr. William Longmire, the chief resident, was first assistant. Charlotte Mitchell was the scrub nurse. After inserting an arterial needle for blood-oxygen tests, Vivien Thomas, who in the dog lab had proved himself a master at vascular suturing, stood by in the event that his advice might be needed. Dr. Denton Cooley administered fluids—he was twenty-four years old.

The tiny, pliable ribs were retracted and the pleural cavity, containing the child's atrophied lungs and small, twisted heart, was opened. Cooley had never seen anything like this—the heart and lungs seemed infinitely more complex in miniature. With the assistance of Thomas, Dr. Blalock found the subclavian artery, clamped it at its origin, and began dissecting away the tissue that clung to it. The instruments were too large and awkward—they had not been designed for this type of surgery —and Dr. Blalock's progress was hampered by the small operating field and his own irascibility. His method was direct and devoid of frills, but his impatience was constantly creating difficulties. In direct opposition to his usual gentleness, in the operating room Blalock was quarrelsome, nervous, constantly complaining about the incompetence and ignorance of his assistants. "My God," he shouted at Longmire. "Do you have any idea what you're doing? Will someone help me, please? *Please*, help me!" Cooley winced.

Using bulldog clamps fitted with rubber tubing so as not to crush the vessels, Blalock, with Thomas's help, carefully prepared a site for attaching the subclavian to the pulmonary artery. A small traverse incision was made between two clamps on the pulmonary artery then, using china beaded silk on fine needles, Dr. Blalock completed the juncture that rerouted the baby's blood. She immediately went from waxen blue to pink. Though the postoperative course was to be stormy, the first blue-baby operation was a success. Being there was a privilege, but to have taken part in the event provided Cooley with a lasting recommendation that was far more important than anything Dr. Blalock could have stated on his behalf.

Dr. Helen Taussig had watched the operation from the head of the table, and as soon as it was finished, she retired to her office in the Harriet Lane Home and added new notes to those she had compiled during the diagnostic and preoperative periods. Dr. Taussig published several articles and follow-up studies on Blalock's blue-baby work, and though he gave her credit in the report of the first operation, his name was not to appear in her subsequent articles. Indeed, on numerous occasions, Dr.

Taussig went so far as to suggest that she had devised the original blue-baby technique. Concerning the controversy, in a letter to Dr. Willis Potts, Dr. Blalock wrote that a description of the pathology was hardly equivalent to its cure. "I must say that if I make a statement to you that you could improve the conditions of patients with aortic stenosis should you be able to find a means to allow more blood to reach the body, I would be far from solving the practical problem."

A month after the operation, Dr. Blalock invited Cooley to lunch in the doctors' dining room. They discussed the basketball season for a while (Cooley was playing for the student-bookstore team, the place where Dr. Blalock had worked as a medical student at Hopkins) and then the topic turned to the pretty girls with whom Blalock had seen Cooley at various parties. Blalock said he could not help but be impressed with the poise and success with which Cooley handled women—a talent that he, Blalock, had never mastered. Most of the cardiologists under Dr. Taussig were women, and Blalock admitted that he could not get along with them. He then offered Cooley a position as house officer on the heart service, with specific duties to serve as a liaison between surgery and cardiology. It was a perfect opportunity to correlate diagnostics with surgical correction, so Cooley accepted. He proved so successful at keeping Dr. Taussig and her group away from surgery that at the beginning of Cooley's second postgraduate training phase he was named as Dr. Blalock's first assistant, a position that was ordinarily held by older, more experienced men.

As an intern, Cooley's opportunities to take part in important operations were relatively few, but his technical skill and calm control, his speed and thoroughness, soon came to the attention of the entire medical school. Destiny, however, had not yet provided him with the opportunity to establish his special importance. One Saturday afternoon during the Christmas season of 1945, that opportunity came.

Dr. Cooley, still an intern, was checking charts on the private service when a nurse called his attention to a male patient who was in a state of distress. The man's pulse was weak and rapid, he was extremely pallid, and was semicomatose and laboring for breath. Ten days earlier, the patient had undergone surgery for a malignant tumor of the sternal cartilages. Dr. Grant Ward, a senior surgeon on the staff, had removed and replaced his breastbone with a stellite vitallium graft; there had been no complications or excessive bleeding. But now the patient appeared to be in severe blood-loss shock.

A stat analysis confirmed Cooley's diagnosis, and on the assumption that over an extended period a small bleeder had been causing the trouble, Cooley ordered a transfusion and had the patient prepared for an emergency exploratory operation. Then he contacted Dr. Grant Ward, who agreed that it was probably nothing too serious.

Cooley and a medical student who happened to be on the floor assisted Dr. Ward in opening the patient. Everything looked all right. But when Cooley and Dr. Ward detached and removed the artificial breastbone, the patient's chest cavity erupted with a gush of blood. Cooley quickly stuck two suckers in the wound, but the chest continued to fill. Whatever was wrong, it was not a small bleeder. They began to sponge as fast as they could. Dr. Ward called for a towel, and then Cooley discovered the source. The metal breastbone had rubbed against the patient's aorta, causing a ballooning weakness in the vessel, a mechanically induced aneurysm. When they opened the chest and relieved the clot compression, the artery had burst, and now the rupture was widening with each thrust of blood.

Before Cooley could say anything, Dr. Ward jammed his finger in the rupture, reducing the blood loss but immobilizing himself as well. Dr. Ward suffered from ulcerative colitis and severe phlebitis that made it difficult for him to stand at the table, and two years earlier he had been operated on for a spinal cord tumor. As a result, the extensor muscles in his left shoulder had been paralyzed. His left arm was now crooked up and out in an aluminum airplane sling and was virtually useless. In a simple operation, he could get by with one hand—but this was not now the case. Dr. Ward was obliged to remain where he was. Meanwhile the patient was bleeding to death.

Without hesitating, Cooley quickly cut a sliver of muscle from the patient's chest, fitted it to the rupture, and began to sew it like a patch over Dr. Ward's finger. When he had attached most of the perimeter, Cooley nodded, Dr. Ward jerked his finger free, and Cooley quickly finished the suture line. But what should they do now?

Dr. Ward was physically incapable of resuming the lead, and it was anybody's guess where to go from here. Since the repair procedure had been successful so far, Cooley was eager to continue. Dr. Ward told him to go ahead.

Under such terrific and constant pressure, the muscle patch would soon give way. An aneurysm could be wrapped with cellophane or wire mesh, but this was a ruptured aortic aneurysm, a deadly tear in the body's main vessel. Such a repair had never before been successfully attempted.

Dr. Ward asked Cooley what he would do if the patient were his—it was not a rhetorical question. Cooley hesitated, looked at the pulsing patch, then replied matter-of-factly, "I believe I would put a clamp on the side of the aorta at the base of the rupture and then oversew all of it."

"Go ahead," Dr. Ward said.

His left arm arrested in that strange, flat salute, Dr. Ward assisted the young intern sew the patched aneurysm to the wall of the aorta.

The patient recovered. The operation was Dr. Denton Cooley's first "first," and his finest performance to date. From Blalock through the medical school faculty and the hospital staff, everyone was pleased. They had expected great things from Cooley; the sole surprise was that he had devised an operation of such far-reaching significance so early in his career. Cooley considered himself lucky to have been with Ward when he was needed, but he was neither surprised nor particularly proud of his performance: several months previous he had concluded that he was the equal of any surgeon at Hopkins, including Blalock, and superior to most. He had needed an opportunity to prove it.

Although Cooley was privately critical of Dr. Blalock's operating style and his habit of abusing his surgical assistants, he was favorably impressed with the man's fairness and his enthusiasm for whatever his students or subordinates accomplished. He was honored to be one of Blalock's "boys"—which, incidentally, came to include some of the finest heart surgeons in the world —and he did whatever he could to unobtrusively impress him. But for Cooley, both his private and professional admiration for Blalock would be tested.

Like Blalock, Cooley enjoyed parties. He liked to drink, but unless he saw the next day was free of responsibilities, he was moderate. However, during a series of parties one Saturday night in the early spring of 1945, the good times made inroads on his judgment and, mixing grape juice and ethyl alcohol punch with bourbon and beer, he got very drunk.

The following morning, he was unable to get out of bed. Jim Davis, his roommate, brought him some orange juice, but he couldn't keep it down. Then he tried a milkshake, but he threw that up, too. Somehow he managed to get dressed and make it to Halstead Library for the meeting that always preceded Sunday morning rounds.

After reviewing some of the cases they would visit, Dr. Blalock called Cooley aside and told him he was looking forward to seeing the basketball game between the student bookstore and the Knights of Columbus that evening. Cooley, who could barely stand, said it would not be much of a game, that Dr. Blalock should wait and come when they were up against stiffer competition.

"That may be," Blalock said. "But I have been trying all year to get Dr. Bard and Dr. Woods to come and see you play, and tonight is the only time we'll be able to get together."

Cooley was on a spot. Dr. Blalock seldom asked a favor of him, and then Dr. Bard and Dr. Wood were influential men. Cooley was in no condition to walk, much less play a game of basketball, but he forced a smile and nodded.

"Don't disappoint us now!" Dr. Blalock added.

Fifteen minutes into rounds, Cooley broke into a cold sweat and had to return to his room. He tried some more orange juice, but it was no use. He couldn't sleep, either. Finally, in desperation, he called Jim Davis, who was interning in the Women's Clinic, and asked if he could come over for an intravenous booster.

After receiving a liter and half of glucose and saline in the treatment room, he felt a little better, but not much. On standing, a wave of dizziness had him momentarily off balance, but he recovered, gathered up his gear, and met the team in front of the statue of Jesus in the main lobby of the hospital. Someone remarked that he looked rather pale, and he blushed himself back to an appearance of health.

The game was in Holy Martyrs Hall, but at the time Cooley was too diminished to appreciate the irony. The team came out on the floor. There was Dr. Blalock and his friends, sitting midway up in the middle of the bleachers, acknowledging Denton with smiles and reserved nods.

The mouthful of paregoric he had swallowed in the locker room had eased his stomach cramps, but he still felt abstracted and out of control. Pretending to work with a malfunctioning shoelace, he managed to avoid warm-ups. He considered faking a charley horse or even a heart attack.

He got the jump, and a warm wave of confidence came over him. His body began to obey him, and then his reflexes began to revive. The Knights of Columbus were tougher than he had expected, particularly under the boards. After the first quarter, he knew he would make it. And after the first half, when his team was eight points behind, to the exclusion of noticing the residue of his hangover or even Blalock and his guests, Cooley focused all his attention on getting the ball through the hoop.

When the final buzzer sounded, the physical horrors that had been held at bay by his determination engulfed him. His stomach turned over. His body was shaken with chills and fever. He had scored forty-two points.

Suddenly Dr. Blalock, flanked by his friends, was shaking Cooley's hand. "Well, Denton," he said, "it was an All-American performance. I don't see how you do it with the hours you have to keep, but I must say you're the finest physical specimen I've seen in a long time."

As they walked away, Cooley thought that it isn't necessary for a surgeon to be a diagnostician.

Following the aneurysm repair with Dr. Ward, Cooley was given more cases than he ordinarily would have received as an intern. He was in subtle competition with every surgeon with whom he worked, yet he was not so confident that he was unwilling to learn. Besides integrating the technical tricks of others in his own evolving style, he profited from their mistakes. It seemed to him that many surgeons, including Dr. Blalock, allowed tension and doubt to interfere with their work. The stereotyped surgeon's ego display, for example, the ranting and raving, did nothing but upset the operating team, distracting them from the operation they were there to assist. Cooley was a rare item: with no less an ego than anyone else, he was able to turn his energy inward and refocus it on the anatomical problem. During an operation he was detached, almost devoid of emotion. He developed mental blinders to everything but the few square inches of diseased flesh before him. It was the same approach he used to defeat his opponents at ping-pong, the same purposely limited vision that had enabled him to transcend a debilitating hangover and score forty-two points against the Knights of Columbus. And as important as the efficiency of his method was the sheer speed that occasioned it. He was clearly the deftest surgeon at Hopkins, yet he never seemed to hurry.

As a basketball star in high school and college, Cooley had been a favorite of the Houston newspapers. He was tall, quietly confident, athletic, brilliant, and unabashedly chauvinistic toward the Lone Star state. He continued to be mentioned in the sports pages for his city-league exploits in Galveston and Baltimore, but when the word got around that as Dr. Blalock's fair-haired boy he had assisted in the first blue-baby operation, his value in column inches increased considerably.

In the fall of 1945, Gaylord Gilliam, the infant son of a Houston war hero, was found to be suffering from tetralogy of Fallot, and the people of Houston contributed enough money to send the child and his family to Johns Hopkins. Aware of the hometown pride for Cooley and the fact that he planned to return there eventually, Blalock arranged for Cooley to operate on the Gilliam infant. The surgery, described by one Houston paper as "more difficult than the classical operation usually performed," was a success. Next to a picture of the angelic Gilliam child was a photograph of Cooley in his San Jacinto High School basketball uniform, looking determinedly in the direction of the goal and, incidentally, of heaven.

It was the first in a long series of Houston newspaper pieces that, heavily spread with references to God and Christ, would report Cooley's future accomplishments. From the outset, this sort of publicity presented Cooley with a dilemma. While he appeared politely indifferent to public acclaim, he had always thrived on recognition. But he did not appreciate the Texas canonization. Regarding his accomplishments in surgery, only his peers, he thought, had sufficient understanding to make meaningful comments.

After reading the article on the Gilliam child, Dr. Blalock told Cooley he understood that in Houston they referred to the Blalock-Taussig procedure as "the Cooley operation." Houston had already begun to consider Dr. Denton Cooley as a natural resource.

Cooley's plans for the third phase of his training program at Hopkins were interrupted by a call to active duty in February 1946. He was twenty-five years old, and though he had never removed a gall bladder, he was already a maturing heart surgeon. The challenge of going into general surgery with little practical experience did not bother him.

A doctor in the service usually considers his tenure a period of enforced inactivity, but for Cooley, who had come so far so quickly, the waste of two years was unthinkable. There was no guarantee he would be allowed to operate, so he asked Dr. Blalock to help him secure an assignment where he would be able to continue his heart surgery. Blalock said he was acquainted with a man in the Surgeon General's office, a surgeon from Cooley's part of the country who, from all evidence, exerted considerable influence in these matters. Dr. Blalock wrote a letter of recommendation, suggesting the type of position he thought Cooley was best suited for. Something at Walter Reed, maybe. Three days later, a letter of introduction in the pocket of his uniform, Cooley went to Washington.

At a time of day when most military doctors would have been thumbing through magazines waiting for the cocktail hour, Cooley found his man surrounded by stacks of reference books, busy at work on a medical history of World War II. Cooley recognized him immediately. They had met before. In fact, Dr. Blalock had introduced them in Atlanta at the Society of Vascular Surgery convention. He was a lung cancer specialist from Ochsner Clinic in New Orleans.

They shook hands—the man behind the desk did not get up —then Cooley handed him the letter. He looked at the letter briefly, then at Cooley. He said he would keep him in mind if anything came up. "I'll think about it," he said, and went back to work on his manuscript.

At the end of the training period at Brooke Army Medical Center in San Antonio, where, in four weeks, doctors were taught to be soldiers, Cooley's orders came through: not only had he failed to get an assignment at Walter Reed, he was being shipped to an outpost hospital in Linz, Austria—Hitler's hometown.

Cooley had guessed that the man in the Surgeon General's office had tossed his letter and his hope in the waste basket, and now he was convinced of it. The man in Washington, executive officer to Surgeon General Kirk, the man who might have helped, was Colonel Michael E. DeBakey. It had been a fitting prologue to the problems they were to have in the future.

Before leaving Brooke, Cooley and Jim Davis, his roommate from Hopkins, stretched weekend passes to five days of swimming and partying at Cooley's father's summer place on Lake Travis. They were reprimanded when they arrived back at the base, but because none of the professional military people took the doctors seriously, the matter was dropped.

The next stop was a staging area at Camp Kilmer, New Jersey. Once again bored with sitting around, Cooley and Davis spent a weekend partying in New York and, once again, they overstayed their passes. They wandered in at four o'clock Monday morning and found everyone in the barracks packing. Their orders had come through; the medical group was shipping out for Bremerhaven in two hours.

Cooley boarded the S.S. *Wheaton Victory* carrying his tennis racket, a dufflebag over one shoulder and a golf bag over the other. The officer in charge dressed him down for being late and confined him to his quarters, where he spent the next five days, on the bottom of a six-high stack of bunks, vomiting into his helmet liner. On the sixth day, he was given a pint of glucose and taken topside. He managed to stand without assistance the day before the ship docked.

Bremerhaven was worse than Brooke and Camp Kilmer combined. Most of the city had been wiped out by Allied bombers, and what was left was dreary and depressing. As soon as Cooley had recovered from the trip over, he and Jim Davis hitchhiked to Bremen, took a suite of rooms in the Bremen Hotel, and drank and played golf for three days. When they arrived back at Bremerhaven, they discovered that their unit had boarded a troop train and departed for Stuttgart. Cooley and Davis rounded up their gear and headed for the station, but after seeing the miserable conditions on the troop trains that were being dispatched south, they bought first-class tickets on a luxury express.

At first, no one in Stuttgart had even heard of their unit, but after an hour of questioning trainmen and military police, they learned that the train they had missed had somehow by-passed Stuttgart and was lost about one hundred miles to the south. Since there was nothing to do but wait, Cooley and Davis checked into the officers' club and initiated a two-day party. Davis remarked that this had been typical of Cooley's thoroughness and luck: his screw-ups were as brilliant as his accomplishments. Cooley arrived in Linz three days late.

The surgical staff at the 124th Station Hospital welcomed the new doctor with beer and wines, Wiener schnitzel, gulas, and frankfurters. According to the scale ratings and ranks, Cooley had the lowest priority on the staff, but the war was over and the doctors there were ready to go home. Consequently, his first day on duty Cooley was appointed chief of surgery by the senior officer, Dr. John Beall. Cooley, of course, had done little routine surgery and it was very unlikely that he would be operating on any blue babies over here, but he accepted the position anyway. At twenty-five, he was to run the operating rooms in a 750-bed hospital, the sole medical facility for a military base of 10,000 people.

Cooley discovered that the facility was not as elaborate as it had first appeared. Since the end of the war, staff and equipment had been cut back so the hospital was equipped for little more than advanced first aid. Most of the doctors who remained were interested more in getting home than in establishing a first-rate medical installation. Among the many discouragements to Lieutenant Cooley, the bleakest was the absence of an anesthesiologist, and for that reason all major surgery had to be referred to Vienna or Munich. But he soon remedied this.

After training a nurse to monitor patients, Cooley began performing routine abdominal operations under locals and spinals. If it was an operation with which he was not familiar, he went to the medical library and read up on the surgical procedure. A month after Cooley arrived, his urologist, who had been fighting a losing battle against VD and chronic prostatitis among the troops, left. Since no one else wanted the assignment, his duties were transferred to Cooley. In time, he became chief of obstetrics and gynecology, chief of orthopedics, head of physical therapy, and coach of the softball team.

Cooley's off-duty activities were equally expansive. Bartering with cigarettes and Meissen china, he managed to get transferred from his regular billet near the Weissenwalstrasse to an apartment in the Villa Guglhof, an elegant private estate that had been converted into an officers' club. There was breakfast in bed, a bar, and a string quartet at lunch and dinner. The chef had been in charge of the kitchens on the luxury liner *Normandy* and was a master at liberating pheasant and venison from the surrounding countryside.

Since the occupation, it had been difficult to secure transportation, but on a tip from an Austrian employee at the PX, Cooley fortuitously attended a surplus auction and picked up a jeep for $170. For two cartons of cigarettes, he had it fitted with summer and winter tops and Mercedes seats. Lieutenant Cooley bartered for most of the goods and services he received. His net pay was $215 per month, $212 of which was deposited in his Houston bank. With the remaining three dollars, he bought PX rations that brought in over one hundred American dollars.

The same afternoon he performed his first brain operation (a depressed skull fracture with a subdural blood clot), Cooley received a call from a Red Cross girl who had transferred to Linz after meeting him in Vienna. The canteen manager was preparing to throw away 134 cartons of stale, water-stained cigarettes. She wanted to know if Cooley was interested.

Cooley counted on the border guards assuming that a jeep so beautifully outfitted belonged to an important military personage. He was right—they moved through customs with ease, the cigarettes cached under the hood. "They're not Lucky Strikes, but they're toasted," Cooley said. In fact, the very brand was suspect, "Virginia Cigarettes."

After arriving in Rome, Cooley and Jim Davis soon located the alley where a number of the 124th Station Hospital personnel had fallen victim to thieves and swindlers. Prices were even better here than in Austria. After unloading the cigarettes, the two men visited Naples and Capri; there and in palazzo apartments in Florence and Venice, they returned their profits to the Italian economy.

Befriended by an impoverished count who had a villa on the Danube north of Linz, Cooley gained access to the private game parks in the countryside, and he skied the mountains and fished the lakes. He toured the Continent, representing the Austrian Theater in tennis doubles, and he was high-scorer for the All-Austrian basketball team. Whenever athletics took him to a major city or a university center, he presented his credentials to the chief surgeon and assisted in operations. He spent six weeks with Dr. Finsterer, the world-famed gastro-surgeon at the Allgemeiner Krankenhaus in Vienna. During that time Cooley learned Finsterer's tailorlike suturing techniques and began to develop his own talent for procedural economy. He also made a study of the residency program at Vienna. The original idea of gathering specialist trainees around a master surgeon had been initiated there by Theodor Billroth in 1880. Dr. John Halstead, who had studied in Vienna, started the first postgraduate residency program in the United States at Johns Hopkins. Dr. Blalock had modified and refined the idea. The chain of influence was interesting. Cooley began to consider the future—the sort of setup he would like when he was finally out and on his own.

During Cooley's absence, an exchange had been arranged between Johns Hopkins and Guy's Hospital in London, where some of the most outstanding heart and lung surgery was being performed. Dr. Blalock was first on the program. Before visiting Guy's, Dr. Blalock made a triumphant tour of Europe demonstrating the Blalock-Taussig blue-baby operation. Henry Bahnson, a junior assistant resident on the heart service, accompanied him.

Lord Brock, director of the Royal College of Surgeons: "Intense interest had already been aroused throughout Great Britain by the reports of Dr. Blalock's successful work on previously hopeless cases of cyanotic heart disease, and everyone was eager to see and hear him. There are two notable occasions that must be unforgettable to anyone who was present.

"The first was when he and Dr. Helen Taussig gave a combined lecture in the Great Hall of the British Medical Association. Dr. Taussig delivered her address impeccably and was followed by Dr. Blalock, who presented his surgical contribution with his characteristic, apparently casual drawl, but really it was a forceful and incisive presentation of his brilliant and impressive results. The silence of the audience betokened their rapt attention and appreciation. The hall was quite dark for projection of his slides, which had been illustrating patients before and after operation, when suddenly a long searchlight beam traversed the whole length of the hall and unerringly picked out on the platform a Guy's nursing sister, dressed in her attractive blue uniform, sitting on a chair and holding a small cherublike girl of two-and-a-half years with a halo of blond, curly hair and looking pink and well; she had been operated on at Guy's by Blalock a week earlier. The effect was dramatic and theatrical, and the applause from the audience was tumultuous. It was a Madonna-like tableau on an epoch-making contribution and left nothing more to be said by the lecturer.

"Dr. Blalock's clinical and operative sessions at Guy's were equally popular and impressive. He had brought Dr. Hank Bahnson with him as his first assistant, and together they operated on ten patients with Fallot's tetralogy. Success was complete.

". . . the outstanding important result of his visit was the firm introduction and launching of his operation in Great Britain and the Continent, acceptance of the immense possibilities of surgery in the alleviation of congenital heart disease in centers previously unconvinced and reluctant."

It was the same in Paris and Stockholm. The low-key lectures and highly dramatic patient presentations brought Blalock and Bahnson acclaim wherever they went. The tour changed the course of cardiac surgery in Europe and, ultimately, around the world.

On this occasion Cooley had failed to take advantage of his

uncanny proclivity for being in the right place at the right time. Prior to leaving for Europe, Blalock had written Cooley and asked him to meet him in London and participate in the surgery. Cooley mulled over the invitation. He wanted to see Blalock, and some heart work would be a welcome change, but he would be returning to Hopkins soon and there would be time for all that. Besides, Cooley had been looking forward to competing in the tennis championships at Bremen—there would be a conflict. So Cooley gratefully declined, thus missing what he came to regard as "the greatest professional opportunity of my life." He felt he could have made his reputation in Europe because Dr. Blalock would have sung his praises and presented him with an opportunity to display his ability. Not only was Cooley convinced that he was quicker and more dexterous than anyone he had seen operate, he felt that the most noted surgeons in Europe would have recognized as much on watching him work.

Following the tennis championships in Bremen, Cooley returned to Linz and his hospital routine somewhat subdued by what he had read about Blalock's surgical exploits.

He had become interested in the surgical vistas opened by battle-field emergencies. Prior to the war, most of the advances in cardiac surgery had been deliberate experiments concerned, as in the blue-baby operation, with the vessels surrounding the heart; no one who had a choice would dare stick a scalpel in the cardiac muscle. But battle wounds necessitated radical operations, and it was soon proved that the heart was not so inviolable as everyone had thought. Over a ten-month period at the 160th General Hospital in southern England, Dr. Dwight Harken, an American, successfully removed 134 pieces of shrapnel from the hearts of soldiers wounded during the D-Day invasion. In June 1947, Dr. Charles Bailey of Philadelphia inserted his finger into a beating human heart and relieved a stenosed mitral valve. Bailey's efforts were rewarded with general censure, but the movement was on and could not be deterred by the conservatism extant in the medical profession. Harken, home from the war, soon began performing mitral valve surgery at Peter Bent Brigham Hospital in Boston. Then Brock developed a similar technique at Guy's Hospital in London. There was no doubt that direct, open-heart surgery was on the horizon, and Cooley was eager to get in on it.

Contrary to what he had anticipated, Cooley enjoyed his time in Austria. He had been determined to gain some medical experience outside his specialty, to slacken the pace he had maintained since high school, and to enjoy life. If Baltimore had broadened his interests, the European experience had lent him a social confidence and security that he had never known. He would never in his life have more freedom, and the will and energy to enjoy it. But it was time to go home.

Chapter 8

Back at Hopkins

During Cooley's two-year absence from Johns Hopkins, the cardiac load on Dr. Blalock's service had increased from a trickle to a torrent. Wartime travel restrictions had been lifted, and the success of the blue-baby operations had received wide publicity. Infant heart surgery—the pristine innocence of the patients, parental anxiety, and the intricacies of the procedures—was ready-made drama for the popular press. As a result, Johns Hopkins had been swamped with patients, visiting surgeons, and reporters. In an unusual move, Blalock opened the observation gallery and, on occasion, the operating room, to anyone who wished to learn his techniques. To some members of the press and the medical profession, this eagerness to disseminate knowledge and exhibit his expertise represented a breach of ethics and, much to his sorrow, Blalock became the object of criticism and censure from several medical societies. Then, too, there was the continuing antagonism between Blalock and Dr. Taussig. Cooley noticed that Dr. Blalock, because of his professional problems and increasingly poor health, was particularly irritable in the operating room.

Dr. Cooley began dating Louise Thomas in the fall of 1948. She was a pretty, soft-spoken blonde with an air of independence. Her father, Dr. Eddy Thomas, was a prominent surgeon in Frederick, Maryland, with wide medical, social, and political connections. Louise was head nurse on Halstead 5, the main surgical floor of the hospital. She was also Blalock's principal consultant on certain personnel matters in the surgical service. In late November, they drove to Frederick and told Louise's parents that they planned to be married. The wedding was on January 15, 1949, and was a major social occasion in that part of the country. Cooley's family and friends arrived from Houston. There were senators from Washington and surgeons from New York. At the reception at the Francis Scott Key Hotel in Frederick, Virginia professors mixed with Texas oil men, ranchers with Johns Hopkins nurses. It was a meeting of the polite South and the friendly Southwest. Later that afternoon, the newlyweds headed south for Sea Island, Georgia, in a green Chevrolet that Cooley had bought with the money he had saved from his military salary. He was twenty-nine years old.

Six months later, Denton Cooley was appointed chief resident of Dr. Blalock's service; it was his final academic goal and without question the most coveted and prestigious postgraduate surgical position in the United States. In many ways Cooley was the finest example of what had come to be known as a "Blalock hand," the formula for which was scholastic excellence and a Hopkins degree, a sharp wit, a sense of humor, athletic competence, aggressiveness, articulateness, technical facility, and a beautiful wife. Unlike many postgraduate medical programs, the Blalock residency was a competition, a contest in the classic style of mental and physical agility. What Blalock wanted, and what he certainly got in Cooley, was an athlete's coordination, drive, and discipline tempered with the judgment and knowledge of a proved scholar. Although Blalock was basically a laboratory surgeon—something that haunted him throughout his professional life—he pressed his men toward clinical rather than experimental and academic involvement. Whether Cooley naturally fit the mold or had conditioned himself to Blalock's notion of the ideal surgeon, he got the job and was to remain true to its conditions.

There were lots of staff parties where the conversation naturally ran to heart surgery and athletics. Blalock established a paternal relationship with many of his men, and there was a wistfulness in his careful concern for them, as though he was hopeful that they might succeed where he had failed. But for some reason—perhaps because of the distance Cooley had always maintained between himself and others, perhaps because Blalock, like Cooley's father, occasionally drank too much— Cooley, unlike so many others, never bent to the father-son relationship. There was gratitude and admiration, but otherwise Cooley remained kindly and politely aloof. Some explained his attitude as indicative of an incapacity for emotional involvement. Others said it was the result of a profound shyness that he had never been able to overcome and which added to his attractiveness. Whatever the explanation, the subtle lack of affection between Cooley and others allowed him to be more objective toward surgical problems. Of all the great heart surgeons Blalock was to train, Cooley was the most decisive and deft. Years later, when two of his former Hopkins colleagues sat in judgment and censured him, he was unable to understand the source of their vindictiveness. Having won the fastest-knife-in-the-West competiton, he failed to realize that according to the story he became the prime target.

Socializing and suturing were not the only areas in which Cooley had gained confidence during his time in Europe. Over the previous three years, he had become bolder and more inventive in his operating. He modified the blue-baby technique while he was still under the tutelage of its originator. A more jealous professor than Blalock would have been resentful; in-

stead, he praised Cooley's brilliance and cool authority whenever he had the opportunity. Cooley appreciated the recognition, but he thought it was his due. Cooley had always received
just recognition for what he had accomplished. Things were
soon to change.

For years following the professional rebuke of Dr. Henry
Souttar, who dared to incise a human heart, cardiac surgery in
England had lagged far behind the United States. But soon after
Blalock had achieved success and fame, Sir Russell Brock broke
the British lock-step and performed a number of daring and
ingenious operations. He developed the valvulotome, an instrument with a retractable, spade-shaped blade, to open the pulmonary valves of children suffering from tetralogy of Fallot,
and a whole range of special clamps and devices for "button-
hole" internal heart surgery. The same exchange program that
had taken Blalock to England in 1947 now, in 1949, brought
Russell Brock to Johns Hopkins.

Dr. Blalock and his staff were making presentations to a mass
meeting of the medical school when they were interrupted by
a slight commotion at the rear of the auditorium. Dr. Brock,
wearing a gray topcoat and a homburg and carrying his own
suitcase, offered a quick smile in greeting and continued down
the aisle as Dr. Blalock introduced him and invited him to give
his opinion of the case that was under consideration. Brock
dropped his suitcase and, without removing his coat or hat,
came up on the stage. He took a stethoscope from his pocket
and listened to the patient's heart. Then, with the aid of a small
pen light, he examined the patient's pharynx. He shook his
head, stepped to the x-ray screen, and measured the shadows
on the film with a pair of calipers he had produced from somewhere. "Coarctation of the aorta," he announced in an almost
incomprehensible Ox-bridge accent. "Surgical correction advised."

Following the conference, Dr. Blalock introduced Cooley to

Brock. Where Blalock was casual and candid, Brock was intense, professional, and formal. Although they were of antithetical natures, Brock was impressed with Cooley as a surgeon. They operated together regularly, and it soon became apparent to Cooley that he was a better surgeon than Brock, manually and temperamentally. Cooley had seen two or three surgeons with left hands as good as his own, but no one had a right hand his equal. But the older surgeon had been inside the human heart, and Cooley hadn't. There was something to be learned from him. Brock believed in a direct attack on the obstructed valves in blue babies; Blalock's operation was a method of circumventing the actual problem by altering the circulation of the blood. Brock had a diagnostic sense (he could recall in detail every case he had operated on over the past twenty years) and a flair for organization that Cooley lacked. Unlike Blalock, Brock was methodical and almost painfully precise.

Before returning home, Brock assured Cooley that if he wanted to do some postgraduate work in London, the door was open. Because of their friendship and the admiration Brock felt for Cooley's ability, Cooley knew he would have more prerogatives there than in any similar program in the United States. He would think about it.

In the spring, Dr. Blalock left for a two-week visiting professorship at the University of Hawaii, and Cooley took over the heart service. A few days later, a man from whom Blalock had removed a coarctation (a congenital narrowing of the aorta) was readmitted to the hospital complaining of severe chest pains. X rays disclosed a massive aneurysm of the right subclavian artery which was possibly threatening rupture. Cooley decided to go in and have a look. A few eyebrows were raised. Dr. Blalock had known about the aneurysm, but because of the high risk involved, he had left it alone and hoped that the lowering of blood pressure on the weakened artery achieved by Blalock's coarctation removal would render it harmless. Cooley thought Blalock had been too optimistic. He was right.

The wall of the pulsing artery had been eroded to paper-thinness and was ready to burst. The standard procedure would have been to wrap the ballooning aneurysm with cellophane or wire gauze, but Cooley was convinced that the least irritation would cause the artery to disintegrate in an uncontrollable hemorrhage. Cooley, who had done a complete coarctation repair before, was not advancing blindly. Improvising with instruments designed to crush rather than contain blood vessels, he clamped the threatening bulb of the artery where it connected to stronger tissue. He touched the aneurysm with the blunt end of his scalpel and it exploded like a blood-filled balloon. Then he sutured up the damage. There were no further complications; the patient's recovery was blessedly uneventful.

On returning, Dr. Blalock presented the operation to the medical and surgical staff at Johns Hopkins. He said his visit to Hawaii had been marred with worrying about this patient; he was not sure if he had done the right thing in neglecting to attempt a repair of the aneurysm. "But that just goes to show: if you are confronted by a serious surgical problem that has no proven solution, take a trip to Hawaii and your resident will handle it . . . that is, if your resident happens to be Denton Cooley!"

The end of Cooley's time at Hopkins was near, and according to a letter from his wife to his mother he was "eager to be the boss and start cutting."

It was true. The almost frivolous extent of his responsibility and authority at Linz had made it difficult for him to subordinate himself to even a man of Blalock's caliber.

He felt, nonetheless, that his training was incomplete. Brock had bent him toward the European tradition, where teaching was part of the complete surgeon's portfolio and where learning was an obligation to his patients and the continuing perfection of his art. Cooley was thirty years old, an age at which by Houston standards (the scale on which he invariably judged his progress) a man of any merit should be financially comfortable. Yet, with his token salary at Hopkins and a monthly GI Bill check, he had just enough to get by. To compound the problem, Cooley had lost none of his ambition to accumulate money, and he still felt that in the United States the index to a man's accomplishment was his income. His wife had been reared in an affluent home. But as a nurse whose father was a doctor, she knew the type of understanding and endurance that was expected of her. The fact that she was going to have a baby seemed to make her no less patient of Denton's relative penury.

There was a job waiting for him at Baylor Medical College in Houston, but he had also been offered the top surgical registrarship at Brompton Chest Hospital in London. Baylor would be the beginning of his true independence, while Brompton Hospital would be valuable experience but more financial treading in place. At Brompton, however, he would be operating with Sir Russell Brock, whose heart and lung service was, to Cooley's mind, the most exciting in the world. When he did return to Houston, the additional prestige of having worked with Brock could not do him any harm.

There was no decision as such; it was simply a matter of working out the details. Dr. DeBakey was willing to postpone Cooley's Baylor appointment. He wrote Brock and accepted.

Cooley had gained much from his association with Dr. Blalock. Though his scenes in the operating room were occasionally unbearable, he constantly drove himself to do better. And when he abused his assistants, he invariably ended up apologizing and admitting that the real trouble was himself. In a profession fraught with jealousies, backbiting, and brutal competition, he had remained a humble and self-effacing gentleman who struggled to gain recognition for the achievements of his associates and stressed the importance of original ideas and intrepid action. He complained that his staff worked too hard, and he never tried to schedule operations or meetings that would interfere with their home life or recreation. Years later, late at night, alone in his study, Dr. Blalock would phone his "boys" to visit about times past and the progress of their lives.

That August, Denton Cooley and his wife and newborn daughter Mary sailed for England on the *Queen Elizabeth*.

Chapter 9

The Brock Influence

LORD BROCK during an interview at the Royal College of Surgeons, November 1969: "Denton Cooley came to Brompton Hospital [in London] as a result of my visit to Johns Hopkins in 1949. As a young man he came to me, I recall, with the great advantage of physique. A very good-looking young man with charming manners and a nice way of expressing himself, all of which were undeniable attributes. It was immediately apparent that his practical performance as a surgeon was in keeping with the high standard suggested by his physical attributes. His title was Senior Surgical Registrar—the equivalent of Senior Resident in the United States—and he was an extremely active worker, operating all the time. A very rapid and able operator with lung as well as heart surgery. I was struck by his extreme restlessness, his pronounced eagerness to do more and better things than anyone else."

There was still a housing shortage in London, but with assistance from the hospital Cooley secured a flat in Latimer Courts, a reconstructed block on Hammersmith High Road, where his wife supplemented the furnishings with bargains from the flea markets in Petticoat Lane and Portobello Road. They bought a gray Hillman Minx car with red leather upholstery, and then Cooley went to work.

Aside from having more opportunity to operate in London, Cooley was particularly interested in learning more about Brock's blue-baby technique and his pioneering in the surgical correction of mitral stenosis. This was heart surgery. But in his own operating rooms, Brock was even stiffer and more autocratic than he had been at Hopkins. While he was not an elegant surgeon, Brock had a well-researched reason for each move he made during an operation. Brock's autocracy, like Blalock's fractiousness, Cooley concluded was sublimated fear and insecurity. But both surgeons were expert at working their way out of trouble, and Cooley learned as much from their mistakes as he might have from their excellence. Still, he could see no logic in endangering the patient out of concern for his life. Despite his experience, Cooley was not yet aware of how rare his own capacities for concentration and calm were.

At Brompton Hospital, Cooley learned fundamental diagnostics, including endoscopy (vascular x rays) and other techniques which, in the United States, would have been performed by specialists.

In England it was once again obvious to him that in terms of technique and temperament he was better than anyone he had encountered. At the same time, and for the first time, he realized that bold confidence was a necessary ingredient for preeminence in the profession, and he assumed that his colleagues felt themselves superior to him. It was, despite the polished manners of the English and their sense of fair play, a competitive business, the type of endeavor at which he excelled.

He was pleased with himself. To heal was one thing; to heal more people with more expertise was quite another. Healing, he decided, was relative; the finest move was only temporizing.

The best he could possibly do was delay death. So his opponent in the game was not death, the predetermined winner, but all other surgeons. As Brock observed, he wanted to outdo everyone. It was true: Cooley thought the surgeons at Brompton Hospital were too slow, and he soon grew impatient with what he termed their "Sherlock Holmes" approach to diagnostics. People were waiting to be operated on.

Cooley was impressed with the British surgeon's dedication to his patients; he was not, however, convinced of its utility. Due to the heavy volume at Hopkins, Dr. Blalock had been unable, and not altogether inclined personally, to follow up each of his cases. That responsibility had rested on Dr. Taussig and, to some extent, on Cooley. Cooley knew well the problems and sorrows of the wards, and he never questioned the therapeutic value of personal attention. Cooley concluded that too much attention from the surgeon could work to the patient's disadvantage. First of all, the surgeon's proper place was in the operating theater; whatever time he spent not operating could work to the detriment of those awaiting surgery. Second, he suspected that a recuperating patient who received excessive personal attention from his surgeon might well develop a psychological dependence on him. For the surgeon there was also the emotional danger of becoming too involved with high-risk cases, the strain of which might impair his judgment, stability, and performance. Cooley liked to operate, but he did not have the talent, patience, or desire to deal with postoperatives. Cooley believed the solution to the patient-surgeon relationship, from the surgeon down to the orderlies, was a highly specialized team. He was aware of being doubly vulnerable to patient demands. Besides being a swift and skillful operator, he possessed a personality and physical attractiveness that fit the layman's most romantic idea of what a surgeon should be. In hope of supplanting awe with respect and confidence, he chose to assume an attitude of professional distance tempered with concern: departmentalize, allocate the time and labor of your specialists, your team. What he envisioned was a sort of mass-produced healing, a surgical assembly line that would free him from all considerations outside an open wound in a human chest. The theory was logically sound, but only Cooley would know how well he managed to limit his emotional involvement with the patients on whom he operated.

Two months after Cooley arrived at Brompton Hospital, Dr. Oswald Tubbs, who was in charge of a surgical firm there, developed tuberculosis of the lung with a positive sputum that made him a carrier of the disease. According to British medical tradition the chief surgeon always operated on his staff members, so Brock got the call. Tubbs's request that Cooley be the first assistant was granted. Two hours before the surgery, he called Cooley to his bedside and outlined the way he wanted the operation performed: in exchange for persuading Brock to crush the phrenic nerve and put the diaphragm at rest (a technique that Brock seldom employed), Tubbs would put Cooley in charge of his firm until he was up and able to operate. Cooley agreed. In fact, to ensure that it was done properly, he reached in and crushed the nerve himself.

As a visitor without authority regarding hospital policy, Cooley had been obliged to go along with the deliberation and short operating schedules of his superiors. But now, suddenly in charge of a major service with a grateful, captive consultant who would back up his decisions, he felt within his rights to put his ideas in action and reorganize the Tubbs firm.

He immediately doubled the operating schedule and began to catch up with the backlog of patients awaiting surgery. He pressed the cardiologists for more rapid diagnoses, mobilized postoperative patients more quickly, and persuaded the operating room personnel to work overtime. Cooley was the first American invited to become a registrar on the new British

National Health Board, and some of the staff began to wonder
if it had been a good idea to give the energetic Cooley his head.
But by the time Tubbs returned, the "Cooley method" had won
the begrudging or enthusiastic approval of everyone at Brompton Hospital.

On a small scale and for a brief duration, his theory had
worked; the experience would prove invaluable to him later.
More important at the moment, he had shown that he was
capable of handling a large operating schedule, and for that
reason he was given all the work he wanted, though not without
stirring resentment.

One day after Cooley had performed three particularly difficult operations (a Blalock-Taussig, a lung removal, and a coarctation), Brock, satisfied that the load on the young surgeon had
been too much to have been borne calmly, asked the head
surgical sister how things had gone. "It all goes very smoothly
when Mr. Cooley works," she replied.

On another occasion a gentleman was admitted for an emergency lung resection. Brock, who was out of the hospital at the
time, was contacted by phone for instructions. Unaware that
the patient was a prominent figure in government or that it was
an extremely difficult case, Brock requested that Cooley operate. The gentleman recovered without incident, but Dr. Seatting, the internist in charge of work-ups on chest patients, had
assumed that Brock would perform the operation. When he
learned it had been Cooley, he became incensed and complained that "rosy-cheeked American boys are apparently handling our most important and most difficult cases now!" As
though underscoring Seatting's observation, a few weeks later,
when Dr. Headly Atkins was having his problems with a new
skin-grafting apparatus called a dermatome, he called on Cooley. Cooley adjusted the machine correctly and cut a perfect
graft. The next day Dr. Atkins sent him a check for ten guineas.

Cooley planned his professional life in much the same way he had planned his academic life—a list of goals on the dormitory wall—so after proving his team theory on the Tubbs firm, he began to think seriously about developing a surgical organization that would permit him to operate from morning to night. His restlessness with the pace at Brompton became more pronounced.

In his personal life, he increasingly wondered if his interests were sufficiently diversified. He began to read more fiction and to attend plays, according to a mentally outlined course of self-improvement. Most of his friends on the hospital staff were liberally educated Oxford and Cambridge men. Cooley requested and received what they had to offer on the arts, but the ambiguities of the subject confused rather than engaged him.

To some of his associates, Cooley came to represent the best of America. A tall, handsome, athletic man; a young surgical pioneer from the American "provinces." He was intelligent and direct, with a penchant for efficiency and an overwhelming ambition to do the most and be the best. Others, whether envious of his coolness under fire or contemptuous of an imagined insensitivity, did not admire him.

Jack Josey, University of Texas Board of Regents: "In the spring of 1951, the Korean war looked bad and I took my family to see Europe while there was still something left. As soon as we checked into the Dorchester, I phoned Denton at the hospital to confirm the dinner and night-on-the-town invitation I had cabled from Houston.

"They were comfortable and happy in their little flat, but Denton, even more than usual, was restless. He had done some new operations over there, and the English doctors were evidently quite pleased with his work. But there was a difference in the way they did things and the way Denton thought they should be done. For example, he saw a disparity in their thorough care of patients and their lack of psychological subtlety. He was critical of their calling an institution 'The London

Hospital for Incurable Children.' Denton thought it indicated a negative attitude and sounded like a throwback to the days of pest houses when you stacked people up to die. It was his relentless confidence—he always thought you should keep trying.

"We went on a delightful pub-crawl up the Thames around Richmond and wound up having dinner at Nelson Inn. But Denton wasn't himself; he was worried about something. He said he had been at Brompton long enough, that he had the feeling he was teaching more than he was learning. He felt he was ready to get out on his own. He seemed to be worried about the war, too; he thought he might have to go back into the service. Then he volunteered some more personal information. He had been eager to go into private practice, but now the time had come he had decided to associate himself with a medical school. He mentioned Baylor, and then said that Mike DeBakey had asked him to come there to help organize a cardiovascular program. I told him I hoped he would. Houston had missed Denton—we needed him."

So Cooley decided to leave Brompton Hospital four months before his tenure would have been fulfilled. He would have more authority at Baylor, more patients. And the more patients he had, the more skillful he would become, which in turn would bring more referrals. First, he liked to operate. Second, he enjoyed the thrill of accomplishment that came with having healed a patient. Third, it was a competition, with routines and rules—a game, perhaps the biggest. And finally, after training and working so long with so little remuneration, in Texas he would have the opportunity to make money according to his ability and willingness to work.

Early in May, Cooley informed Russell Brock of his intention to return to the United States.

Lord Brock: "Denton Cooley was eager to return home for two reasons: there was the Korean war—which may have been an excuse, though he was liable to military duty—and then it was admittedly the restlessness of his nature. He believed he had gotten as much in nine months here as the average man would have gotten in a year—which was probably true. It stands to reason that the world will not produce a second Denton Cooley; and, frankly, I have my doubts if the world could handle another one. He spun in and out of here like a whirlwind, though not without leaving his mark—indeed, several marks."

Cooley had learned the tricks of organization and had benefited a great deal from Brock's genius in lung surgery. He learned to study medical histories and the postoperative courses of patients as they would be pertinent to subsequent cases.

Unlike Blalock, Brock had been proud and somewhat pompous. He was ambitious, and he rationalized his shortness with his staff by declaring that he was a man of destiny. In a controversy with a physician over the treatment of a patient, Brock had insisted on his approach to the problem. "If two men are to ride the same horse," he said, "one must ride behind"—an attitude Cooley was to emulate.

Essentially, Cooley was to choose the middle ground between his two mentors: self-certain humility. It was a way to avoid conflicts. Besides, by nature, Cooley wanted affection and admiration from everyone—a need that was soon to be tested to the limits. As for surgical technique, he relied on dexterity and calmness; these he had learned from no one.

On June 1, 1951 they closed their flat in Latimer Courts. With his wife and child, his savings all but depleted, Cooley sailed for his first civilian job as a surgeon. He was nearly thirty-one. His salary at Baylor would be five thousand dollars a year.

Chapter 10

The DeBakey Influence .

THE complex problem of returning to one's hometown is no less difficult for being an old and familiar one. Usually the attractions are the security afforded by one's family and friends, a sense of place, and happy memories. But more often it becomes apparent that the selectivity of one's memory has discarded a lot of unpleasant truths. The sanctuary is violated by reality and the result is disillusionment and frustration. Denton Cooley's homecoming was different.

His personal polygraph of acceptance and accomplishment had always been at a steady level along the top. What he was seeking in Houston now was an opportunity to push the tracings off the paper. That evening earlier in the spring at dinner in the Nelson Inn, Jack Josey had remarked, "If you do come home to Houston, Denton, you'll have the whole town at your feet." The administration at Baylor had made the same observation.

Two days after arriving in the United States, Cooley drove to Baltimore and spent the afternoon with Dr. Blalock discussing his time at Brompton Hospital and his future at Baylor College of Medicine. Blalock agreed that under the circumstances—the stir in the medical profession caused by another war—Cooley had been wise to return before the conclusion of his registrarship. Cooley was, Blalock assured him, a fine surgeon with a good future in Houston. The city, which had a reputation for philanthropy, was booming, its pockets bulging with money. If the long-range plans for the new medical center there were realized, it would rival any facility in the world. Blalock looked at Cooley—vibrant, supremely trained, whetted to an edge of readiness. "Tell me, Denton, can you still knot a suture inside a matchbox?" "With either hand," he said.

Ten miles west of Monroe, Louisiana, on the way to Houston from Baltimore, Cooley rounded a curve and met a truck stopped dead in the middle of the road. He swerved to miss it and skidded sideways, then fish-tailed to avoid an oncoming car and struck a culvert, smashing the windshield and sending luggage flying from the roof rack.

Louise Cooley had thrown herself across the baby. Her back was riddled with fragments of glass from the shattered windshield; the baby was screaming but unhurt. Wrapping his fingers in a clean handkerchief, Cooley removed the larger pieces of glass from his wife's back and told her to sit tight against the seat to retard the bleeding, then he wrapped her and the baby in his raincoat. The truck had disappeared, but the man Cooley had swerved to miss returned and sped off for an ambulance. Louise Cooley was two months pregnant.

There was a downpour. Cooley removed his raincoat from his wife and the baby and covered the windshield opening with it, then he spread a blanket from the trunk over them and stood in the rain, waving on cars that slowed down to see what had happened. With a sense of revelation uncharacteristic of a man whose well-planned life had been smooth and devoid of personal trauma, the threat of tragedy came home to him. He recognized the possibility of loss over which he had no control.

And briefly, before dismissing the thought in favor of the business at hand, he considered the families of the patients who had died and would die on his operating table. But Cooley did not believe in portents or, for that matter, apt preludes.

Michael DeBakey was born in 1908 in the Cajun country near Lake Charles, Louisiana, where his father, a Lebanese immigrant, ran a small drugstore. As a child, Michael DeBakey was small for his age, rather studious, and played the violin. At Tulane University in New Orleans, DeBakey majored in science, graduating in 1930 with above-average marks. He then entered Tulane Medical School, where he came under the influence of Dr. Alton Ochsner, a noted surgeon. After finishing his medical degree and a two-year residency, DeBakey received an M.S. degree and left for Europe, where he studied for two years at the University of Strasbourg and the University of Heidelberg. He then returned to Tulane as an instructor in surgery and became a member of the staff at Ochsner Clinic, where, as Dr. Ochsner's protégé, he soon established a considerable reputation as a lung surgeon. It was under Ochsner that DeBakey began to develop his talent for organization.

From the beginning of his medical career, DeBakey was a prolific writer in medical journals, a strong believer in self-promotion through the proper channels. In 1932, he devised a flange to anchor rubber tubing in the roller pump. Although the pump itself had been patented in the 1860s, it was DeBakey who popularized the device and promoted its use in the early heart-lung machines, a project for which he was later to share the coveted Lasker Award for Clinical Research.

In 1942, Dr. DeBakey entered the Army as chief of the general surgery branch of the Surgeon General's office; he subsequently became director of the surgical consultants division. His job was to report on wounds of the chest, arterial injuries, and other aspects of medicine as it was being practiced by Army physicians and surgeons.

In 1946, DeBakey was discharged from the Army with the rank of colonel. On the recommendation of his political contacts in Washington, he was instrumental in planning the postwar medical research program of the Veterans Administration.

DeBakey returned to Tulane for two years and then went to Baylor Medical College as chairman of the Department of Surgery. He continued to be active in politics, serving on the Hoover Commission and the Democratic party platform committee. On behalf of the National Heart Institute, he appeared before several congressional committees. He was an adviser for the National Institutes of Health, the National Research Council, and the United States Public Health Service. To many senators and congressmen in Washington, Dr. Michael DeBakey came to represent the primary liaison between the medical profession and the federal government, and he learned to use that influence well—to his own and Baylor's advantage.

The administration at the new Baylor College of Medicine was eager to establish the school as superior to the University of Texas facilities in Galveston, and they believed DeBakey, with his access to federal funds, was the man to do it. DeBakey had foreseen the rising national interest and opportunities in the field of cardiovascular surgery and had invited Cooley to join the Baylor staff for the expressed purpose of organizing a comprehensive heart program. Though the development of a heart-lung machine had been interrupted during the war, he knew a reliable device was close at hand and that with its perfection, heart surgery would, literally, open up.

Besides being young and attractive, Cooley was experienced in cardiovascular work and also a native of Houston—a fair-haired boy who held the admiration of some of the wealthiest and most important people in the state. DeBakey had expanded his political associations from the Surgeon General's office to the agencies that distributed federal grants, but with a few exceptions* he had neither the time nor the temperament to meet and socialize with the moneyed people of Houston. Where DeBakey was solitary, intense, and physically unprepossessing, Cooley was the affable, casual, tall Texan. Thus, DeBakey's influence in Washington was complimented by Cooley's connections in Texas. If, in time, the medical world would stand in awe of Cooley's ability as a surgeon, they would be no less impressed with, or envious of, the medical-political power DeBakey came to wield. Certainly DeBakey was a fine surgeon, and Cooley was not altogether naïve in the subtleties of persuasion and power, but their fame in the medical profession was to be: Cooley—surgical genius *and* organizer; DeBakey—genius organizer *and* surgeon. Perhaps the key to the problems of their relationship was that each tried to beat the other at his own game. At any rate, what was to become the most celebrated and stormy partnership in medical history began on a series of sour notes.

It was June 11, 1951, Cooley's first day at Baylor. Dr. DeBakey, bespectacled and hawk-nosed, his head thrust just forward of his body, led his staff on swift morning rounds through the corridors of the old Jefferson Davis City-County Hospital. He stopped outside the door of room 411 and explained, briefly, that the patient, Joe Mitchell, age forty-eight, had a syphilitic aneurysm of the aortic arch. The conventional cellophane-wrap method of repair had proved unsatisfactory, and the prognosis was poor: the weakened artery would rupture and the patient would quickly bleed to death.

Dr. DeBakey checked Joe Mitchell's chart, felt his pulses, and listened to his chest, pointing out significant irregularities. In the corridor, DeBakey suddenly announced, "We have a new

*Notably Ben Taub, the philanthropist for whom the city-county hospital in Houston was named.

man with us today. Dr. Cooley, what would you do in the case of Joe Mitchell?"

"I think I'd try to take it out," Cooley said.

Someone muffled a laugh.

"What exactly do you mean?" DeBakey asked.

"The aneurysm. I think if you put a clamp across the base of it, you could take the thing off and the man would recover. He sure doesn't have a chance lying there in bed."

"You would remove it. And you've done this before?"

"As a matter of fact, twice," Cooley said and recounted his experience with Dr. Grant Ward, who held his finger in the ruptured aneurysm while Cooley repaired it, and the massive aneurysm he had removed from Dr. Blalock's patient when Dr. Blalock was in Honolulu. The staff was astonished. Dr. DeBakey turned and continued leading rounds.

Two days later, Cooley operated on Joe Mitchell and removed the aneurysm from his aortic arch; it was the first such operation in Houston, possibly the first anywhere. Mitchell's recovery was complete. The following week DeBakey sent a file of 700 lung cases to Cooley's office, with a request that Cooley continue the follow-ups on the patients. The operations had been performed in New Orleans, before DeBakey's move to Baylor. Cooley was annoyed at DeBakey's assumption that he was available for paperwork. He was the most junior man in the department, but he considered himself a surgeon, not a secretary. This was the time, at the outset, to declare his position. He put the files away and forgot about them.

Blalock had paved the way for Cooley. Brock had been obliged to recognize his excellence and bend to his will. But it soon became apparent that DeBakey would do neither. Cooley was out in the world now, and this was the sort of competition he had been trained for.

That fall, DeBakey presented Joe Mitchell to the general meeting of the Southern Surgical Society. The paper, a beautifully written, comprehensive effort, was received with great enthusiasm, and DeBakey was immediately established as *the* aneurysm surgeon, the man who was intrepid enough to make a direct attack on a lesion that had previously meant certain death for countless patients.

Cooley, who was not yet a member of the organization, had sat in the audience and listened to DeBakey give the details of the work he, Cooley, had done—or at least the work they had done together. No, DeBakey was not Blalock.

In fact, according to the protocol of scientific reporting, De-Bakey had been well within his rights. A principal scientific investigator or the chairman of a department in a medical school has the option of stamping his name on whatever work is done under his jurisdiction. Some investigators see that their staffs are justly recognized for personal accomplishments and contributions. Others do not. Ideally, the contribution is more important than individual recognition. However, as a practical matter, particularly among surgeons, such is not often the case. "If two men are to ride the same horse, one must ride behind."

Nonetheless, Cooley thought DeBakey's aneurysm paper neglecting his own major role in the historical Mitchell operation was bad form (one thing about British medicine that had favorably impressed Cooley was its celebrated sense of fair play), and he resolved never to represent another's work as his own. Consistent with the stereotyped image of the heart surgeon, Cooley and DeBakey both had huge egos, the difference being that DeBakey, who virtually lived in the hospital, had no reason to mask his. So Cooley had met his match. DeBakey was bright, accomplished, and ambitious; moreover, he was clever in the methods he chose to achieve his ends. The problem was, if you were inclined to dislike him, DeBakey's ends were eventually for the good of humanity. Nor was he impressed with Cooley's charm.

The operation on Joe Mitchell was followed by more successful attacks on aortic aneurysms. Referrals began coming in from all over the country, and soon DeBakey and Cooley were working side by side as full partners in consultation practice. Baylor was rapidly becoming recognized as the leading institution in vascular research and surgery. But there were problems.

What was needed in aneurysm surgery was a reliable arterial graft. In instances where the diseased section of the artery was not too extensive, Cooley would remove it and suture the ends of the vessel together. But when the diseased portion involved a segment so large that on its removal there would not be sufficient slack to effect an end-to-end anastomosis, Cooley would bridge the gap with a cadaver artery, a homograft. Usually it worked, but it was not good enough. It was discovered that the aorta (approximately an inch in diameter; the artery arches from the left ventricle of the heart and descends along the backbone) would regenerate if given a proper surface to "grow" on.* After experimenting with several new materials, Dr. Oscar Creech, a researcher at Baylor, and a patent engineer who owned a necktie factory came up with a crimped Dacron that filled the bill: unlike a homograft, it was easily tailored, demanded no preparation, and formed a perfect lattice for arterial regeneration. To fertilize the surface for regrowth, the semiporous graft was soaked in the patient's blood. It was sutured in place, and a vine of human flesh grew from either end over and inside the pliable plastic cylinder until the span was completed and the artery as good as ever. "When they dig you up a thousand years from now," Cooley would say, "and your flesh and bones have long since rotted and turned to dust, that piece of Dacron I put in you will still be in good shape."

DeBakey reported the results of their aneurysm surgery in journals and at medical meetings throughout the country. And

*Dr. Harry Schumacher made a cloth graft at the University of Indiana, Dr. Paul Sayer had one of Orlon, and Dr. Shelby Edwards had been using a crudely woven nylon graft since 1955.

while some doctors were critical and incredulous, referrals increased. By July 1955, Cooley and DeBakey had performed 245 aneurysm repairs, far surpassing any other series in volume and success. That August, they toured Europe, lecturing and demonstrating their operations, thus popularizing aneurysm surgery as Dr. Blalock, ten years earlier, had popularized the blue-baby procedure: two of the most significant developments in cardiovascular surgery, and Cooley had been on the ground floor both times.

Once again, Cooley became restless and increasingly resentful. During these first few years with DeBakey, he learned the meaning of total dedication. DeBakey seldom slept more than three hours a night and was virtually a stranger to his family (DeBakey, the studious professor, had all boy children; Cooley, the athlete, had all girls). DeBakey would rise at four in the morning, do paperwork in his study until six (the study at home and his offices in the Medical Center were locked when he was not in residence), and then speed to the hospital (grateful patients kept him in new Cadillacs) and start operating. His tirades in surgery made Brock and Blalock look like schoolboys. (A resident who had worked under both surgeons said, "DeBakey shoves and pushes his men to better efforts; Cooley's guys follow him.")

Cooley recognized DeBakey as a good surgeon, though not as good as himself; he thought DeBakey's temperament worked to everyone's disadvantage. The operating room was in constant turmoil. When an assistant made a mistake, DeBakey reprimanded him before his fellows and sent him from the room—occasionally never to return. When a Cooley assistant made a mistake, he got an ice cold stare followed by a long silence. While he remained associated with DeBakey in a partnership, Cooley knew that he would be the junior man. Somehow he would have to strike out on his own.

Over the years a number of instruments had been developed

which permitted surgeons to operate "blind" inside the heart, but the repairs had been minimal and the more complex lesions remained uncorrectable. Dr. John Gibbon had been working on a heart-lung substitute since 1937. In 1953, using a large cumbersome machine that had been built to his specifications by IBM, Gibbon and his colleagues at Jefferson Medical School performed the first human application of a heart-lung by-pass. The results were not encouraging. But a few months later, Dr. John Kirkland of Mayo Clinic had better luck with a similar apparatus and shortly initiated a full-scale open-heart program there. This was it—what Cooley had been waiting for.

Dr. Denton Cooley: "I had been trying to develop a heart-lung machine using plastic screens, but I wasn't getting any place with it. Then John Kirkland came up with a copy of Gibbon's machine that worked. I realized then that if I kept trying for something unique, I might lose out altogether, so I dropped my research and tried another approach.

"It was in 1954, at the Southern Surgical Society meeting at the Homestead in Hot Springs, Virginia. I told Dr. DeBakey in front of Jack Gibbon that he should do as Kirkland had done and copy Gibbon's machine—time was wasting. Dr. DeBakey said no. He said that he and Dr. Stanley Olson and Dr. Hebbel Hoff [a DeBakey appointee who, fifteen years later, was to head the Baylor committee that investigated Cooley's use of the artificial heart] were working on a pump of their own and if they needed my assistance or advice, they would call on me. That, of course, was a blind alley.

"When I got back home, I decided that the Gibbon pump was too expensive to build without some sort of institutional funding. C. Walton Lillehei and Richard DeWall had developed a simpler, less expensive machine at the University of Minnesota and were going at it full tilt. After discussing the feasibility of the venture with Joe Latson, a cardiologist at St. Luke's, I phoned C. J. Tibideau, a Houston oil broker and a close friend, and said that I had decided to build a heart-lung machine on my own. He asked me how much I needed. I said three or four thousand should do it. He sent five thousand out by messenger that afternoon, with a note assuring me that there was more when I needed it.

"Dr. Latson, Dr. Keats, and Dr. Leachman helped me. We were able to secure most of our materials from hardware stores; what wasn't available there, we had made in metal shops. Commercial Kitchens did most of the major custom work; for that reason, I guess, they called it the 'Cooley Coffee Pot.'

"We tried it on a number of dogs and all of them died. Anyone who has worked in an animal lab knows how easily an animal dies, particularly dogs. They're fragile. They are not endowed with a constitution or a will to live and, consequently, are poor human substitutes. For that reason, I wasn't too discouraged.

"Then one day I got a phone call from Dr. Sidney Schnur. He had a patient with a perforated septum between the ventricles that had been caused by a heart attack. The man's name was Sommerville, and he was dying. Dr. Schnur asked me if my machine was ready. I thought it was, but because of the dog tests I didn't give him a direct answer. He assured me that the case was hopeless without immediate surgery, so I said okay. At the time, less than fifty open-heart operations had been done with a heart-lung machine.

"We put Mr. Sommerville on the pump and I patched up the holes in his ventricular septum. He survived for six weeks before dying of an infection, but that was time enough to get us on the road. Before he died, we did six more, less difficult operations and, because of Mr. Sommerville's courage, we were in the open-heart business. Referrals began to pour in. We modified the machine so the components could be cleaned and reused—the first one included a lot of expensive, disposable parts—and I put in an order for two more.

"I heard Dr. DeBakey had scrapped his plans to build a heart-lung machine. Then one afternoon I was told that he had scheduled an operation using my machine and pump team. I went to his office and told him I thought it wasn't right for him to do such a thing without consulting me. He said it wasn't my machine, that it belonged to the Department of Surgery. I disagreed and reminded him how and why I had built the thing on my own. Finally he said he had planned to do the case with Dr. Crawford, but that he would be willing to step aside and let me do it with Crawford. I asked Crawford, and he said he had not wanted to do it in the first place. So I ended up doing it myself—closing a ventricular septal defect in a child."

This was the true beginning of heart surgery—the first time in history that this mysterious muscular organ, the source of life's pulse, could be arrested, cut open, repaired, closed, and restarted. And Cooley took advantage of the situation. He operated constantly at that steady, controlled pace, with an unprecedented level of success, until he had soon passed everyone in volume and variety of interventions; indeed, by his reckoning, his personal series was, and perhaps still is, greater than the combined efforts of the entire cardiovascular staff at Mayo Clinic.

Added to his adult cases, Cooley's infant heart surgery, a field in which he has always been the unrivaled master, raised his patient volume until Methodist Hospital was literally not large enough for him and DeBakey. There was an ongoing struggle for beds and operating rooms, so Cooley quietly moved his infant and children's service across the yard to Texas Children's. He was operating in both hospitals, walking, sometimes running, the hundred yards between them as often as fifteen and twenty times a day.

He and DeBakey agreed that the department should be expanded, that they should take on more surgeons; they also decided that it would be in the best interest of the college if they

dissolved their consultation partnership. Though both had been guilty of pettiness, they had always avoided a face-to-face confrontation. More than anything, their relationship had been a quiet combat of two extremely dedicated and ambitious men, and the end of their formal partnership was to mark an upsurge in competition and production. Cooley was a full professor now.

Cooley was quickly gaining a reputation as one of the finest —and wealthiest—surgeons in the world. Although 50 percent of his income went to Baylor College of Medicine, and many of his patients were "courtesy" cases, his gross income was immense, and he was not yet working at capacity. The year of the Mark-Cooley heart-lung machine (he received no remuneration for the use or the sale of the device), Cooley became a director of the Bank of Texas; locally, his fame as a land speculator very nearly equaled his fame as a surgeon.

His speed and dexterity were without peer—he patched, recirculated blood flow, grafted, and virtually rebuilt hundreds of tiny infant hearts with apparently no more difficulty than he operated on adults. There were photographs of Cooley vaguely nonplused in a recovery room filled with squalling babies. Understandably, his public image was almost Christ-like. But, similiar to the situation in London, there were reservations among his colleagues who believed that a surgeon should concern himself equally with operating and research. Cooley had a firm scientific background, and his participation at medical conventions indicated that he kept abreast of what was happening in the world's laboratories, but he had a tendency toward specializing within his specialty, concentrating his attention more and more on the patient on the operating table. This was not traditional, but then Cooley was just beginning to impose his own ideas on the profession. When a former Johns Hopkins classmate asked how much time he spent in the animal lab at Baylor, Cooley replied, "I follow the films and the reports, but

I'm often obliged to experiment inside the heart of a patient whose problem hasn't yet been worked out in a dog." This sort of self-assuredness piqued many of the physicians and surgeons who heard the stories at third-hand.

In 1956, Cooley was named one of the ten outstanding young men in the United States. The awards were featured in *Look* magazine; it was his first national recognition in the popular press. The event was not without incident: several newspaper reporters covering the banquet were critical that an enterprising French public-relations firm had given each of the honorees a magnum of champagne. Cooley parried with the observation that France had produced Carrel and Leriche, two of the most outstanding cardiovascular pioneers in history; to have ignored a gift from their homeland would have been an insult to their memories. Eleven years later, Cooley won the coveted international René Leriche Prize for his own contributions to cardiovascular surgery; soon after, Leriche's grandson came to the United States to study with Cooley. The basic experiments in cardiac transplantation, the field in which Cooley was to gain his widest fame, were performed by Dr. Alexis Carrel.

Cooley brushed up on his Spanish and, in 1957, took his heart-lung team on a tour of South America, performing scores of operations, offering advice on the establishment of surgical programs, and extending invitations to surgeons who were interested in visiting his operating rooms in Houston. His "coffee pot" was adopted by several hospitals, where it is still in use. Wide news coverage of the tour brought in numerous referrals and a wave of young surgeons who came to the United States as fellows in Cooley's program. He was knighted or otherwise decorated by five countries.

Cooley was invited to participate in the Japan Surgical Congress in late 1957. Since no American surgeon had ever operated in Tokyo University Hospital, the invitation was particularly flattering. There were to be meetings and research papers, and the congress was to present the first medical color-television broadcast in Japan (Cooley had taken part in the first such program in America at Johns Hopkins in 1949). Three surgeons were scheduled to perform before the cameras: Japan's celebrated Kimoto and Nakayama, and Cooley of Texas.

The day began with morning rounds. There were over a hundred Japanese students and residents in the entourage, complicating a language barrier that would have been formidable in a quiet room. To make matters worse, Tokyo Hospital had been built to accommodate people of considerably shorter stature than Cooley, and he was constantly banging his head on door jambs and apparatus suspended from the ceilings. Finally Cooley met his patient and reviewed her history and x rays. He explained to Dr. Kimoto that the operation might be complicated by the fact that the patient was no larger than an American child and yet her condition necessitated a type of procedure that he had only performed on adults. They were discussing the matter when two nurses approached and began encircling Cooley with tape measures—one stood on a chair. Kimoto apologized, there had been an oversight: they had not planned on the doctor's being so large. The nurses were measuring him for a surgical gown they were fashioning from bed sheets.

The cameras and lights were set up in the operating room. There were photographers and newsmen and a crowd of chattering residents and technicians on the floor. The amphitheater was jam-packed above them. Each surgeon was allotted an hour on camera. Cooley, as their guest, was to go first.

The patient was wheeled in and prepped. She had an aneurysm of the abdominal aorta extending from the middle of her spine to the bifurcation (the junction of the aorta and the leg arteries) and out into each thigh. Under normal conditions it would have been a tedious and touchy operation. But the patient, as Cooley had observed, was extremely small; moreover, the scrub nurse was unfamiliar with his style and had a short reach, the instruments were small and of a different design from what he was used to, the surgical gown didn't fit, and Cooley knew only the Japanese word for scissors. Despite the fact that he had to scramble around for his instruments and virtually assist himself, in a flash of the scalpel he opened the patient's belly from her diaphragm to her pubic bone, removed and replaced the ruined artery with a Dacron graft, and sutured shut the wound in fifty-five minutes—a skin-to-skin procedure that would have taken the average surgeon, under ideal conditions, three to four hours. He received a standing ovation.

Professor Nakayama congratulated Cooley on a grand performance, commenting that American surgery was very effective and meticulous. To Cooley's mind, a meticulous operator was picky and overly cautious. He had never been called that, but he smiled and accepted the remark as a compliment.

Professor Kimoto was next. He had developed a technique for cooling the brain by circulating chilled blood through the neck arteries, thus allowing him to stop the heart with a minimum of danger to the central nervous system.

Kimoto was not a rapid operator; even so, he repaired a septal defect in a patient's heart in forty minutes. To Cooley's amazement, when Kimoto had closed only the heart, the patient was removed from the table and another, his chest already open and his brain already cooled, was wheeled in. Kimoto quickly patched the defect, dropped his instruments, and stood back from the table and bowed to the applause. He was one minute under his hour limit. Cooley was startled and a little confused, but he said nothing.

And then the legendary Nakayama from Shiba University. He was expert in the surgical resection of stomach and esophageal cancers and had a reputation as one of the fastest surgeons in the world.

The first patient had cancer of the lower one-third of the

esophagus. Nakayama removed this and two-thirds of the stomach, tailoring what remained of the stomach into a tubelike channel which he then sutured to the abbreviated esophagus. The patient was quickly removed and replaced by another. Nakayama resected the cancerous portion of the second patient's esophagus, bringing the upper end out of the neck and the stomach opening out of the abdomen. By any standards, one such operation was a long, tiring affair, yet Nakayama had done two within an hour.

Later, in a communal bath with the entire surgical team, Cooley announced his conclusion that the Japanese definition of "meticulous" was "slow." He did not say that compared with the delicate and idiosyncratic human heart, he thought gastrointestinal surgery (and, indeed, much of peripheral vascular surgery) was more like plumbing.

As Cooley became more widely recognized and exercised his newly found independence, his problems with Dr. DeBakey increased. Possibly, the differences between the two surgeons could have been amicably resolved had it not been for certain extenuating circumstances. The *mano a mano* competition in Houston divided much of the nation's medical community into Cooley and DeBakey camps. A few optimists foresaw the rivalry as a situation from which patients and the profession would benefit, inasmuch as each man was driving the other to ever-increasing heights of accomplishment. But hardly anyone outside of Houston knew, or apparently cared to know, the truth.

Because of the eminence of both men, the situation had been oversimplified and amplified out of all proportion. DeBakey was not the tyrant his detractors portrayed him as being, nor did Cooley fit the DeBakey-camp notion of him as a disrespectful, slash-happy glamour boy, though, oddly enough, both men tended to conform to their popular images. Perhaps it was a strange twist of ego, a concession to recognition. Whatever, the controversy mounted noticeably in the late 1950s. As a close observer who worked with Cooley and DeBakey remarked at the time, "Surgeons are egocentric, everybody knows that. But these two exist on a level that surpasses the imagination. The difference is the types of egos. DeBakey is an introvert whose ego is so strong that he seeks only self-satisfaction; he has what I would call negative charisma. Cooley's ego is just as big, but it's more conventional. He needs admiration and recognition, love, and huge amounts of it. Yet, he's essentially a shy man and, in his own way, as solitary as DeBakey. It will be interesting to see what happens when Cooley receives all the recognition he desires (though he'll never really be satisfied) and probably deserves. I mean, how will it affect each of them?"

The afternoon of September 3, 1959, Cooley was summoned from surgery to receive an emergency phone call. It was his wife. At Poe Elementary School, where three of their daughters were students, a man had just thrown a bomb onto the playground. The dying and injured were everywhere.

Cooley, still in his scrub suit, knelt on the playground and did what he could until the ambulances arrived. The Cooley girls had escaped injury, but three adults and three children had been killed, and a number of others near the blast had been seriously injured.

Joe Glenny, a Houston realtor: "If Dr. Cooley has any emotional vulnerability, it's children. The tragedy at Poe School really got to him. The father of one of the dead children, a little boy, was a friend of Dr. Cooley's. He was afraid the man would get the news over the radio and no one would be there to talk to him and explain what had happened. He grabbed his medical bag and went down to the father's office and told him, point blank, that his son had been killed. They sat and talked for a long time and Dr. Cooley did what he could to comfort him. It's the same way with a death notice at the hospital. There's a rule that Dr. Cooley always delivers the bad news. I suppose he feels he can handle situations like that better than anyone else. Over the years, he's gotten pretty familiar with death."

That year Dr. Cooley received the Humanitarian Award of the Variety Clubs International, an honor that in the past had been bestowed on men such as Winston Churchill and Albert Schweitzer.

Although Cooley and DeBakey communicated politely and avoided any direct confrontation over their differences, the people who surrounded them enjoyed a continuous turmoil of hospital gossip and second guesses. If you were from Baylor and attended a medical convention, you would usually be asked more questions about the squabbling surgeons than about your own specialty. No one, in DeBakey's presence, would risk stirring his ire. But Cooley, being less irascible, met with some direct opposition.

He had finished his day's surgery at Methodist and was on his way to Texas Children's when one of Dr. DeBakey's cardiologists asked Cooley if he had a minute to look at an x ray. The cardiologist pointed out a shadow on the film and asked Cooley if he had ever seen an aneurysm in this particular area before. Cooley, who as a surgeon was not overly impressed with the conservatism of "medical men," said no, adding, "And neither has anyone else, because that's not an aneurysm." The cardiologist begged his pardon too politely. "You can beg anything you want to," Cooley said, "but it won't make that an aneurysm."

The cardiologist insisted that Cooley was mistaken. Cooley offered to bet him a hundred dollars. He declined; he said he was not a betting man. Then Cooley offered to bet him a coke. The cardiologist said that the amount or denomination made no difference, he simply did not believe in wagering. Cooley, angered by the man's superciliousness, said, "If that thing's an aneurysm, I'll eat it!"

The following morning Cooley received a phone call at Texas

Children's from the cardiologist's secretary. "The doctor said to tell you to get your knife and fork ready. The x ray you were discussing yesterday? Dr. DeBakey just took an aneurysm out of the patient."

"Where is it?" Cooley asked.

"Where's what?"

"The aneurysm."

"In the OR or in pathology, I guess. Why?"

"Do me a favor," Cooley said, "find it and tell them to put it in alcohol, not in formalin."

Cooley sent an orderly across the street to borrow a tablecloth from the Cathay House Chinese Restaurant and had Mary Lou Budd, his best-looking nurse, tape up the hem of her scrub dress to miniskirt length. Then he phoned Medical Photography and told Fred Gygli to bring a movie camera and some lights.

A table set up in the central hall of the surgical suite was spread with a red checkered tablecloth. The glass was a beaker. Instead of a knife and fork, there was a scalpel and a pair of forceps. Lights, camera. Cooley entered and sat down. A surgical mask dangled from his neck like a napkin. Mary Lou, affecting a wiggling walk, placed a plate covered with an inverted steel basin (the kind that was later used to carry donor hearts for transplanting) before him. With a flourish, she removed the basin. And there, centered in the plate, was the bloody pulp of the questioned aneurysm. Cooley put on an expression of mock dissatisfaction. Ah! Mary Lou raised her finger and produced salt and pepper. Cooley seasoned the aneurysm and then, holding the rubbery vessel with the forceps, dissected off a hardy bite and ate it.

"Did you get that?" Cooley asked.

"In sixteen-millimeter color," Gygli said.

"Okay. Develop it and deliver it to my cardiologist friend over at Methodist. Tell him Denton Cooley is a man of his word."

Whether or not it was really an aneurysm that he ate (some say it was; others say it was a cleverly carved piece of chuck roast) the incident demonstrates the enigma of Cooley's personality.

A witness to the unusual brunch: "Cooley is unpredictable inside his steadiness. The aneurysm lunch was a good example. His authority was questioned, undiplomatically, by someone he disliked for no other reason than that someone disliked him. He went out on a limb to dispute his adversary and made a casual, rash commitment. But when he was proved wrong and his hand was called, he honored his word. And by honoring his word so cleverly and with so much style, he pulled defeat from the fire and emerged the victorious cavalier. He is full of arrogance, honor, purpose, and fun—each edging the other. The problem is you're never sure about the proportions of the mix."

From its advent in the spring of 1959, the Starr artificial heart valve had been a stock item in Cooley's surgical armory, but he was not altogether satisfied with its efficiency; so when Dr. Domingo Liotta arrived at Baylor in the spring of 1961, Cooley enlisted him to help develop a better valve. They did, and the result was another increase in Cooley's patient load and more wrestling for space in Methodist.

When he hired Liotta away from Cleveland Clinic, Dr. De-Bakey was laying plans for a center that would deal with every aspect of cardiovascular disease from surgery to the prevention of heart attacks, but as yet there was no program for cardiac assistive devices or for total cardiac replacement. This was Liotta's specialty, the reason he had been brought to Baylor.

Liotta was interested in continuing his research on an artificial heart, but DeBakey thought he should spend his time building a simpler device. Under a grant from the American Heart Association, and with the sponsorship of Cooley, Liotta created the left ventricular by-pass—an extracorporeal, one-chambered plastic pump that was designed to relieve the load on the heart's main chamber. Cooley contended that the device was ingenious, but the premise—given a rest, the heart would heal itself —was at best unproved and very likely absurd. DeBakey disagreed. Liotta neglected his artificial-heart research and kept working on the partial assist pump.

From whatever point of view, as long as he had any patients at Methodist, Cooley knew he would be second man. Simple arithmetic told him he was wasting too much time trying to be in two places at once, so he moved his adult patients into St. Luke's, which adjoins Texas Children's. He was happy to have all his work under one roof and to be separated from DeBakey, but he had another, more professional reason for making the move.

Traditionally, pediatrics had been divided from the rest of medicine by a distinction purely of age, which disregarded the common denominators children and adults share by their being members of the same genus and species. Cooley thought this distinction was a barrier to a surgeon's gaining comprehensive experience in the nature of heart disease. In order to understand heart surgery thoroughly, he felt a resident should be exposed to every variation of congenital and acquired cardiac malfunction, from the grotesque lesions of the newborn to the faulty valves and atherosclerotic problems of the middle-aged and the elderly. It was the way he had been trained at Johns Hopkins.

Dr. DeBakey's administrative responsibilities had increased to such a degree that he was now doing vascular surgery almost exclusively. As a consequence, Cooley's pediatric service at Texas Children's and his adult service at St. Luke's represented the most active cardiovascular program in the world; it seemed only logical that the two hospitals should combine as an institute. Cooley's London dream of a massive attack on diseases of the heart and blood vessels was beginning to come true.

What Cooley learned from DeBakey differed radically from the lessons of his previous chiefs. While Blalock and Brock were dedicated men, DeBakey was driven. Blalock's ambition was to satisfy his curiosity, to experiment. Brock assumed himself to be a man of destiny, the surgeon who would reestablish the British lead in chest surgery. But DeBakey was obsessed with accomplishment and a desire for professional recognition. His method, though ostensibly simple, demanded power, persuasion, vision, and perseverance: adopt a project of international magnitude, surround yourself with experts, and direct them toward your goal. As he had told Cooley in the early days, "It is not the man who has the idea so much as the man who convinces the public and the profession of its importance and validity." On the basis of this rationale, the Department of Surgery at Baylor was run like a Park Avenue corporation and on a level of efficiency unprecedented in the medical profession —the best medical artists, the best photographers, excellent writers, and a highly organized public-relations office.

So it was from DeBakey that Cooley learned to sell an idea. His natural approach had been to throw out a thought to the public and let them do with it what they would, but he soon realized that this was a sure-fire way for him to be forgotten. Great people, DeBakey had said, could be recognized by the number of enemies they had accumulated. In time, Cooley was to test this theory.

Chapter 11

The Cooley Influence

COOLEY'S extensive work in pediatric surgery had already changed the reputation of Texas Children's from that of a general hospital to one specializing in cardiovascular surgery, and there was little doubt that his massive adult service would have a similar effect at St. Luke's. The combined bed capacity of the two hospitals was less than four hundred; Cooley had been pressed for room in the one-thousand-bed facilities of Methodist. He would need at least three of the six operating rooms and as many beds as he could get. Then, too, the research space was limited. Understandably, several members of the St. Luke's and Texas Children's surgical staffs were resentful at being eased aside.

Cooley's move stirred interest beyond his differences with Dr. DeBakey. The University of Texas controlled only two major hospitals in the Medical Center: M. D. Anderson Hospital and Tumor Institute and Hermann Hospital. Although the University of Texas had medical schools in Galveston, Dallas, and San Antonio, the Board of Regents were determined to take advantage of the high patient volume in the Medical Center and establish a teaching institution there. For years, Baylor had been able to keep the university out, but pressure was increasing and it appeared only a matter of time before the University of Texas built a medical school on its property across Holcomb Boulevard from St. Luke's. One major concession was certain: Baylor College of Medicine was a private corporation, only loosely associated with Baylor University in Waco, Texas, and as such it was constantly burdened with financial problems, and it was fearful that the University of Texas, with its almost unlimited funds, would, if given a foothold, soon control the entire Medical Center. To avert this, Baylor had exacted a promise from the Texas Board of Regents that it would not entice Baylor faculty or Baylor-affiliated institutions to join the Texas group.

Two of the most influential members of the Texas Board of Regents were Jack Josey, chairman of the Medical Affairs Committee, and Frank Irwin, an associate of Lyndon Johnson's who was soon to become chairman of the board. Both were life-long friends and former classmates of Cooley's at the University of Texas. They were aware of the prestige, power, and income his presence would bring to a new medical school. Even though Cooley was still a member of the Baylor faculty, as were most of the staff and personnel at St. Luke's and Texas Children's, Josey and Irwin were deeply interested in the long-range results of his move from Methodist.

Dr. Denton Cooley: "In 1962 I decided to do something about my idea that the Medical Center needed an institution dedicated to the treatment of heart and blood-vessel diseases. All we had were general hospitals, and it was apparent to me that this cardiovascular center should embrace three of them— St. Luke's, Texas Children's, and Methodist—and that the hub of the complex should be Children's. Such an institute that didn't deal with children's heart diseases would be sadly lacking, like others in the country where they emphasize only adult surgery. So my idea was to get the three together.

"Then one day I heard a rumor that they might get a cardi-ovascular unit at Methodist. I was told that Mrs. W. W. Fondren, who had spearheaded the Methodist plan, was going to put the unit on the other side of Methodist, far removed from Chil-dren's, when I thought it should be in the parking lot between the three hospitals.

"When I realized that they were going to do something soon and that I was not going to be consulted, I decided we should get our own heart institute for St. Luke's and Children's. At the time, we were doing three or four times as much heart surgery as they were doing at Methodist—more than anyplace in the world.

"Using seed money from the Denton A. Cooley Foundation, I got together with Starr, Rother, and Howes, an architectural firm, and asked them to draw up a rendition of a wing to go on the back of St. Luke's–Texas Children's. They made a model for me and I presented it to the joint boards of the two hospitals at a luncheon at the Ramada Inn. I explained this addition, what I wanted housed in it, and talked to them about the concept of a comprehensive heart institute. At that time, the two hospitals were having trouble with their building programs; things had been dragging along for four or five years, and no one had raised any money. I said if they would let me build this heart institute, we could relieve the bed shortage, take all the cardiovascular patients out of the hospitals and leave the rest for general use. The cost of the new wing would be $4.5 million. I told them I felt I could raise this money myself. I had the idea in the back of my mind that my great benefactor Mr. Benjamin Clayton would support me in a very substantial way. I first knew him after I had operated on his chauffeur, Richard, a fine man who had been with Mr. Clayton for over forty years. It was one of the early vascular cases. I peeled an occlusion out of Richard's iliac artery and he was able to walk again. As a result, Mr. Clayton began supporting my program for taking care of indigent patients, and he gave me fifty thousand dollars for an angiocardiograph to use at Methodist.

"So, I put my proposal before the joint boards. I felt that St. Luke's couldn't afford the additional expense of a cardiovascular unit, which is a losing proposition financially. I wanted to see if I could get enough outside help to make it self-sufficient. The joint boards gave me their approval and told me to get on with it. Then I went out confidently to raise money and met with no success. Mr. Clayton, unfortunately, was not interested in brick and mortar. A modest man, he didn't want his name identified with anything. There was nothing I could say.

"We floated along in the doldrums for a while and then decided to develop an extended plan which would include the expansion programs of St. Luke's and Texas Children's and the incorporation of the Texas Heart Institute. This was something of a disappointment to me because I thought we might lose our identity in a huge hospital complex. But it seemed the only way. Certainly it combined the efforts of everyone and satisfied those who had misgivings about the possibility of the Texas Heart Institute's becoming a separate, autonomous hospital."

In 1963, while Cooley was busy developing plans for his institute, Dr. E. Stanley Crawford attached Liotta's left ventricular by-pass to a patient. There was little publicity. The operation, unfortunately, was not ultimately successful, but the pump had worked long and well enough to satisfy Dr. DeBakey that Liotta should continue to refine it. In exchange for dropping the privately funded American Heart Association grant (which, with Cooley as a sponsor, had been backing Liotta's research since he arrived at Baylor) for a federally funded National Heart Institute grant (where Dr. DeBakey was the principal investigator) Liotta was made an assistant professor of surgery at Baylor.

Although Cooley was having problems raising money for the Texas Heart Institute, his surgical practice was soaring and so was his reputation. In November 1963, at the Pan-Pacific Surgical Congress, he caused a stir by predicting heart transplants, an artificial heart, and prenatal surgery. The following year he performed the first resection of an aneurysm on the primary artery to the liver. Hardly a week passed when he did not devise some new technique in refining cardiac surgery. Houston's Hobby Field was busy with chartered planes bringing patients to him from around the world. The Shamrock Hotel, two blocks south of the Medical Center, became known as the Cooley Hilton and ran a special limousine service for his patients. Indigent children were flown in by the United States Air Force. In November 1964, Cooley operated on the left arm of Whitey Ford, the New York Yankee's ace pitcher. "Now I know how the surgeon who operated on Caruso's vocal cords felt," Cooley said.

In the meantime, Dr. DeBakey was moving ahead at flank speed. He had operated on the Duke of Windsor and Billy Rose, but on April 21, 1966, at 7:30 A.M. he opened the chest of an Illinois coal miner who was to be his most famous, and most controversial, patient to date.

The evening before the operation, over a hundred newspaper and television reporters were called together for a briefing by Methodist Hospital's public-relations staff. Some of the reporters had been waiting around the hospital for weeks and were tired and disgruntled. They had not been given enough information to sustain their interest; they complained that the entire setup was frustratingly amateur. No one seemed to know anything except Dr. DeBakey, and he wasn't available. A patient was to receive an artificial cardiac device that had been developed by Dr. DeBakey and an Argentinian, Dr. Domingo Liotta. The reporters had interviewed the people who were to assist in the operation, but none of them, including Dr. Liotta, had known the name of the patient.

As the operation got under way, Dr. John Lancaster, who was

seated in the amphitheater, provided a play-by-play description of the proceedings over a public-address system in the press room. Dr. DeBakey would replace the calcified mitral valve in the patient's heart with a plastic valve; if that was unsatisfactory, he would attach the left ventricular by-pass, an auxiliary pump that would "give the heart a rest and allow it to heal." Ralph Morse, the only news photographer in the operating room, had been authorized by *Life* magazine to take pictures which, after editing, would be available for general release. Everyone was to get the same news simultaneously.

Dr. DeBakey put in the plastic valve and then attached the by-pass to the patient's left atrium and ascending aorta and started the carbon dioxide from the power console. Dr. Lancaster's voice boomed over the speaker in the press room, "The artificial heart is working!"

For twenty minutes the by-pass worked, then suddenly it stopped pumping. The patient was returned to the heart-lung machine that had taken over while the mitral valve was being replaced. The patient had suffered right heart failure. By 2:00 P.M., six and one-half hours after the operation had begun, the by-pass was pumping again and the patient's chest was closed.

Dr. DeBakey, still wearing his blood-spattered surgical gown, left the operating room and was met in the corridor by Jules Bergman and an ABC crew who had somehow managed to set up television cameras in what was supposed to be a restricted area. Dr. DeBakey stripped off his mask and gave Bergman an optimistic, exclusive interview.

Disorganization bordered on chaos. Having been promised equal treatment, the newsmen were incensed. The public-relations office was confused. No one connected with the hospital seemed to know what to do without Dr. DeBakey's authorization, and he was unavailable. Morse's photographs went out unedited.

The patient, Morris DeRudder, never regained consciousness. Over a five-day postoperative period, his kidneys failed and his blood had to be cleansed by dialysis, he bled internally, and he finally succumbed to a massive lung rupture.

Dr. DeBakey was to perform seven more attachments of the left ventricular by-pass. Two of his patients would survive. None of the records were to appear in the Baylor surgical files, and none of the results were to be published in medical journals.

The operations brought Dr. DeBakey fame that survived the criticism of his peers, but the relevancy of the precedents he set in the use of artificial cardiac devices in humans was not to be fully apparent until the aftermath of the operation when Cooley implanted the world's first artificial heart in Haskell Karp.

Ancient Chinese legend has it that in 300 B.C. two sick travelers, Kung Wu of Lu and Chi Ying of Cao, called on the surgeon Pien Ch'iao for medical treatment. Ch'iao gave the men sleeping potions and then interchanged their hearts and stomachs. Three days later the patients awoke fully recovered and were sent their separate ways home. 2,267 years later, Denise Ann Darvall and her mother were struck by a car while crossing Pretoria Street in Capetown, South Africa. Mrs. Darvall was killed outright. Her daughter, whose skull was crushed, was removed to Groote Schurr ("Big Barn") Hospital where Louis Washkansky had been hospitalized as a potential heart transplant recipient. Following a tissue type and blood match between the donor and recipient, Dr. Christiaan Barnard removed the heart of Denise Darvall and sewed it into the chest of Mr. Washkansky. The public was stunned. The medical world was surprised—that is, with the exception of Dr. Norman Shumway, a clinical surgeon and researcher at Stanford University School of Medicine.

Pien Ch'iao aside, the scientific era of organ transplantation was ushered in by Dr. Alexis Carrel, who in 1912 won a Nobel

Prize for the first reported heart and lung transplantations. His patients were dogs. In 1957, Norman Shumway and Richard Lower, his associate, picked up where Carrel had left off and extended the research toward solving the three most crucial problems related to transplantation of the human heart: the development of a workable surgical technique for implantation; an accumulation of knowledge as to how well a heart cut off from the central nervous system could maintain circulation; a means to arrest the body's natural tendency to reject foreign tissue. By the summer of 1967, they had made the initial breakthroughs, and Shumway granted an interview to Duke Yates of *The Journal of the American Medical Association.*

Shumway told Yates that the time was ripe for a human heart transplant, the required conditions being that a recipient and a compatible donor turn up simultaneously. Shumway did not tell Yates that he had a suitable recipient waiting at Stanford University Hospital. The patient, a thirty-five-year-old man, had an irreparable cardiac ailment; moreover, because he had undergone extensive x-ray treatment for Hodgkin's disease, his rejection processes had been arrested and his body was more apt to accept a foreign heart. Shumway was eagerly awaiting a donor.

The interview was published in November. In view of the fact that Shumway was the world's foremost authority on heart transplants, his declaration meant that the race was on. The green light was no sooner given than Dr. Adrian Kantrowitz, a cardiac assist and transplant researcher at Maimonides Hospital in Brooklyn, New York, sent out five hundred telegrams in search of a donor. But Barnard beat them all on December 3.

Dr. Denton Cooley: "Like most surgeons, I was dumfounded when I heard that Chris Barnard had done a transplant, and I immediately predicted failure within forty-eight hours. The truth is, I was envious of Barnard. I wished very much it had been me, but since it wasn't, I was eager to participate. I discussed the matter with my associates. I told them I was contemplating doing a transplant and to be on the lookout for a donor. Tooling up was only a matter of minutes. And we always had more than our share of potential recipients."

Dr. DeBakey commended Barnard's accomplishment as a "real breakthrough in the whole field of heart replacement." He then organized a transplant committee at Baylor to study the ramifications of the matter. Cooley, who had performed more heart operations than anyone else in the world and had a celebrated knowledge of the organ, was not invited to become a member of DeBakey's committee, and he was momentarily crestfallen and furious.

Kantrowitz found his donor, an anencephalic infant with a badly deformed head and virtually no brain, and transplanted its heart into a two-day-old baby. It was a tedious nine-hour operation, and the tiny recipient died on the operating table.

Meanwhile in South Africa, Louis Washkansky was being constantly monitored in sterile isolation. His mattress and bedclothing were autoclaved and changed regularly. The air in his room was mechanically circulated and disinfected, and the walls and floors were scrubbed with phenolic solution. Swab specimens were taken from the skin, throat, mouth, and rectum of everyone who attended him. He had daily blood cultures and his scrotal area was periodically dusted with Mycostatin powder. Despite all these precautions, the immunosuppressive drugs and radiation therapy which were administered to ward off rejection of the transplanted heart severely reduced Washkansky's ability to react against microorganisms and infections. One week after the transplant, his blood showed an increase in white cells, including lymphocytes, the type of white cell that the body manufactures to attack and destroy foreign tissue. Barnard stepped up the drug dosages and increased the cobalt treatments.

While Washkansky was fighting for his life, several thousand miles away, at the Plaza Hotel in New York City, an international panel of heart surgeons was meeting to discuss the ethical implications of his transplant. Dr. Charles Bailey, who in the early 1950s had incurred the wrath of the medical profession for his hospital-to-hospital rush to perfect a controversial heart valve procedure, declared the Washkansky transplant ten years premature. Dr. Jacob Zimmerman, a colleague of Bailey's at New York's St. Barnabas Hospital, agreed, adding, "It is medically and morally wrong for us as doctors to stand by a dying patient's bedside, hoping he'll get it over with quickly so we can grab his heart." Zimmerman predicted despotic rulers taking the hearts of political enemies for transplants. "I will never participate in such surgery," he said. Dr. Donald Ross of London, a South African by birth and a former classmate of Barnard's, and the great Swiss surgeon, Ake Senning, said not only would they perform transplants, they were optimistic that heart banks would be established where organs could be stored. But the American conservatism prevailed; throughout the country plans were abroad to declare moritoria on the new operation. Dr. DeBakey's committee at Baylor concluded that heart transplants were as yet untenable. Despite the questionable merits of the left ventricular by-pass, DeBakey, who had a large government grant for its development, still believed that mechanical devices were the answer. The Baylor committee recommended a local moritorium on heart transplants. On learning of their decision, Cooley doubled his efforts to find a donor.

Washkansky took a turn for the worse. Uncertain whether he was developing pneumonia or rejecting the transplanted heart, the Barnard team loaded Washkansky with penicillin and white blood cells. Seventeen days after receiving the first heart transplant, Louis Washkansky died. There was evidence of pneumonia in both lungs, but no signs of rejection. Barnard told newsmen, "As soon as the occasion arises, we will do the next transplant."

Moments before that press conference, Barnard had told a potential recipient in the cardiac ward of Groote Schurr that Washkansky was dead. He asked the patient if he would be willing to go through with the operation when a donor was found. Dr. Philip Blaiberg said yes.

On December 28, Dr. Donald Frederickson, director of the National Heart Institute, and six of his lieutenants met with fourteen federally supported transplant specialists at Chicago's O'Hare Field. The purpose of the three-hour conference was to assess the heart-transplant scene and discuss the prospects for financial support from the National Institutes of Health. Cooley, who had never received a government grant, had not been invited. Nor had Christiaan Barnard. However, when CBS heard that the meeting was forthcoming, they paid Barnard's way and arranged for him to attend as a personal guest of Dr. Adrian Kantrowitz.

The focus was on Barnard—handsome, self-certain, arrogant. He discussed the Washkansky case as a therapeutic procedure intended to prolong life. But the majority of those present, several of whom were rankled at Barnard's recent publicity, contended that the operation was still essentially experimental. Unruffled, Barnard made several personal appearances on American television, visited LBJ's ranch, and then flew back to Cape Town. The day he arrived, a twenty-four-year-old factory worker named Clive Haupt suffered a massive brain hemorrhage while sunbathing on a Cape Town beach. When his condition was declared hopeless, he was removed from Victoria Hospital to Groote Schurr, where Barnard removed his heart and placed it in Dr. Philip Blaiberg.

Shumway had been disappointed that another surgeon had anticipated him. That the surgeon was Barnard, a classmate of Shumway's at the University of Minnesota, was in no way ameliorative. In addition, Barnard had spent three and a half months in the transplant laboratories of Dr. Richard Lower, Shumway's coresearcher, just prior to the Washkansky operation. Finally Shumway got his chance.

Three days after the Blaiberg transplant, Mrs. Virginia May White collapsed at a party while celebrating her twenty-second wedding anniversary. The next afternoon Shumway transplanted her heart into Mike Kasperak, a fifty-four-year-old steelworker. In opposition to Barnard, many in the American medical profession were counting on Shumway to make a gloriously successful entry into what was becoming a transplant derby. But it was not to be. Although there was no question that Kasperak received the most sophisticated and thorough care available, the aftermath of his transplant was a nightmare of frustration and suffering.

The cavity left after Kasperak's diseased heart had been removed was three times too large. Five hours after the operation, he was returned to surgery, where his chest was reopened and drained of blood and excess fluids. Two days later, his liver and kidneys failed and his intestines began hemorrhaging. To cleanse his blood of the poisons left by his shut-down kidneys, the surgeons opened Kasperak's abdomen and filled the cavity with an absorbent solution of salts and sugar. He was given continuous transfusions of whole blood and blood platelets. The crises seemed to be abating when Kasperak fell into a coma. The surgeons opened him a third time and removed his gall bladder.

After fifteen days, Kasperak died. His hospital bill, which included $7,200 for 288 pints of blood, was $28,845—nearly $2,000 a day. Though not exceptionally high for an early transplant (Cooley eventually reduced the cost of the procedure to $250 a day), the Kasperak expenditure brought a barrage of criticism from those who felt that the money might have been better spent on research toward preventing heart disease—a manifestation of the traditional differences between the surgeons and the researchers.

Three days after the Kasperak transplant, Adrian Kantrowitz tried another one. The operation lasted nine hours—six hours longer than the patient survived. Kantrowitz withdrew from the race. Then P. K. Sen in Bombay lost a patient on the operating table. At the Hôpital de la Pitié, hours after the French Cabinet ruled that a donor is legally dead when his brain waves are flat, Dr. Christian Cabrol put a new heart in a truck driver who died without regaining consciousness.

After the initial shock, the interest of the press was directed toward clinical justification of the operation and whether or not all the people who were attempting heart transplants were equipped to do so.

By medical tradition, innovative procedures and discoveries are not aired before they have been perfected. But nothing on the scale of a human heart transplant, with its drama and hints at patchwork immortality, had ever confronted the medical establishment. It would have been impossible to avoid the onslaught of the news media. Besides, the time lags inherent in the traditional reporting in the professional journals forced most engaged medical people to turn to newspapers and magazines for up-to-date information. One of the most interesting revelations of the heart transplant controversy was that surgeons often worked in competition with one another, not only for the good of humanity but for the gratification of their own egos. The contest wasn't limited to two Houston surgeons after all.

Dr. Denton Cooley: "Some of the news reports were fine, but others were so confusing and inventive, I came to rely on the press for little more than general information. I was vitally interested. My first concern was saving the lives of sick people, but it would be untrue to say that I was not eager to take part in this, the most exciting development in cardiac surgery.

"The delay of my entry into heart transplantation is easily

explained. We couldn't find any donors, and we suspected that they were being purposely denied us. I could respect, if not agree with, the contention of some people that the spirit or the soul or what have you resides in the heart. But it was impossible for me to in any way agree with those otherwise enlightened people who chose to relegate the viable organs of their loved ones to dust when those same organs would have provided hope for people who were dying in wait. It was frustrating as hell. Finally, though, we got our chance."

May 1, 1968. Mr. Newell France, administrator of St. Luke's–Texas Children's hospitals, informed Dr. Cooley that he had their full support and approval to proceed with a cardiac transplantation program. The following day, while Cooley was attending a medical meeting in Louisiana, Katherine Martin, age fifteen, arrived at the emergency room of Ben Taub Hospital, one of the Baylor-associated hospitals in the Medical Center. During an argument with her nineteen-year-old husband, the girl had put a bullet through her right temple. The physicians at Ben Taub declared the wound mortal. Katherine Martin was without reflexes and her brain waves remained flat, though her heart activity continued with mechanical ventilation and injected vasopressers. When Dr. Cooley's two associates, Grady Hallman and Robert Bloodwell, received news of the girl's condition, they requested that she be transferred to St. Luke's to be considered as a potential donor for a heart transplant. Her family agreed, and at 6:00 P.M., her cardiac function being maintained by portable support apparatus, the child bride was moved across the street to St. Luke's.

Mr. Everett Thomas, a forty-seven-year-old accountant from Phoenix, had been admitted to St. Luke's on April 28 for evaluation and support in preparation for the surgical replacement of three heart valves damaged by rheumatic fever. He had had two serious heart attacks. As a result of residual liver and lung damage, he had suffered two blood clots to the brain, causing partial paralysis of his right side and temporary blindness in his right eye. He had been bedridden for five months. The prognosis was extremely poor; nonetheless Thomas was scheduled for surgery Friday morning, May 3.

Dr. Cooley: "When I learned that a potential donor was in the hospital, I immediately thought of Thomas. He was comparatively young, and other than a ruined heart and some paralysis, the rest of his body was in pretty good shape. The young lady, of course, was hopeless. She was decerebrate and the bullet was lodged in the base of her brain.

"It was a peculiar coincidence that this girl should arrive as a potential donor. Not only was the timing remarkable, I had operated on her for a coarction of the aorta when she was nine. At that time, her heart had been enlarged from the stress caused by the constricted aorta. But now, as a replacement for the diseased heart of a large man, this cardiac enlargement was so much the better to handle his circulation."

Cooley explained the situation to Thomas and his wife. A triple valve replacement was one of the riskiest operations he performed, and if Thomas made it off the table, his chances would be extremely slim. There was a potential donor in the house. If the valve replacements did not appear to offer hope of life, there was an alternative: a transplant. He asked Thomas and his wife to discuss the matter and let him know their decision. At 6:30 P.M., half an hour after Katherine Martin had arrived in OR Two, Everett Thomas agreed to accept her heart.

Although Cooley had not definitely decided to proceed with the transplant, at 7:15 that evening he met with Newell France, the hospital administrator. Cooley said that much of the criticism resulting from DeBakey's use of the left ventricular bypass in 1966 was attributable to poor press management on the part of the Methodist Hospital public-relations staff. "I'll do the surgery, and you handle the circus," Cooley said. France agreed and called a meeting of his staff for 9:00 P.M.

In the meantime, Katherine Martin had failed to respond to the Cooley team's continuing efforts to resuscitate her. There had been no activity on her EEG since her admission to Ben Taub more than six hours earlier. Her pupils were dilated and fixed. She had no breathing reflex. Dr. Robert Jones was the fifth neurologist to examine the girl and he, like the others, declared her beyond recovery.

Up to this point, the case of Katherine Martin was not unlike many in which the patient has suffered massive, irreversible brain damage. But rather than turning off the respirator and discontinuing the drugs, two surgeons wheeled her through the inside corridor from the recovery room to OR Two. Everett Thomas, whose condition was rapidly deteriorating, was moved into OR One. Through the windows of the scrub room between them, Thomas, who was semiconscious, could see Katherine Martin's head swathed heavily in bandages. The pumping of her respirator sent echoes of amplified breathing throughout the surgical suite. Thomas, a large, bald man with a heavy jaw, lay back and closed his eyes. The nurses and doctors felt puzzled by the combined atmospheres of tragedy and hope: a young bride who had killed herself in a fit of passion; a man in his forties whose will to live had been relentlessly challenged by progressive illnesses that had finally reduced him to little more than will.

The meeting took place in the conference room adjoining Newell France's office. There was France, two assistants—John Creighton and Bonnie Woolridge—Armen Jorjorian, the chaplain, and Dr. Cooley, who was in and out between surgery. The purpose of the meeting, as France explained it, was to anticipate the public-relations impact the transplant might have on the doctors, the patient and his family, the donor's family, and the hospital. The first question was whether there should be a complete news blackout, the drawback of which was to make likely inaccurate reporting based on leaks and speculation.

What's more, being denied information, the press might respond hostilely. No one, including Cooley, was eager to hazard a proclamation as to how the matter should be handled.

Shortly before midnight, Dr. Cooley drew a scalpel down the center of Thomas's chest, sawed open the rib cage, and attached the heart-lung machine. Then, assisted by Robert Bloodwell, he cut through the thick heart muscle and began to explore. The calcification of the aortic valve extended up into the artery. The dense calcification of the mitral valve had spread into the septum between the heart's chambers and into the conductive system (the natural pacemaker) of the ventricles. The damage was too extensive to repair.

During the induction of anesthesia, it had been impossible to raise Thomas's blood pressure above seventy-five. Katherine Martin was in total respiratory arrest. At 1:01 A.M., Cooley called across to Grady Hallman in OR Two and told him to take the girl's heart out.

Rather than cooling the patient and the recipient as Kantrowitz had done, or perfusing the donor heart with blood from the heart-lung machine as Barnard and Shumway had done, Cooley would rely on his speed and skill to get the donor heart in place with a minimal amount of tampering. With the entire upper right chamber and segments of the ascending aorta and the pulmonary artery intact, Hallman brought Katherine Martin's heart across from OR Two in a steel basin. Detached, bodiless, it continued to beat beneath a sterile towel.

The left upper chamber of the donor's heart was open at the back, leaving the overlapping tissue necessary for attachment. Cooley opened the right upper chamber, a modification of his that preserved the auricular nodes, the independent nervous system of the heart. There was a gaping dark hole where Thomas's heart had been. Cooley lifted the glistening donor heart from the basin and began an inside suture joining the left upper chamber with the corresponding remnant of Thomas's heart. Then in the same manner, rolling the heart over and into the chest, he joined the right chambers. He quickly anastomosed the pulmonary artery and the aorta and checked all the suture lines for leaks. When the vascular clamps were removed, the heart shuddered into ventricular fibrillation. Cooley held the defibrillator paddles tight to the quivering muscle. After a single jolting countershock, the heart resumed a regular beat and Thomas's blood pressure found a normal level.

It was 1:36 A.M. The actual transplant had taken thirty-five minutes, a fraction of the time previously required by other surgeons. When the drains were in place and Thomas's chest was closed, he was taken to OR Six, which had been converted to a sterile intensive-care unit. Katherine Martin's body and the ruined heart of Everett Thomas were removed to the pathology laboratory in the basement.

The surgical team and France's group spent the early hours of the morning establishing guidelines for a press release. At 6:30 A.M., the press and wire services were notified and the hospital was almost immediately inundated with reporters and photographers. By 9:00 A.M., calls were arriving regularly from around the world. Berlin wanted to know Cooley's age, height, and weight. A Louisville man requested a penis transplant. There were threats from the emotionally unsettled, congratulations from other surgeons and well-wishers, and importunate calls from referring doctors and patients with wasted hearts and new hope. James Cobb flew in from Alexandria, Louisiana, on a jet provided by his congressman. James Stuckwish, an Alpine, Texas, hospital administrator whose condition Cooley had declared inoperable a few months earlier, arrived the same day. They both wanted new hearts.

Meanwhile the press scramble continued without abatement. As more newsmen and television crews arrived, they were moved from the administrative conference room to the Texas Children's auditorium. An effort was made to relate developing news to the local papers first, then to the wire services, networks, and the nation's metropolitan newspapers and major magazines. But priorities became confused. Miriam Kass, a medical reporter on the Houston *Post*, became friendly with Mrs. Thomas and got an exclusive interview. A Milan reporter broke his leg in the melee, was hospitalized, and got exclusive interviews with the patients and the surgeons. The auditorium buzzed with angry accusations.

In the midst of the press uproar and the confused elation of the tired hospital staff, a call arrived from Methodist. A fifteen-year-old boy had been transferred there from Conroe Hospital. He had been in a motor-scooter accident. His spinal cord had been severed at the base of his brain, and his parents, personal friends of Cooley's, wished to make him available as a donor.

Because James Cobb was fourteen years younger than the other potential recipient, James Stuckwish, Cooley, unavoidably cast in a God-like role, decided that Cobb should get the heart. At 8:45 that Sunday evening, less than forty-eight hours after the Thomas transplant, the young accident victim was pronounced dead, Hallman carried his heart across from OR Two, and Cooley put it in Cobb.

But James Stuckwish didn't have to wait long. At 2:00 P.M. Tuesday, May 8, Cooley gave him the heart of Clarence Nicks, who had been beaten in a brawl. He was transferred from Methodist to St. Luke's as a potential donor, but because a homicide charge would likely be made against Nicks's assailant, if indeed his flat brainwaves indicated legal death, the Harris County medical examiner urged Cooley not to proceed with the transplant. Cooley argued that Nicks was dead and that another man's life was in the balance. Under the circumstances, Cooley said, he was going ahead with the operation. At 2:00 P.M.

that same day, Cooley transplanted Nicks's heart into James Stuckwish.*

Within seventy-two hours, Cooley had performed three heart transplants. True to form, he made the operation his by refinement and modification. He neither cooled nor perfused the donor hearts, he avoided clotting by removing a particular portion of the recipient's heart, he was the first surgeon to use antilymphocytic globulin, reducing the risk of infection and allowing patients to be up and about forty-eight hours after surgery.

James Cobb died three days later of leukopenia, pneumonia, and a sepsis infection. James Stuckwish lasted seven days, then his kidneys and liver shut down. But Everett Thomas survived his body's initial attempt to reject the foreign heart. Four days after the operation, he was ambulatory—the first American transplant who had made it, though no one knew for how long.

Louis Fierro, whom Cooley transplanted May 21, came along as well as Thomas. On June 12, with a dying patient on his hands and no human donor available, in a desperate emergency measure, Cooley put a ram's heart in a forty-eight-year-old man. Rejection was immediate—the ram's heart literally shriveled and died as it was being sutured in place, and Cooley didn't have a chance to use the pig's heart he had ready as a backup. Despite large numbers of violent accidents in Houston, donors were already becoming scarce. St. Luke's and the surrounding motels were filled with people waiting for hearts. Some got them, many more died waiting.

By the middle of August 1968, Cooley, with nine transplants, was far in the lead among the world's surgeons. The subject of television interviews with reporters from Europe and Asia, he was an international celebrity. And because of his articulateness

*Two years later a grand jury indicted Robert Patterson and Alfred Barnum for the murder of Clarence Nicks.

and his established reputation as a great cardiovascular surgeon, he soon supplanted Barnard as the recognized spokesman
for those who had participated in transplants. He enjoyed the
limelight immensely, but there were problems. There was dissent among his cardiologists as to whether or not he should be
doing so many transplants so quickly. Others on his team
thought Cooley was working in an optimistic euphoria borne of
this new power to give life.

"Cooley quickly had the surgical technique down pat," a
member of the team observed, "but the other end of it—postop
care, how to avoid infection and rejection when the patient's
natural defenses were reduced by drugs—was mostly guess-
work. Sometimes it was pretty depressing. But he believed in
what he was doing, and he believed the other problems would
be solved with experience. A few people were simply jealous:
they got ticked-off when they heard about him hob-nobbing
with royalty. They missed him in the coffee room."

At his wife's insistence, on August 17, Cooley and his family
flew to Acapulco for a week's vacation. He was unpacking his
bags at a villa lent them by a former president of Mexico when
a call came from Houston. An eight-year-old boy who had fallen
from a tree and crushed his skull had just arrived at St. Luke's.
His parents wanted him to become a donor. He was a suitable
match for Maria Giannaris, a lovely, doomed five-year-old. She
was a favorite of Cooley's. He took the first plane to Houston.
Following her transplant, Cooley took an unusual personal interest in little Maria.

Richard Hudson, independent oilman: "That next morning
he called me about eight o'clock and asked if I wanted to go to
the football game with him. I said I thought he was in Acapulco
—the morning papers weren't out yet—and he told me he had
come home to do a transplant on this little girl named Maria.
He sounded upset. I asked him if he wanted to come on over
now, and he said no, he'd been at the hospital all night and he

thought he'd go home and get a little sleep. I told him he was going to ruin himself sleeping so much. He said other people didn't seem to mind.

"After the football game, we went to the hospital. There were doctors working around the little girl, and Denton was very concerned. He kept saying, 'Maria? Maria, honey?' And you could tell by his tone of voice and the way he looked at her that this was more than the usual doctor-patient relationship. She knew who he was, too. She recognized him."

Cooley did another transplant that evening, and the next day, satisfied everything was being handled correctly, flew back to Acapulco. Four days later, Cooley's youngest daughter, Helen, fell from a twelve-foot diving board and struck her head on the side of the pool. Cooley pulled her out. She was unconscious, with a deep gash in the side of her head. Cooley tied the wound shut with strands of her hair and drove her to the small hospital in town. While he was waiting for x rays and working over her, he wondered at the tragic irony should his own daughter become a heart donor. Since his return to Acapulco, he had been thinking about Maria Giannaris.

After an hour or so, Helen came around. It was a minor skull fracture; she would be all right. The next day there was a call from Houston: Maria Giannaris was dead.

No sooner had Cooley returned from Acapulco than the De-Bakey team launched into the transplant business with a surgical spectacular. Perhaps because Barnard had garnered first glory or because DeBakey had spent his influence promoting cardiac-assist devices, DeBakey had been reluctant to enter the race; he agreed to the necessity of clinical trials, but insisted on the most careful, objective evaluations. It was a safe, sane, though somewhat uncharacteristic position he assumed.

Meanwhile, unbeknown to DeBakey, Dr. Ted Diethrich—a brilliant young surgeon-researcher on DeBakey's staff who, for his ambition, was locally recognized as a slightly scaled-down, latter-day Cooley—had been laying out a detailed master plan for multiple transplantations from the body of a single donor. The recipients were ready, the donor arrived (ironically, like Cooley's first donor, she was a teen-age suicide), and Diethrich, organized and set up down to the last suture, approached De-Bakey for the go-ahead. The publicity prospects were overwhelming. DeBakey agreed, and at 2 A.M. on August 31, Diethrich initiated a simultaneous series of operations that took the heart, one lung, and both kidneys from a single donor and transplanted them into four recipients. The headlines were: DEBAKEY TEAM OF SIXTY PERFORMS MULTIPLE TRANSPLANT. In time, Diethrich would follow *his* first heart transplant recipient to Phoenix and, emulating the model of Cooley's Texas Heart Institute, organize and head the Arizona Heart Institute.

Whatever disillusionment and melancholy Cooley might have felt following the death of the Giannaris child faded in the light of the spectacular challenge from Methodist. The De-Bakey team did its second transplant on September 5, but the patient died of cardiac arrest eight days later. The following morning, Cooley took the heart and lungs from a one-day-old anencephalic female baby and transplanted them *en bloc* into the tiny chest of a two-month-old female infant with incurable heart disease and atrophied lungs. No one had ever before attempted such an operation. Surgically, it was a near perfect procedure, but the postoperative complications proved insurmountable, and after fourteen hours, the child died of pulmonary insufficiency. It was Cooley's tenth transplant and although he was to perform eleven more, at this point, appalled by the mortality rate and the paucity of donors, he began to think in terms of alternatives.

Having done five transplants in less than a month, DeBakey had committed himself to the new operation and, consequently, began to neglect the importunings of Dr. Liotta, whose cardiac-assist research was failing for want of funds. It was then

THE COOLEY INFLUENCE   169

that Dr. Cooley made an astounding statement to UPI: Due to the lack of donors, he planned to build an artificial heart "on another basis" from the one Dr. DeBakey was interested in. Though he elaborated no further, what Cooley had in mind was a plastic device for *total* cardiac replacement rather than an auxiliary pump on the order of the left ventricular by-pass.

Two of Cooley's transplants died in October, and many of those who had been waiting for hearts that never appeared left their motels and hopes in Houston and returned home to die. Then Everett Thomas, who had been the star of Cooley's showcase, the longest surviving American transplant, checked back into St. Luke's exhibiting the unmistakable signs that his body was rejecting the heart of Katherine Martin. DeBakey did three transplants that month; Cooley, one.

On November 20, after all efforts to reverse the rejection process had failed, Cooley did a second transplant on Everett Thomas. He survived three days. There were two more recipient deaths that November. It had been the world's busiest heart transplant month (Cooley had done five) and the period at which public interest in the most publicized and controversial operation yet devised peaked and began to pale. Regardless of what had been learned and what was left to be learned (a year and a half later a National Heart Institute task force was to pronounce the operation worthwhile), without public support the moment would be lost.

Throughout the world, there were twenty-six heart transplants in November 1968. Six in December, none by Cooley. Instead, that Saturday morning before Christmas, Cooley summoned Dr. Domingo Liotta to his office in the basement of St. Luke's Hospital and they laid plans for the construction and first implantation of a total replacement artificial heart.

Part Three

Chapter 12

Going to Houston

$W^'E$ were living in St. Louis when Dr. Cooley put the artificial heart in Haskell Karp. The press had pretty much botched the beginning of the transplant era, so it was understandable that they were more restrained in their coverage of the first mechanical heart. The tenor of the news on Karp as he lay in Houston with a plastic device circulating his blood was one of guarded hopefulness: a wait-and-see attitude that was so remarkably different from the sensational manner in which the first heart transplant had been reported, that I wondered if Dr. Barnard's accusations of the irresponsibility of the media had not been accurate. At any rate it seemed that the newsmen and the public were on their way toward recognizing that medicine is a developing discipline, and that doctors, rather than being sacrosanct miracle workers, are human beings and subject to error. But heroes fall hard because their descent proves the vanity and ignorance of those who created them. When Haskell Karp died, the trouble began. The complex physiology of human heart transplantation, the welter of moral-ethical problems related to it, and the number of participating surgeons presented the world's journalists with a starburst of moving targets. The situation did not lend itself to easy conclusiveness because no one had a comprehensive knowledge of what was happening. Four days after Barnard's first transplant patient died, before the press or the public or the medical profession had yet had a clear shot at him, he did another, and the world competition was on. The critical focus was obliged to widen and lessen its force. But Cooley, whose use of a mechanical heart represented a technical achievement that in many ways surpassed the exchange of one natural organ for another, had been alone at center stage, in full view of a world somewhat vindictive and more sophisticated than Barnard's.

I had kept up with Dr. Cooley over the years. Once in a while someone who needed an operation and had heard about my experience in Houston would telephone. It was usually, but not always, a heart problem. My high school football coach, for example, suddenly began developing blood clots in his legs and no one could figure out what the cause was. After a clot migrated to his lungs and almost killed him, he checked out of the local hospital and settled at home with a TV Guide and a bottle of bourbon, resigned to go out in that pose. His situation was similar enough to what mine had been that I was able to persuade him to see Dr. Cooley; but there was a condition. It was late Saturday night; he would go only if Dr. Cooley would see him the following Monday. So I phoned Dr. Cooley and he agreed. That Tuesday he performed an exploratory operation on my friend, found the problem (a partially withered kidney had been generating the clots), and fixed it.

I suppose I was proselytizing. But my faith in Dr. Cooley was based on fact, on practical results. If I ever considered the possibility that there had been anything fortuitous or mystical about the circumstances of our initial meeting, unlike many of the patients and families I was to see in Houston, I kept it to myself.

When Dr. Cooley made national headlines by performing three heart transplants during the first week in May 1968, I sent him a congratulatory telegram and followed his career through that year and into the spring of the next. Before the transplants, it had been difficult to identify Cooley to a nonmedical person without relating him to DeBakey. But that suddenly changed. Everyone knew who Cooley was. And it was significant that toastmasters at various medical meetings began telling this anecdote: Late for an operation, Dr. DeBakey was speeding through the Texas Medical Center in his new Ferrari when a police officer stopped him. "Do you know who I am?" the speeder fumed. "I'm Dr. Michael E. DeBakey." "Look, fellow," the officer replied, "I don't care if you're Dr. Denton A. Cooley, you can't drive fifty in a ten-mile zone."

One Saturday night in late April, we gave a small party to celebrate a new book by a friend, Stanley Elkin. Elkin brought William Gass with him. Gass was a writer too, and they were both professors at Washington University in St. Louis.

The only remarkable thing about the party—and I recall having thought so at the time—was the coincidences that precipitated the main topic of conversation. A few months earlier, Elkin had had a heart attack, and he was obsessed with his diet and cigarette regimen. My main concern was our second son who, after suffering a severe case of rheumatic fever, had just been released from St. Louis Children's Hospital, a subsidiary of Washington University Medical School where, nineteen years earlier, my first heart ailment had been diagnosed. As if that wasn't enough, Gass gave an impromptu reading from his story, "In the Heart of the Heart of the Country"—the only existing piece of literature with "heart" in the title twice.

Inevitably, I told a few Cooley stories, but there was something different in the way they were received. Cooley had come to be more than a heart surgeon—he was a personality. Someone, perhaps it was Elkin, was interested in the man behind the anecdotes. None of the news stories had offered a single insight into Cooley's character, no answers to the implicit question, Why? More than that, one story seemed to have been spun off another, presenting a stock profile of him as simply a tall Texan who was, by all reckoning, the best heart surgeon around. What was even more startling, and somewhat disappointing, I had little more to add. I had always believed that I excelled at understanding people, and yet, except for a few personal stories that I had probably pruned to inaccuracy, I knew no more about the man to whom I owed my life than what a few reporters had observed and passed around for paraphrasing. It was good that Cooley's abilities as a surgeon had finally been recognized by the public, but no one seemed to know how he had gotten there. Indeed, sidetracked by the sort of egocentricity that life-and-death scenes prompt, and the continuing spectacular that brought Cooley to notice, no one seemed to care.

After everyone left, I sat down and tried to distill what I actually knew about Denton Cooley from the embellished stories I had so often told. It was all pretty impressionistic. I remembered the deep green tropical hedge that lined the walk to the building where his office was. He had a crew cut in 1957, and his sideburns were graying. He wore the type of iridescent suit that you associate with the garish tastes of wealthy Texans. And a swirling bow tie. And black-and-white spectators. He was certain, casual, indifferent, and shy. I thought he exhibited a mandatory, professional concern that had been calculated to permit him to test a patient's awareness—if you believed the pose, it was reassuring; if you didn't, you gained his respect.

The night before my operation Dr. Cooley took my wife into the hall and told her that I might come out of the surgery paralyzed from the waist down. "... from the waist down," she repeated to me, holding back her tears, and added, assuming in her innocence that she was changing the subject, "He's the most attractive man I've ever seen in my life."

To me, everything about Cooley raised competitiveness. After he did a cut-down in my arm for a dye study and suggested that I take a cab back to the motel, I insisted on walking and passed out halfway there. In another ego confrontation, I sat up on the operating table and, aware that he himself had never been where I now was for the second time, feigned cool interest as he pointed to an x ray with a scalpel and explained exactly what he was going to do. I had a lucky penny in my ear; the circulating nurse secured it with a strip of tape.

Until that evening after the party, I had purposely forgotten these things, because it had been far simpler and more acceptable to present Dr. Cooley, at least implicitly, as my hero. In fact, I was deeply and secretly, even to myself, locked in a dilemma concerning how I felt about him.

The next morning at a Quaker meeting, a pathologist from Washington University gave me his underscored collection of Cooley-damning articles. That afternoon I called Houston.

In a lethargic, cultured drawl, Dr. Cooley said today he had played tennis for the first time in seven months, taking three sets from a local "hot-shot," though not without some effort. The weather was as lovely in Houston as it was in St. Louis, but in Houston they often enjoyed the same sort of day in January.

I said I had some business to discuss with him.

"For God's sake, don't come down here and commit suicide so I can use your heart in a transplant!"

No, but I did want to come down there.

He paused. "All right," he said. "We'll talk about it. Call me in three weeks."

Before two weeks had passed, I read in the paper that Dr. Cooley was going to speak, of all places, at Washington University School of Medicine. The cardiologist who had treated our son told me who was in charge of Cooley's visit. But when I phoned the man, he wouldn't tell me when Cooley was arriving or where he would be staying. Such security seemed odd and overly dramatic. But at the time I had no way of knowing about blood maniacs and how they had responded to the more macabre and ghoulish aspects of transplants and mechanical hearts.

An hour before the lecture was to begin, most of the middle section and the lower side seats in Clopton Auditorium were taken. A large group of nurses' aides and auxiliary ladies in scarlet aprons were munching sandwiches from the canteen. The medical students were distinguishable from the professors for their youth and practiced severity. All the seats were soon taken or saved, and three rows of folding chairs were filled as quickly as they were set up. When the word was mumbled along that Dr. Cooley was on his way, the aisles and steps were loaded four abreast and the exits were packed. Then Cooley entered.

A fashionably dressed man wearing French glasses began the introduction. Dr. Cooley, elegant and insouciant, sat in the front row, his legs crossed, bouncing a black monk's strap loafer. No one was listening to the introduction. They were all looking at Cooley.

Cooley rose to the applause and clipped a microphone around his neck. His tan was accentuated by a white shirt and, when he smiled in the corner of his mouth, by even whiter teeth. He was a startlingly handsome man. This, combined with his professional reputation and rumors of his considerable wealth, led one to the quick conclusion that Cooley had everything and, of course, prompted a subtle compulsion to dispute his excellence. It was a brief, petty reaction, but, as I was to discover, widespread and integral to an understanding of the man and his relations with others.

"Dr. Evarts Graham, after whom this lecture series was named, was a great surgeon and a fine gentleman. But perhaps a more meaningful tribute than mine would be that of the late Dr. Alfred Blalock, my mentor, whom Dr. Graham recommended for the Chair of Surgery at Johns Hopkins in 1938." The lights went out and a slide was projected on a screen behind Dr. Cooley. Dr. Graham and Dr. Blalock were laughing and drinking at what appeared to be a night-club table. "I believe this picture illustrates not only the intense nature of their consultations, but also Dr. Blalock's high esteem for Dr. Graham. If you look carefully, you will notice that Dr. Blalock is offering him an unfiltered cigarette. Friendly, professional competition . . . we know all about that!"

Four patients from Children's Hospital were presented to Dr. Cooley. All of them had undergone surgery for congenital heart defects. Three were well enough to stand. One, a pale, spavined infant, fought the air as his mother rocked him and listened with anxious pride. Remarking about similar cases of his own, Cooley corroborated the diagnoses and treatments without being expansive or overly complimentary. In style and substance, he knew what he was doing. His muted enthusiasm, his smooth interpolations and changes of pace were stage perfect. Those I spoke with later were surprised and impressed with his medical sophistication, his ability to diagnose as well as correct rare deformities and malfunctions. He was a great surgeon, hence the average doctor was delighted to assume that he neither knew nor cared about any other facet of medicine. My pathologist friend was in the front row.

Cooley narrated a movie on the implantation of the artificial heart. Just as the film ended, he said, "The controversy and criticism precipitated by this operation have caused me grave concern. As a result, I now make it a point to consult with my colleagues before performing any operation that's in the least out of the ordinary." The concluding slide was an arm-locked circle of naked men and women in group therapy.

The audience stood. The applause began at a crescendo and stayed there a full minute before Cooley, having returned to his seat, half lifted himself up on the chair arms and made a slight bow. Appearing faintly bewildered, he looked to his host as if for support or an explanation. Then he rose to his full height and turned to the audience and smiled. And then he blushed. That did it. While the applause could not have grown louder, it accelerated until the staccato was lost in a steady roar.

If this had been a lay audience sympathetic with Cooley and angered by his recent press, their response would have been understandable. But these were not sentimental people. The dramas of medicine were commonplace to everyone here, and yet they were obviously overwhelmed. The subject had been spectacular, historical. The performance flawless. No actor could have had a better knowledge of his audience. No rhetorical apologist could have presented his case more persuasively. Still, it was Cooley—articulate, irreverent, at once certain and shy—whose presence had carried and then loomed over the message.

When the doctor with the French glasses began to ease Cooley away from the medical students who were questioning him, I moved down in front. He inquired about my wife and family. The doctor with glasses approached and lifted his hand as if to place it on Cooley's shoulder, but smiled and cleared his throat instead.

"So, you come on down to Houston," Cooley said. Then he turned and straightened his tie in the glass of the exit door. One of the entourage opened it, and the others, trying hard to appear unimpressed, followed Cooley's lanky shamble down the hall.

May 1969. Coming in on Route 59 past miles of dozer-tracked clearings and the skeletons of new motels, the northern edge of Houston was mostly warped frame houses and junkyards with hubcap displays. The freeway dipped to a series of exits, and then, beyond a labyrinth of unfinished interchanges, the city appeared. In the early evening the buildings resembled huge cracking towers sprinkled with lighted windows and topped with the emblems of Gulf, Texaco, and Humble, all in a haze of yellow smog blown in from the refineries farther south.

The major streets ran one-way from Court Square on the bayou. I turned off there and headed south on Main, past the movie theaters and the ironwork balconies of the Rice Hotel, the fashionable Warwick Hotel, and the art museum at the Montrose fountain roundabout, where the street was lined with hibiscus and lattice trunked palmettos.

But to backtrack and approach the city again from a different point of view. Dr. Cooley had speculated on much of the land the dozers were clearing, and he had an interest in a large motel going up out there. Just west of the junkyards were the decaying mansions of Houston Heights, the residential subdivision that Cooley's paternal grandfather had developed at the turn of the century. And D. D. Cooley School and the church he founded. It was rumored that when the officials who planned this highway discovered one of the interchanges would be over a parcel of land that Dr. Cooley owned, they altered the master blueprint, converting an acre of land worth only its assessed valuation into prime commercial property. Then Dr. Cooley gave away the deed. And the buildings: L. F. McCollum, chairman of the board of Baylor Medical College, held the same position at Texaco. The president of Gulf and Western was on the board of Cooley's Texas Heart Institute, as was Gus Wortham, president of American Standard Life and one of the wealthiest men in Texas. Cooley's uncle had founded the Security National Bank, while Cooley himself was on the board of the Bank of Texas. Shortly after their marriage, Cooley's mother and father had lived in the Rice Hotel, site of the first capitol of Texas. Now, Governor John Connally, along with the rest of them, was on the Texas Heart Institute Board, too. Denton Cooley's influence in Houston was seemingly limitless. As a crack athlete–businessman–heart surgeon, Houston born and bred, he had fulfilled the Texas dream. He was the most respected and popular man in the city. But, with fame, Cooley had begun consorting with movie stars and kings and queens . . . and Houston wasn't too sure about that. The Karp controversy came at a time when some of the local people thought Cooley was getting too self-important. The question was whether their criticism was grounded in fact.

For several blocks past the Montrose fountain, both sides of Main Street were so dense with foliage that the street lights were all but obscured with leaf shadows. Then it was Texas Medical Center territory—drugstores, surgical supply, uniform and medical bookstores, restaurants, and motels—and there were hearts everywhere. A bumper sticker on a lopsided Cadillac in the front rank of Big-Hearted Bert's Used Car Lot: THE HOUSTON SCHOOL BOARD NEEDS A HEART TRANSPLANT. Past a drive-in bank with a neon valentine sign—IN THE HEART OF THE MEDICAL CENTER—was a low green-and-white structure where you could donate any or all of your organs to medical science.

I pulled up beside the bank on the narrow concrete island that separates Main Street and Fannin Avenue. Across Fannin, the twin nine-story wings of Methodist Hospital rose from a blue mosaic mural of Christ that covered the façade of the building. Dr. Michael DeBakey was chief of surgery there. South across a parking lot, at a forty-five-degree angle to the street, was the beige brick and steel Texas Children's side of the

St. Luke's–Texas Children's combine. And beyond there, specifically planned to be the tallest medical building anywhere, the superstructure of the Texas Heart Institute rose into the dark above the floodlights. Already it was called the Cooley Tower, just as the Shamrock Hotel, where Cooley's wealthier patients awaited surgery, had come to be called the Cooley Hilton. Methodist Hospital had 1,000 beds. St. Luke's–Texas Children's had 650, but with the completion of the Texas Heart Institute, the tri-hospital total would exceed 1,300. Until the Baylor investigation began in April, Dr. Cooley had thought he was chief of surgery here, but now there was some question if in fact he ever had been.

Cooley still housed some patients in Methodist Hospital when he operated on me in 1957, but I did not remember much about the place. Seven years earlier at Mayo, I had almost become addicted to morphine. It had been such a horrible experience that I had asked to receive a minimum of drugs after the Cooley operation. Consequently, much of my awareness had been consumed by pain. And to compound the situation, when Dr. Cooley took the aneurysm out of my chest, it had been necessary to sever a nerve that controlled one of my vocal cords.

I left the motel at daylight and drove north on Main toward the hospital. The idea of a comprehensive medical center in Houston was first planned by the trustees of the M. D. Anderson Foundation in 1941. They purchased a 134-acre tract of city land and presented the deed to Dr. Robert Bertner, the first president of the center.

In 1949, Baylor College of Medicine built Methodist Hospital and brought in Dr. Michael DeBakey as their first chairman of the Department of Surgery. Now more than twenty major facilities—general hospitals, research laboratories, and specialized clinics—representing investments of nearly $200 million and serving over a million patients a year, encompassed a huge courtyard of esplanades and parking lots, and the sounds and dust from new construction were everywhere. Methodist and St. Luke's–Texas Children's were staffed exclusively by Baylor, while the affiliations of the other institutions were equally divided between Baylor (where Dr. DeBakey had recently been named president) and the University of Texas, Dr. Cooley's alma mater. For years, the University of Texas had been trying to establish a medical school in the center, but Baylor had been able to keep them out. However, once again, the events of April were to change things. On May 7, Dr. Cooley had delivered the main address at a testimonial dinner for Leopold Meyer, a local philanthropist and president of Texas Children's. Mr. Meyer was a member of the pro-Cooley faction and Dr. Cooley's closest adviser. Cooley's address that evening did much to dispel any doubts about his integrity. A psychiatrist in the audience said it was the most brilliantly persuasive appeal he had ever witnessed, "a masterpiece of sentimentality and common sense." One guest estimated the combined wealth of those in attendance at something over six billion dollars. The most influential men in Texas were there, including Jack Josey, oilman, rancher, vice chancellor in charge of medical affairs at the University of Texas, and Cooley's fraternity pledge father. He had just been given the go-ahead to build a medical school in the center, and he was determined to take advantage of the current controversy and persuade Cooley to leave Baylor and become its president.

It was seven thirty. Already the parking lots were practically full, and the sun was boiling the dew into one of those unbelievably humid Houston days. A Shriner in a spangled fez and a clown suit was driving a crimson antique car around the drive at the entrance to St. Luke's, waving and tooting his horn for the amusement of the patients standing at their windows. After checking my credentials carefully, the auxiliary lady at the information desk directed me to Dr. Cooley's basement offices.

I opened the door to a seductive aroma of lemony perfumes

and coffee and introduced myself to the three attractive secretaries who handled patient and visitor relations and served as
liaisons between Cooley's Texas Heart Institute and the fifteen
surgeons who were there on fellowships working for him. The
bulletin boards around the room were bordered with cutout
flowers, and there were daisy-blossom ballpoints and paper-clip
boxes covered with bright prints. The woman I needed to see
before going up to surgery, Elaine Revis, Dr. Cooley's private
secretary, was out for the moment, so I should make myself at
home.

Seven more attractive secretaries in two adjoining rooms
were surrounded by ceiling-high cabinets full of patients' files.
Near the hall exit was a fan-file display of surgical slides of
excised hearts and arteries, an infant with a grotesquely deformed head (presumably the anencephalic baby whose heart
and lungs Cooley used in the first *en bloc* transplant), a light
table, and desks where two surgeons in blue-green caps and
scrub suits were preparing articles for publication. Bill Ha-
maucher, one of two Americans among the THI fellows, was a
colonel in the Air Force. He was slender and slightly sycophan-
tic, an incessant gum-chewer, a racer of Porsche automobiles,
and a favorite of the nurses who were not overwhelmed by the
more severe foreign doctors. The other was Bruno Messmer, a
blond Swiss. He was on leave from a hospital in Zurich. We
arranged to talk later in the morning.

Opposite a small anteroom, Dr. Cooley's private office was
carpeted in bright blue and paneled in walnut. Thirty thick
green volumes of his publications lined the far wall. Amid a
montage of diplomas and citations, there was a poem written
in pencil on notebook paper: "My Best Friend," by Helen Cooley, age eight. Whoever arranged the room had stopped just
short of excess.

The redhead from the outer office excused herself as she
stepped around me and counted three one-hundred-dollar bills

from the lower righthand drawer of the desk. She explained that neither the hospital nor the local banks would cash checks on foreign accounts. The families of patients from other countries were often distressed and disoriented, particularly if they didn't speak English, so in order to help them out, Dr. Cooley provided this service. The check was drawn on a bank in Athens. I asked if they ever bounced. She smiled and locked the drawer.

An ostrich egg on the desk had been signed by the world's heart-transplanters during the 1969 Capetown convention, where Dr. Cooley had presided and thereafter become a spokesman for the group. Dr. Christiaan Barnard had inscribed the egg: TO DENTON COOLEY, THE FINEST SURGEON I KNOW OF. Later, in his autobiography, *One Life*, Barnard was to expand on this.

In Houston, I found that Dr. Wagensteen was right about Dr. Cooley. It was the most beautiful surgery I had ever seen in my life. Every movement had a purpose and achieved its aim. Where most surgeons would take three hours, he could do the same operation in one hour. It went forward like a broad river—never fast, never obvious in haste, yet never going back. Some surgeons drove themselves, their hands groping for a solution to the imbalance before them. Dr. Cooley's hands moved effortlessly, as though he was simply putting everything back in place. This allowed him to make direct and often dramatic entries that would seem daring if done by anyone else. In dissecting the femoral artery, for example, one normally would make a small cut, then another and another, until it was exposed. Dr. Cooley simply made one slit, and the femoral artery lay open. No one in the world, I knew, could equal it.

Elaine Revis was a small, well-tailored brunette with a firm handshake and a hint of ward-room toughness. As a child she had danced in the *Our Gang* comedies. At fourteen, she had flown a biplane under the McAllen Bridge.

"Whoever he recommends is acceptable to us. But I want to warn you, Dr. Cooley is a good man. He trusts people because he has nothing to hide, and he's always getting taken advantage of. We deal with suicidal maniacs, religious fanatics, gypsies, cranks, reporters, politicians, cracked inventors, and exhibitionists—every kind of freak you can imagine. See, Dr. Cooley will listen to any son of a bitch who can find the hospital. He's too nice for his own good. That's why we're here. Tommy?" She called to a young Oriental who was sorting mail at the light table. "Bring me the nut file." He nodded and brought her four thick manila folders. "Look through these when you get a chance. You'll see what I mean. Take Tommy there, for instance. Ten years ago he was flown in here from the Philippines on an Air Force jet. Poor as Job's turkey, dying of a heart condition. Dr. Cooley did him for nothing, a courtesy case, and saw that his hospital bill was taken care of. But when it came time to leave, Tommy wouldn't go home. He followed Dr. Cooley everywhere he went. The administrators tried everything, but he wouldn't budge. Finally Dr. Cooley gave him a job as a houseboy, but he couldn't hack that. Now he's settled in as a messenger.

"Then there was the guy who escaped from East Berlin and stumbled into Methodist, half-dead, saying whatever the German word for heart is over and over. They took him up to DeBakey. He handed DeBakey some sort of clipping from a German newspaper that turned out to be about Dr. Cooley." She laughed and lit a cigarette. "So they hustled him over here and Dr. Cooley operated on him.

"What I'm getting at, it's hard for Dr. Cooley to say no. His time is important to lots of people. We're here to look out for him . . . to try and protect him. Take the nut file if you want to, you'll see what I mean."

I walked up the stairs to the main floor and took the elevator to the third, where twenty-five or thirty relatives of the patients Cooley was operating on that morning were waiting. After phoning downstairs for clearance, the lady at the desk let me pass.

The long corridor from St. Luke's to the Texas Children's side of the hospital was lined with gurney carts. Past the recovery room on the right, a pair of double doors led to the surgical suite. On the Texas Children's side of the restricted area, a huge police officer leaning over a coffee vendor looked back at me and jerked his thumb toward a door with a Texas Heart Institute plaque and a white-on-red plastic sign: OBSERVATION GALLERY. DENTON A. COOLEY, M.D. ABSOLUTELY NO ADMITTANCE. I climbed the three steps up to the juncture of two narrow passageways with inside glass walls and small offices at each end. An operation was in progress. I was right on top of it.

It must have been a subconscious ploy that caused me to observe the scene on the other side of the glass as an illusion, a soundless motion picture framed by the long cineramic window. And to avoid another shock, I looked at everything in the room before looking at the patient.

Twenty visiting doctors in green caps and masks and short-sleeved scrub suits were gathered two and three deep around three gowned surgeons, a heart-lung technician, and a scrub nurse at the foot of the table just below where I stood. In their loose, wrinkled uniforms, they were anonymous of shape and sex and blended with the soft greens and blues around the room. A circulating nurse opened plastic packets of sutures on a table ranked with bright scalpels and forceps. The operating lamps suspended from the ceiling were like eyes with pupils of pure light focused on the bisected chest of a child who could not have been more than seven years old. The scrub nurse handed the surgeon on the right a steel retractor shaped like an H with a high horizontal. He fitted the sides along the edges of the incision. He turned the gear handle with his index finger, and the wound slowly opened, displaying a tiny muscle pumping behind a milky membrane.

My own heart began to beat harder, and I suddenly felt like an intruder upon some occult investigation into the mystery of life. Despite the sophisticated apparatus, it all seemed primitive and ritualistic. I wanted to leave. But then the surgeon turning the retractor saw me and all the eyes in the room looked up. I felt that I had been discovered. For no particular reason I opened my notebook and began to write my name.

When I looked again, the surgeon turned from wiping a smear of blood off the retractor and nodded hello. He looked at the clock and sighed. The scrub nurse smiled with her eyes. The pump technician, wearing owl-frame glasses and sitting tight-kneed on a low stool, slipped a pair of hemostats under his cap and scratched his head, then got up and walked out. In a few moments, he stepped into the gallery and handed me a cup of coffee.

"Well, god*damn*, don't just stand there! Get on a suit and come down where you can see." His name was Euford Martin, his accent was pure Texas prairie. He was the brightest, most aware person I was to meet in Houston. "Son of a *bitch!* Doesn't Dr. Cooley realize we have more important things to do than putter around here all day? It's eight thirty and we haven't started the second pump yet."

Martin gave me a brief rundown on the organization of the operating rooms. The surgical team consisted of Dr. Cooley, his associate Dr. Grady Hallman (first trombonist and leader of the Heartbeats, a Medical Center orchestra for which Cooley played bass), Dr. Domingo Liotta, and the fifteen THI fellows headed by Dr. Dave Horton, an Australian, the chief resident from Baylor. Dr. Cooley did all the open-heart surgery, while Dr. Hallman did most of the peripheral vascular cases. Liotta assisted with operations that were specifically related to his artificial valve and heart research.

Prior to founding the Texas Heart Institute in 1962, Dr. Cooley had drawn his assistants from a federally funded program at

Baylor which was closed to foreigners. As chairman of the Department of Surgery, Dr. DeBakey had gotten first choice of all
fellows and residents, so Cooley's staff had often been limited
in numbers and experience. But the THI program, backed with
private money, was open to everyone, and some of the finest
young surgeons in the world came here to work with Cooley.
The advantages were obvious. In an average week Cooley
would perform more heart surgery than the cardiovascular
staffs of most major hospitals would do in six months. Over the
period of a year (a full fellowship ran from July to July), a for-
eigner here on a fellowship would assist in and witness more
open-heart operations than he was likely to perform during the
rest of his life.

Then there were the anesthesiologists—Dr. Keats, Dr.
Strong, and their staff. And surgical nurses—the scrub nurse
holds gowns and gloves for the surgeons and hands instruments;
the circulating nurses keep a running record of the procedure
and watch over the nonsterile section of the room. And the
recovery room personnel.

"Then, finally, at the *end* of the roster"—Martin fitted a stick
of gum into his mouth—"Mary and I run the pumps for Dr.
Cooley *and* Dr. DeBakey, oh yes. Of course, we interpret in-
nuendos and carry scurrilous tales back and forth across the
DMZ—the parking lot between here and there! All that sort of
crap. Come on. Get a suit on."

He took me to the doctors' lounge, an indoor-outdoor carpeted dressing room with lockers, and gave me a pair of scrub
pants and a shirt. The floor below the lockers was lined with
pointed European shoes. A tiny man, the cuffs of his trousers
bloused with strips of tape, swaggered by and began combing
his bushy sideburns in the mirror above the lavatories. "Caps
and masks in the hall," he said.

In the coffee room next door, a drug salesman was distribut-
ing cupcakes and scratch pads to a group of nurses and doctors

lounging on naugahide sofas and chairs. Half the recessed
fluorescent lights at the ceiling were burnt out. Four or five
"Great Moments in Medicine" illustrations hung askew on the
walls. I accepted a scratch pad and the drug salesman's last
cupcake, then suddenly everyone was quiet. Dr. Cooley
grabbed a dirty cup from the trash barrel, sloshed in some
coffee, and tossed it down. He looked at the cupcake in my hand
and said it was good to see me. I held the cupcake out to him.
He smiled, pealed down the pleated paper and took a large bite.
Then he handed it back to me and, before a hawk-nosed visitor
with a name tag marked Minneapolis could finish introducing
himself, wheeled off in the direction of the scrub room, nodding
as he chewed.

"That cup!" The nurse in the corner shook her head. "I mean
to tell you, Dr. Cooley don't waste nothing. He says the germ
theory is something cooked up by the mouthwash people. Hell,
he'll use anybody's toothbrush!"

The open area of the suite was loud with nurses shouting
orders, ringing telephones, and the cacophony of opposed
stereo systems in ORs One, Two, and Three. There were more
gurney carts and green oxygen tanks against the walls, and two
heart-lung machines which compared with the one in the OR
seemed obsolete and absolutely worn out. Beside them,
beneath a fitted plastic cover, was a complexly retracted apparatus for lifting a movie cameraman over an operating table.

A bald man with his hands folded over a sheet-draped mound
of stomach studied the flow of the ceiling as a tall orderly
wheeled him in. The double doors from the corridor had not yet
swung shut when a masked nurse, smoothing the hair of a tear-
ful young mother, took her baby—"Such blue eyes!" she said—
and bumped open the door to OR Two with her hip.

Whether out of dedication or a need for the diversion of
work, everyone seemed extremely busy. If there was ever a
time and place to ponder life without risking your sophistica-

tion, this was it. But no one seemed to bother. Maybe there wasn't time, or the place appealed to a type of intelligence that didn't lean toward metaphysics. Or perhaps they disguised their true feelings as they did their faces, for there was certainly a measure of emotional security in hiding behind a mask, as there was physical safety here in the midst of the expertise and equipment to meet any personal emergency.

Four visiting doctors were discussing a mimeographed operating schedule taped to the tile wall across from where Dr. Cooley was scouring his forearms with yellow lather.

"Okay, let's see here . . . " One of the doctors ran down the list with his finger. "One two three four five six seven. Seven open-hearts, including a tet and a Mustard*—I want to see that. One biopsy. Three aneurysms. This is impossible. Impossible! How in the hell . . . " He shook his head. "No wonder they rotate assistants. Nobody but Cooley could stand on his feet that long. What do you suppose the fees amount to?"

"I don't know," one of the others said, "but for the price of an open-heart in San Francisco you can fly down here and get Cooley to do it and still have something left. I've made the referrals."

Two visitors with long blond hair trailing out from beneath their caps were busy drawing diagrams and taking notes on everything from the brand of the autoclaves to the labels on a row of saline bottles. I asked one of them where I could find the child who was to have the tet later that morning. He looked up from inspecting one of the worn-out heart-lung machines, smiled apologetically, and pointed to his name tag: U.S.S.R.

The entrance to the scrub room was blocked by three doctors gesturing and clearing their throats in an effort to interrupt the polysyllabic diatribe of the Minneapolis surgeon who had followed Cooley from the coffee room and now had him cornered

*Tet is tetralogy of Fallot. Mustard is a transposition of the major heart vessels, named after the Canadian surgeon W. T. Mustard.

at the sink. He had developed a new antirejection serum and wanted Cooley to try it on his next transplant. As Cooley scrubbed, he nodded. "A guy from a surgical supply house was in here last week. Said he heard I had a twelve-inch instrument and wanted to put it in mass production." His eyes suggested a smile behind the paper gauze mask. Cooley tossed his head in the direction of a large man with pale, hairless arms. "Tiny here has put himself on a regimen of scrambled egg whites so his wife won't reject him." But the man from Minneapolis would not be deterred.

"Good God!" Euford Martin whispered over my shoulder. "Will you take a look at *this?*"

A few steps away a doctor who had examined the first astronauts and handled the delicate job of administering anesthetics to fifteen of Cooley's transplants stared abstractedly at a castered steel table. His cap was tipped level with his eyebrows, a soiled surgical sheet folded and held out before him. "Ojo, Toro!" He sailed the sheet aside, executing a perfect veronica and revealing a pair of skinny calves angling out from his rolled-up scrub pants. "Bravo!" The THI fellow for whom he was performing clapped silently, unenthusiastically.

The other visitors gave up and filed into OR One, but the man from Minneapolis still persisted, "So the summary of my experiments in a wide spectrum of—"

"You know something?" Cooley closed the flow lever with his elbow. "It sounds like you've hit on the greatest thing since Bardahl."

A nurse was trying to explain to the bald man on the gurney cart that an x ray taken this morning indicated his blood clot had dissolved overnight and he wouldn't need an operation after all. But the man didn't understand. Leaning back on his elbows, he shook his head and looked from her into OR Three, where a woman, the insides of her thighs and calves split to the bone, was having her iliac arteries removed and replaced with Dacron grafts.

"Who around here speaks Spanish?" the nurse said. "Get me someone who speaks Spanish."

"I'll get José." A tall orderly ran off toward the coffee room and returned shortly with a slight, dark-haired man carrying a half-eaten, triple-decker bologna sandwich which he stuffed in the pocket of his white coat.

"You speak Spanish?" the nurse asked.

José nodded and wiped a slash of mustard from his mouth. The man on the gurney launched into a rapid monologue, jabbing his finger toward the woman on the table in OR Three. José continued nodding.

"All right," the nurse said, "now tell him that the medications he got last night dissolved the clot in his leg and we won't be operating on him."

"Cómo?" Jose grimaced and shrugged.

"What's the matter?" the nurse demanded.

José looked to the tall orderly for help. "Hablo español, sí. Pero no hablo inglés, amigo!"

"Wukash has already taken over as chief resident—I'm leaving in the morning—but I'm sure the kids with the tet and the Mustard got the same mental and physical prep as the rest of them." Dr. David Horton fitted a black Flair pen in the pocket of the white jacket he wore over his scrub suit and leaned back in the bottom bunk in the residents' quarters. Twenty-eight years old, Horton had a ruddy complexion and a pleasant, constant smile. He spoke with a pronounced Australian accent. "Miss Conroy is the RN here trained in medical psychology. The night before an operation she shows the kids and their parents a doll outfitted with all the paraphernalia they'll have on him in the recovery room—trach tube, needles, and all that stuff. Even if you're an adult, it's a shock to wake up with a piece of plastic down your gullet and be surrounded by a lot of weird equipment and bleeding people. She familiarizes the kid with everything, and the parents, too, so they'll know what to expect when they go in the recovery room to visit him. She also stresses the point that the pain and anxiety are only temporary and well worth suffering in order to have the child well again. In this case, though, he won't be well *again*, because his heart has been a mess since he was an embryo. It's interesting, I guess, and useful, but incidental to the actual surgery. Without Cooley, all the preop psychology would be wasted motion."

I asked if there was any difference between Cooley's approach to children and his approach to adults.

"It's a mistake to assume, as some do, that Dr. Cooley is more compassionate toward children. There's less levity abroad when he's operating on a kid because it's damn hard work. The parts are smaller and, as you'll see, exposure is extremely difficult. In the second place, these children are almost all very high-risk affairs and their hearts are unpredictable as hell. Then, Dr. Cooley is not known for his cheerful disposition early in the morning, which is when we do kiddies. Cooley is a strange guy —the tougher it is, the better he likes it. Which is one way of explaining why he has such marvelous results with kids. He's the original cutting horse, and he turns out some true masterpieces on cases nobody else would touch. He once told me he got more pleasure out of a tet or a Mustard than anything else he could do with his clothes on!"

I asked about Dr. Cooley's motivation, the long hours he worked, and how the current Baylor investigations into the Karp operation were affecting him.

"Those brutal schedules, Jesus, I don't purport to know what drives him. He would have to love what he's doing, and then, I suppose, like everyone else, it's a desire for fame and fortune. For a guy who says he doesn't believe in do-gooders, he does an awful lot of good.

"Heart surgeons are all egocentric competitors, and Cooley, of course, is top gun. He's come in for criticism because he's been so damn successful, professionally and financially. An example of a rub against him is his idea regarding the surgeon-patient relationship. It's a great emotional advantage for a surgeon to walk into a room where the patient as a personality is blocked out and the surgical problem, the operating field, is framed with towels. When you're operating, the patient is no longer a person—he's an anatomical problem. You have a job to do, and you try to do it the best way you know how. That's Cooley's idea—there is no good argument against it.

"Cooley doesn't have the personality for being a psychiatrist. He's personable, yes, but he's not interested in sitting on the bed and shooting the shit with a patient. And he's not interested in praise or backchat from them, either—these people telling him he's some kind of god, kissing his hands and all that. He wants to establish his authority, then get the hell out and get down to the business of fixing what's wrong. He won't be encumbered with emotional involvement, and, regardless of what they might say, the patients believe in him for that very reason. Listen, one of the quickest ways to lose a patient's faith and respect is to offer him unqualified sympathy. It's better for everybody if you hold your distance.

"As for the Karp thing and all this furor, everyone has a different theory according to his personal capacity for envy. Dr. Cooley was well advised to try something because Karp had already had it. Advances are made by people who aren't afraid to try—ask Dr. DeBakey—but I'm not sure Cooley didn't do himself something of a disservice in this controversy by being too available and too direct with the press—they're not used to that. But it was no more of a show than those ventricular by-pass deals over at Methodist. It's a shame, this split between Cooley and DeBakey. But the way they have crowded each other through the years has been to the advantage of medicine. Coo-

ley is a Texan; few Americans and no foreigners understand
what that means. Your country and in some respects my own
country, Australia, were built by men like him.

"Anyhow, Dr. DeBakey often becomes personally involved
with his patients and, for their benefit, he has this additional
motivation to wring a first-class performance out of himself and
his associates, which is where he gets the reputation of being
such a bastard. He has five guys over there who perform the
same operations he performs. Cooley, on the other hand, does
everything here but sweep up. He doesn't have anyone to
blame or bitch at because he seldom lets another surgeon into
a patient's heart. What it amounts to, DeBakey has a tendency
to kick his people along, while Cooley pulls his. But no matter
how many run-ins they might have had with him, DeBakey's
people invariably have a sneaking affection for him. And, of
course, all the young heart surgeons—and, I suspect, if the truth
were known, many of the old ones—want to be just like Denton
Cooley. DeBakey's surgical competence is excellent. But Cooley is unbelievable. He has programmed himself and designed
his surgery to get the job done as thoroughly and as quickly as
possible. He's a safe corner-cutter. There's never a wasted motion. He has the unique ability to expose tissue by himself, with
a minimum of help from his assistants. He can pass through one,
two, three layers of tissue in a single hit, rather than picking up
his needle and fitting on each successive piece. Bang-bang-
bang, exposing for himself, suturing with a single motion. Always a sure, delicate control, he just whips it on in there."

I asked how it was to train here.

"Everybody does a good job. It's part of the follow-the-leader
atmosphere Cooley creates. The THI fellows come here from
around the world. Some of them can't speak English, but as far
as I'm concerned, they are all extraordinarily talented people.
And dedicated to learning, in a European sense. Most young
American surgeons are eager to set up on their own as soon as

they finish their residencies; they're not interested in fellowships. But the surgeons from other countries tend to seek out
the best training available and continue learning under what
they call 'masters,' sometimes for several years. Cooley helps
lots of them financially. He has put unpaid fellows on the payroll
many, many times."

What was it like to work with Dr. Cooley?

"Every once in a while he comes out with some words of
compassion, though not very commonly. I remember the first
time I assisted him in an open-heart operation. I was shaking
like a leaf. He looked over and said, 'Don't be nervous.' Later
I was complaining to the senior resident about coming unglued.
He said, 'Well, when you're assisting the greatest surgeon in the
world you should be nervous.' Then it dawned on me. I understood."

Outside the coffee room Don Wukash, a former heavyweight
boxing champion at the University of Texas who had just replaced Horton as chief resident, was handing out the day's
assignments to several THI fellows. He was a soft-spoken blond
with a slight stammer and a quick, somewhat uneasy smile.
Someone had forgotten to refill and turn on the coffeemaker.
They were all drinking tea from the Vendo-Matic in the hall:
Michi Vucinic, a balding, mustached Yugoslav with a bullet
crease in his head sustained during a raid on a Red Cross operating room in Biafra; Chafizadah, a talkative, peripatetic Persian;
Martin, grandson of the famous French surgeon Leriche;
Tanaka, a stocky karate black belt and protégé to Dr. Juro
Wada, who had developed the valves Cooley used in the artifi-
cial heart; Sechas, a handsome Greek; Havananda, a Thai.
There were others from India, Venezuela, Afghanistan, Italy,
Germany, and Switzerland. And Dr. Arthur Killen, an associate
professor at Vanderbilt University.

Two human hearts smelling strongly of formalin were in a

porcelain tray on the counter below the window in the observation gallery. The child I had discussed with Horton was brought into the operating room. Far too frail for a normal six-year-old, already sedated with scopolamine, he struggled half-heartedly and turned down the corners of his mouth. Dr. Strong, the middle-aged matador from the hall, smoothed back the child's fine blond hair and briefly lowered his surgical mask so the child could see the reassuring smile on his face. Strong held the black inhalation mask to his own face and then handed it to the child. As the child held the mask to his face, Strong bent down and whispered in his ear. In a few moments, the child's eyes rolled back and his arms went limp, and Strong began inserting arterial and venous needles in his wrists and brightly colored EEG leads in his scalp and ear lobe.

Killen and Vucinic gently eased the child over onto his right side. His left elbow lifted behind his head, his right arm taped to a fold-out extension, the child was braced on both sides with cushioned sandbags. As the scrub nurse brought in steaming instrument packs, the child's body was swabbed golden with Mercresin. Under anesthesia, male children often have erections; the nipples of female children contract. His bladder was tapped with a narrow gauge catheter. A rectal thermometer led to an elevated heating mechanism that activated a flow of warm water through a green rubber blanket that was placed over the draping sheets; the blanket was magnetized to hold instruments.

With one motion, Dr. Killen made an incision from the breastbone back along the third rib space and up to the shoulder. Another, deeper. The larger vessels, spurting blood, were clamped with miniature hemostats. The smaller bleeders were cauterized with an electric needle.

Finished in OR Two, Cooley was back in the scrub room, surrounded by visitors.

Dr. Bruno Messmer, whom I had met earlier in the basement

offices, entered the observation gallery. He was a small man with strong features and a flamelike fringe of blond hair. "Senning. You know Senning? The great Swiss surgeon who did the first transposition of the great vessels in 1959? Dr. Senning sent me here from Zurich. He said I would see the most in the shortest time. There is no place like this anywhere in the world —I know because I have been there. In Europe things are so much slower. Nobody does anything unless he is told. Here everybody does his job and then looks around for something else to do. And still they only do what is necessary. Nothing wasted—not a minute or a suture. Even the patients are more positive here, more eager to get back to normal. Dr. Cooley always goes forward, forward. Always.

"Senning says Cooley is the finest surgical technician in the world, and he is right. All you have to do is watch another surgeon, any of them. The difference is between night and day. Senning himself is an example. He does an aortic valve replacement in one hour—very fast. Cooley does one in thirty minutes. And Cooley, operating on the most difficult cases you can imagine, has the lowest mortality rate of all. I don't just read the figures, I've been keeping them for over a year. He has an average eight percent mortality compared with the others' fifteen to twenty percent. His success with Fallot's tetralogy is an unbelievably low twelve percent—one of the most difficult operations there is. Other surgeons regularly have complications with tets. Cooley?—almost never. Others let the heart beat and still get heart blocks. Cooley stops the heart and never gets blocks. Who knows how he does it.

"One thing, he has everything standardized. Everyone knows exactly what to do, how to do it, and when. He attaches the heart-lung machine the same way, always. Over the years, he has reduced his movements to an art. I say to you, you can walk into an operating room and tell exactly where he is in a procedure by the way he is standing at the table.

"He is always exploring with those big hands. His left hand is always in there exposing the operating field. He can do so much with no assistance. Other surgeons use twice, three times as many instruments as he does. Cooley, he sutures without pickups half the time—they get in his way. It's like he wants to feel what's going on with his own hands. And he improvises quickly and well, somehow anticipating problems before they happen. After so many thousands of hearts, he has a touch that can be gotten no other way. The other day he was tightening a tape on a major artery, and a visitor asked him how he knew when the tension was right. Dr. Cooley held up his index finger.

"He learns from experience when others don't. He's never in bad trouble technically. When he goes in, he comes out. At times there is nothing he can do, but when he starts, he finishes. A lot of people walk out of here who by rights should have left feet first."

I stood at the head of the operating table to the left of Dr. Strong. His arms held up, dripping water from the elbows, Cooley stopped short of the instrument table and the circulating nurse fitted a pair of antique wire-framed glasses on his nose —they were a gift through the mail from a horse-and-buggy doctor in south Georgia—and secured them with a strip of tape. As Cooley slipped into his gown, thirty visitors moved in around the table. Five of them were standing on high stools and hanging from the light tracks for balance. Cooley turned into the blue-green surgical gown, catching and tying the sash as he stepped up to the table.

With forceps he lifted the pericardium like a tiny membranous tent and scissored it open. Dr. Strong pressed a lever with his foot and raised the table. The assistants stepped up on metal stools. Cooley bent toward the wound. I leaned over the table (the unmistakable smell of entrails mixed with the astringent odors in the room) but the operating field was so restricted, the child was so small, excepting the swell of pink lungs framed by the steel retractor, I could see nothing.

Guiding his moves by touch and staring at the ceiling, Cooley suddenly came up with a tiny heart contained in two fingers. Sensing the thrill of the minuscule vessels, he looked at the clock across the room. And then, as though having determined the direction he would take from here, he quickly and effortlessly attached the narrow gauge cannulae from the heart-lung machine. The little heart struggled in his fingers and went flaccid . . . still. The onlookers strained for a better view, Cooley tapped a small scalpel against his gown and made a one-stroke cut that laid open the ventricle.

"Say, will you please give me a little help?" Cooley mumbled. "No, look. The other hand." He flipped a needle holder back on his wrist and adjusted Vucinic's hold on the retractor. He adjusted the light by a saber-grip handle and began stitching a white Dacron patch between the ventricles as he mumbled something to Dr. Strong. Strong called out the blood pressure and Euford Martin raised the heart-lung frame to increase the gravitational flow.

After trimming off and tailoring a square inch of the child's pericardium, Cooley sutured it over the incised seat of the faulty pulmonary valve. There was no apparent speed, and yet the circulator and the scrub nurse rushed to keep him in needles.

The FM on the wall was barely audible. The only other sound was the steady snapping of the Russian visitors' cameras. Then Cooley abruptly shifted to one leg and, arms outstretched, broke into an atonal, baritone sing-along with the voice from the radio. The puzzled visitors looked at one another. The assistants breathed sighs of relief.

"That's Vicki Carr's 'Sign Your Name' divorce song," Dr. Strong explained. "Dr. Cooley can't make it through the 'curl your hair' line without his sterile Kleenex."

"Uh huh." Cooley resumed sewing. "That Greek kid. Tell
Keats he doesn't have bronchitis, just a big voice. I heard him
on rounds last night and thought we had a soul singer in the
house. Pull down his diaper and ten-to-one you'll find a handsome set of outsized testicles."

The last stitch in place, Cooley stroked the small heart gently
with his finger. The circulator stood by the defibrillator, a red
light on the console indicating full charge. But it was not necessary. As Cooley smoothed the heart, the ventricles began to
contract, first irregularly then with a flowing motion until the
rhythm was steady and full.

Cooley pulled in the purse strings and sutured up the femoral
artery. He touched the heart here and there and watched its
rolling beat. There was no bleeding. He wiped his fingertips
lightly on his gown and took two stitches in the pericardium.
"Thank you, gentlemen." The visitors parted and looked after
him. "Dr. Cooley, it is a poem," Dr. Kato, a Japanese surgeon,
said.

While his assistants were opening another patient in OR Two,
Cooley grabbed a white coat from the rack across from the
coffee room and, speeding through the central corridor of the
surgical suite, leaving questions and congratulations on the lips
of visitors, headed for the recovery room. It was there that
Wukash and five fellows, unable to match his long-legged stride,
caught up with him.

The recovery room contained twenty beds, each with its own
life-support systems and monitoring equipment. The catheters
leaked urine, the chest drains leaked old blood into graduated
bottles beneath the beds. Oxygen tents, the overlapping hiss
and suck of respirators, the heart action of each patient bleep-
ing across the screens of their oscilloscopes. Nurses were giving
injections and words of encouragement and scurrying from bed
to bed checking the drainage bottles. The maze of blood lines
and electric leads, the corrugated breathing tubes resembled

the works of a huge mechanical womb. A transition back to life. The blood was going brown on their bandages. Their faces were struck with pain and bewilderment.

Cooley moved quickly from one patient to the next, checking charts and altering medications. "Everything went fine. You're going to be all right." A pat on the leg. Their mouths were filled with plastic trach tubes. They could not speak. Instead, they nodded or blinked their eyes. There was a visible easing of restlessness and anxiety in the wake of Cooley's movement down the line of beds.

Back in his gallery office with a cup of black coffee, Cooley complained about the slowness of those opening for him in OR Two. Watching the progress of the orderlies disinfecting OR One before the next case, he dictated four quick letters, accepted a referral call from Puerto Rico, another from Honolulu, autographed a cloth dachshund for a nine-year-old girl being released today, and corrected the grammar of a paper on the artificial heart that he was co-authoring with Dr. Domingo Liotta.

They were not yet ready in Two. Cooley phoned Joe Glenny, his real estate broker, about a parcel of land adjoining his ranch south of Houston.

Joe Glenny: "Dr. Cooley has a great ability to size up a real estate deal. I give him what I think are the facts, and in five minutes he's found all the loopholes and figured out ways they can be worked around. It's speculation, pure and simple, but with his success, it seems more like a system. Sometimes what I see as a hard risk, he sees as a sure thing. Then he gives me his reasons and I understand. His average is high. That's why he can borrow the way he does. One time he kept the most powerful man in south Texas waiting in that cubbyhole office at the hospital for an hour. Dr. Cooley came in between operations and in a whirlwind of fancy dealing borrowed over a million dollars from the man. Dr. Cooley told me I looked peaked and sent me to get an x ray. Later that afternoon, after he had looked at my x ray, he told me I had a bad gall bladder and there was no profit in fooling around and postponing an operation. Two hours later, I was on his table. Decisiveness. It takes the same thing to make a go of it in land speculation."

Ready in Two. Cooley sidled through the visitors and began to scrub again.

Two secretaries from downstairs brought armloads of memoranda and sorted mail to the gallery office. There were two eight-inch-square boxes. One marked RUSH from a physician in New Jersey; the other was from Cutter Laboratories in California. Incoming calls blinked on three of Cooley's four lines.

A delivery boy arrived at the coffee room with fancy cakes and cookies—there was no card. Another brought sacks of Po'-Boy sandwiches from Antone's. Still another brought a huge steak complete with trimmings and asked directions to Dr. Cooley's office—there was a card. "That Mafia lawyer in 406," Dr. Shanbag said. "The local boss is so thankful of the job Dr. Cooley did on him, he sends up a super steak every day."

A portly staff surgeon who was cursing the Kennedys lost his audience to Dr. Vucinic's dark good looks and more interesting accent. "This prejudice is a strange thing." Vucinic's eyes danced. "I marry my wife, Lutzia. My parents say, 'What you mean you marry this Lutzia? Is a *Serb.*' She is not Serb. She has Serb name—Lutzia. 'No. Is a Serb,' they say. 'How many boy children in this Serb family? How much land, horses?' You see? A boy is a gun is a power. Like the land. But no Serbs. Say, 'Next you tell you marry Albanian.' This is worst of all. Every Yugoslav *knows* this Albanian is, you say, lazy, no good. Good only for peasant, huh?" He smiled.

"What kind of Communist are you, anyway?" the portly staff surgeon asked. "Russian or Chinese?"

"Me? I tell you I am Yugoslav."

Having finished a valve replacement in Two, Dr. Cooley got

a list of family names from Wukash and struck out for the family room. Euford Martin and his team, sitting on carts and window ledges in the hall, complained good-naturedly about the number of today's pump cases as he passed. Group by group, Cooley called aside the relatives of each of the morning's cases and explained what he had done and what the prognoses were. He was certain rather than optimistic, but when their response was more than a cursory concern and thank you, he quickly called the next name. Several were reduced by his impersonality—he seemed not to notice—but they quickly recovered in the light of good news.

Perhaps it was facing the real, basic world of the laity after a series of sessions within the number-fast and logical safety of technology or, perhaps more likely, a lack of understanding and a distaste for the capriciousness of human emotions, but Cooley was markedly ill at ease in the family room. He was eager to get out, and he did as quickly as possible.

A brief THI meeting with Henry Reinhard in his main-floor office, another with Dr. Leachman (who appeared pleased that Cooley avoided the smoke from his cigar) in Cardiology, and Cooley returned to his gallery office where, over a half pint of pineapple yogurt, he examined the heart rushed from New Jersey. He put down his plastic spoon and removed the specimen from a bottle of preservative. Three months following a mitral valve replacement, the patient had died of an embolism, a blood clot. He peeled open the upper chamber and inspected the plastic valve. "I remember his operation," he said. "The seat of the mitral valve was so densely calcified I couldn't clear it well enough without endangering the aortic valve. Well, son of a bitch, there's nothing left to do here, is there?" He was not talking to me.

An attractive nurse, a wedding ring pinned to her scrub dress, brought him a jar of homemade chicken soup, two packets of crackers, and another plastic spoon. She waited until he ate it.

In a sharp monotone that could be heard in Texas Children's reception room, Cooley began dictating replies to the stack of letters his secretaries had brought. His wife phoned about a party tonight. Nodding to the mouthpiece and rolling his eyes, he split open the box from Cutter Laboratories and took out the latest modification of the artificial heart—the first artificial heart ever produced by a commercial manufacturer. He blew into the power source tubes and the four-way diaphragm closed in a wide H. "I've just discovered the portable power source," he said. "No. Nothing. Go on, I'll meet you there. Good-bye, good-bye." He hung up the phone and studied the ventricle, then blew on the tube and turned it to me. "Does that remind you of anything you've chased after and felt good in? These women are more than just behind you, you know!"

Chris, a surgical nurse, stopped by to show off her new baby boy. "Be careful," Cooley said. "Don't drop little Denton on his head. That's what happened to Mary Lou." A reporter from the *Wall Street Journal* was next. He asked perfunctory questions and got perfunctory answers. A member of the ladies' auxiliary requested an autographed picture for her cleaning woman's birthday.

Ready in One . . . and then in Two.

Dr. Strong and Dr. Liotta came into the gallery office. Liotta looked at the floor. Strong pulled off his cap and tossed it in the wastebasket and caught his breath. "Well, the buzzard struck. The Emory girl is dead." Liotta mumbled to himself in Spanish, from a sense of loss and perhaps to offset Strong's drama that was embarrassing to him and to Cooley. Cooley appeared to be caught between natural resignation and the sort of response Strong was soliciting. "Just now?" he asked. "Two minutes ago," Strong said. "There wasn't much hope to begin with, Denton." It was the first time I had heard anyone call Cooley by his first name; assuming safety in the face of death, Strong was trying

for nearness. Liotta shook his head. Deep down everyone knew
what was happening on the vehicle of tragedy and passed it off.
Liotta shook his head. "Here." Cooley handed him the artificial
heart from Cutter and left for the family room.

At four o'clock, all but the last pump case was done, and the
heart-lung team, with the exception of Euford Martin, left.
Three other operations remained to be done. In One, Cooley
was performing a biopsy on a two-year-old child dying of an
incurable, degenerative heart disease. A teen-age girl with
moist blue eyes, her auburn hair drawn back to a neat bun,
watched intently from the gallery.

"Who in the hell is that one?" It was the nurse who had
brought the chicken soup. "These people just wander in and out
of here at random."

Cooley glanced up at the girl in the window. She smiled
demurely.

"Maybe she's a spy from you know where!" Euford Martin
said.

"By the way, Euford, how are things over at the Big Top?"
Cooley asked.

"Slow, Dr. Cooley. A veritable snail's pace."

A friend of Louise Cooley's is in Two; she has a breast tumor.
After prepping and draping her himself, Cooley dissected out
a piece of the tumor and took it to the pathology lab where Dr.
Garland McKinney, a taller man than Cooley, prepared a slide
from the tissue. McKinney corroborated Cooley's opinion that
the tumor was malignant, and Cooley returned to the operating
room and performed a mastectomy.

Dr. Chafizadah, a Persian THI fellow: "It was the most beautiful surgery of that kind I have ever seen, not to mention the
speed. So clean, so very fast."

Unlike most surgeons, Cooley operates on his friends and his
family, whether it is a gall bladder or a heart. He believes he is
the best; it makes no sense to trust anyone else.

Richard Hudson, a childhood friend of Cooley's: "My mother was ill. I called Denton. He came to the house in an ambulance and carried her downstairs himself. At the hospital, he called me into the scrub room and told me it was just like operating on his own mother. He didn't want to do it, I knew that. But he felt it was his responsibility and he wanted me to share the burden with him."

Most of the visitors were back in their hotel rooms having drinks. After finishing his last vascular case in Three, Dr. Hallman left for the cardiology office to catch up on his paper work. Liotta retired to his small laboratory on the seventh floor.

Eighteen years earlier, the elderly woman on the table in One had undergone a palliative operation for a thoracic aneurysm. Because there were no arterial grafts then, the surgeon had been unable to remove the weakened segment of her aorta and had done the only thing he could do at the time: he opened her chest and wrapped the ballooning artery with layers of steel fabric. It had saved her life, but now after so many years, residual fibrous tissue had impregnated the mesh until the upper lobe of her left lung was completely eroded and half her chest was filled with a tumor of steel wire.

Cutting and tugging, after a thirty-minute wrestling match that had Cooley bracing his legs and lying across the table with both hands deep in her chest, he came out with a huge ball of wire and yellowish tissue that filled a large basin. Rosa, the scrub technician, turned her head and retched. Cooley soaked a seven-inch graft in blood drawn from the patient's aorta and then sutured it in place. "This is the greatest thing since rubber gloves," he said. "It ranks with the invention of the wheel"—whispering—"the bottle!" The patient was seventy six. Cooley's oldest open-heart was eighty eight; his youngest, thirty six hours. *C.H,*

Before leaving for home, Euford Martin went up to the gallery to phone his wife, Rana, for grocery shopping instructions.

The young girl with auburn hair was still there. She was trim and pretty in her pink and white uniform, and as she spoke, she looked down at Dr. Cooley.

Her name was Susan. She was nineteen and from Long Island. She said she had always wanted to be a nurse, but that last spring when Dr. Cooley had been so much in the news with transplants, she became particularly interested in his work and his life and she decided then that her one ambition was to scrub for him, to become part of the great things he was doing. Because they offered two years training in the Texas Medical Center, Susan had enrolled in the Nursing College of Texas Women's University. It was, she thought, an omen that the university was located in Denton, Texas. She said she had so looked forward to watching him operate, but now—she sniffed, there were tears in her eyes—the supervisor had scolded her and told her not to come back. "If I could just talk to him for a minute," again she looked down at Cooley, "I'm sure he would understand. He's such a wonderful man."

Uncertain how to handle the situation, Martin began to explain that the supervisor was always mindful how last summer the gypsies took over the hospital when their king came in for surgery; that since then she had been anxious about visitors.

Then Dr. Cooley came up the steps. Martin was blocking one aisle, Susan the other, and there was a pursuant family in the hall behind him.

Susan beamed and wiped her eyes. She asked Cooley for a handkerchief (he didn't have one) and then began to tell her story. When she got to the part about Denton, Texas, she burst into tears and moved close to Cooley. He put his arm around her, blushed, and shrugged hopelessly for the benefit of Martin and the nurses watching in One.

The previous week, a pretty coed from the University of Houston had cornered him downstairs with a proposition: if he would allow her to write a magazine article about him, the money from its sale would permit her to finish college. If she could just be around him for a few weeks . . . get to know him.

Cooley patted Susan on the shoulder and eased her away. He said he understood and was impressed with her ambition. He was certain she would make a wonderful nurse. She turned her eyes up to him and smiled. He wished her best of luck with her studies, and then, rushing more than was necessary, returned to the sanctuary of the scrub room.

The last scheduled case for the day was a ventricular aneurysm—a weakening in the heart's main chamber. It was the same operation he had performed on Haskell Karp before using the artificial heart. Cooley had saved this patient till last because he knew the odds were strong against the man's coming off the table alive. There was a slim chance and without an operation, the patient's heart would literally explode.

Cooley looked across the patient's open chest to Bruno Messmer, who was standing on a high stool, resembling a child in a gown several sizes too large for him. "This man is in his early forties." Cooley shook his head. "It's a damn shame we don't have a transplant or an artificial heart to offer him."

Everyone was quiet as Cooley cut out a large bulbous portion of the heart and drew what was left into a trident-shaped suture line. Little more than half of the left ventricle remained. But when Cooley placed the defibrillator paddles, the countershock sent the heart into regular rhythm. There were sighs of amazement.

Cooley quickly ordered Strong to inject more stimulants and began to double stitch the incision. "Come on, fella," he mumbled. "Hang in there now. Keep it up. Don't quit."

When the partial heart began to falter, Cooley sutured with one hand and massaged it with the other. He curled the needle holder back over his thumb and looked at the heart. It shuddered like a motor out of balance, but it got stronger with each beat.

"This guy's going to live," Cooley said. "He's going to make it. Come on, let's hurry up and get the hell out of here."

"It makes you have faith in something," Messmer said.

"I believe in the Big Dipper." Cooley reached over and steadied Messmer's hand.

Cooley, relying more on touch than on the monitors, checked each patient in the recovery room. One of the valves was bleeding too much. The little two-year-old girl who had had the biopsy was no better or worse. She looked the picture of health; it would have been difficult to believe that within a few months she would be dead. A portable defibrillator and a bow-shaped device for external heart massage were beside the bed. Everyone else was complaining—a good sign. Once again he reported to the relatives in the family room. The first postoperative day was most crucial, he said, and they should not be upset by the scene in the recovery room. The men with their hats in their hands, the women wiping away their tears, filed in to visit their loved ones.

The THI fellows had changed to ties and white coats and were meeting in the coffee room. With information from Cardiology and Admissions, Don Wukash had compiled tomorrow's schedule. The patients had already been examined by the fellows who would present them to Dr. Cooley. Cooley flashed by in a long, white coat. There was a scramble to toss down coffee and extinguish cigarettes, and grand rounds began.

Tanaka had been stationed to hold the elevator, but there wasn't room for everyone and the stragglers had to take the stairs. In Radiology, Cooley reviewed a wall full of chest films. Challenging a diagnosis as though asking advice, he directed a question to José Gubiera and waited patiently through his Spanish-English reply. Despite his nervousness, Gubiera was correct. Bruno Messmer reported his cardiac catheterization studies.

Cooley smoothed back his hair in the dark view screen. Wukash opened the door, and they left.

Outside room 201 A, Dr. Martin moved to the front of the group and gave the patient's history and examination results: a fifty-year-old physician from Florida. He fell unconscious during a family outing. Rheumatic fever, a history of high blood pressure and coronary heart disease in his family. Complete exhaustion upon moderate exercise. Stenosis and malfunction of aortic, mitral, and pulmonary valves. Opposed to transplantation. Cooley was familiar with the case. They entered the room.

The patient looked nearer seventy than fifty. He was very thin, and his complexion was greenish. Gasping for breath after each word, he said he wasn't feeling well. Cooley and four of the fellows listened to his heart. Then Cooley said he would do his best.

In the hall Cooley said the only hope for the man was a transplant. Everett Thomas's life had been extended for nine months. "Three artificial valves in a worn-out heart doesn't hold much promise," Cooley said. "You know, they have the world's annual triple-valve convention in Atlantic City . . . in a phone booth."

There were two more mitral valves, two aneurysms—one extending from the groin to the heart—and a handsome Ivy League hippie who was in for an abdominal exploration and seemed more concerned with the metaphysics of Pentothal than his own well-being. Presentation, examination, corroboration—rounds continued.

Wealthy patients often pique Cooley's competitiveness with their forced familiarity. Others, rather than respecting his work as he would prefer, hold him in awe. "Doctor, cue bello! You are even more beautiful than your pictures," an Italian wife said as she kissed his cheek. A buxom Greek lady whose little boy was recovering after a difficult time cornered Cooley at a nursing station. "Your hands." She kissed his hands and held them to her breast. "They are the hands of a god." He had not learned to manage such scenes; his blushing only made matters worse. And though he had secret routes through the hospital and sent decoys ahead where demonstrations seemed likely, he was unable to avoid a number of emotional responses from thankful people.

A tet, a septal defect, a coarctation. In the gaily decorated rooms of Texas Children's, there was less talk, more directness and deeper faith among the parents of the young children.

Rounds were over.

The mitral valve in the recovery room had continued bleeding. Cooley decided that the patient must be redone. They set up in OR One and in fifteen minutes Cooley had unwired the patient's chest and stopped the hemorrhage.

At 9:45 P.M., a two-way radio clipped to his belt, Cooley put on a blue blazer and backed his black Toronado out of his parking space at the entrance to Texas Children's. He was two hours late for a small dinner party and dance at Robert Herring's, president of the THI board. The maid would serve him a plate from the warming oven.

At midnight, a call came from Dr. Messmer. There was a rule at the hospital that only Dr. Cooley delivered death notices. Messmer had broken that rule.

Dr. Cooley: "I like to save lives. On the other hand, when I lose a patient it's a great disappointment to me. It's a reaction I've never been able to overcome. I keep thinking maybe there was something I might have done—I might never have operated in the first place.

"You hear all this talk about being a great surgeon. But even the greatest surgeon in the world can be neglectful of a patient or can make a mistake. You can't see everything. You must be determined to do what's right by a patient, but sometimes you lose them. I want to talk to families because just seeing me means a great deal to them. Very, very rarely do I get a resentful response, but when I do it really wrecks my conscience. I think—I can't help it—maybe I have done something wrong along the way. This is how I take defeat. I can't be very philosophical about it for some reason. Other doctors seem to be able to, but as much as I wish I could, I can't think my way around failure.

"Once you've got the reputation I have, you don't refer away anyone. If it's cardiovascular, it's my problem. And that's all there is to it. Occasionally, I'm exploited and asked to do impossible things, but I'll try—I always have, I always will."

The two-year-old girl with degenerative heart disease had arrested and died. The father of the child had threatened Messmer and was still in the hospital.

Dr. Cooley went immediately to Reverend Jorjorian's office where the child's mother was being comforted by the chaplain. He was halfway across the room when the father, a husky young man in a white tee shirt and Levi's, jumped in front of Cooley and shook his fist.

"Who in the hell do you think you are?" he shouted. "You think you can take advantage of people like this? What did you do to my baby?"

Cooley made a move toward the mother, but the father stepped in his way. Then Cooley explained. He said he was terribly sorry. Everyone had known that the child was mortally ill and he had done everything he could, but there wasn't much to be done. He told the father he would like to speak with his wife privately.

"Get out of here. I don't want to look at you," the father shouted. "You killed my baby."

"I'm sorry you feel that way," Cooley said.

"I said get out, you son of a bitch! Now, right now! We don't want you around."

Cooley hesitated, then said he would talk with both of them tomorrow.

Twenty minutes later, the young father and his brother, a large man in a denim jacket and cowboy boots, stormed into Cooley's gallery office.

"You didn't think I was through with you yet, did you?" the father said.

Cooley asked them to leave.

The brother said they weren't leaving, not until they'd settled this. He reached down and shut the door.

There was no way out except over both of them. Cooley stood. "Now, let me tell you something," he said. "First you tried to assault my colleague, a man half your size. Thirty minutes ago you cursed me and tried to order me out of my own hospital. And accused me of killing your child. Let me remind you of something. I didn't father that baby. When it was born, it was your responsibility. The baby was sick—it couldn't have lived. But I shared your responsibility when I tried to fix her. I wanted the baby to live, just like you and your wife did, but she died. And now you come to me like this.

"I've been pushed as far as I'm going to be pushed. You've already upset the whole hospital. If you're looking for physical satisfaction, you and your brother come on out in the parking lot with me. If not, I advise you to get out of here right now, because I'm calling a security officer."

Dr. Cooley was home in bed by three o'clock.

Part Four

Chapter 13

Ethical and Legal Complications

On April 8, 1969, Dr. Ted Cooper, director of the National Heart Institute, wrote a letter requesting that the Baylor administration answer a number of questions pertaining to the origin of the artificial heart that Cooley used. That same day, Cooper phoned Cooley and assured him that his interest in the matter was strictly routine. However, prior to the letter and the phone call, a committee headed by Dr. Harold Brown and appointed by Dr. DeBakey had already launched a fact-finding investigation for the Baylor Board of Trustees.

On April 9, a spokesman for the NHI was quoted as saying, "We have no reason to assume that there was any violation of the tenets of the federal grant to Baylor." But Dr. Frank Hastings, head of the NHI artificial heart program, assumed a different position: "Any medical innovation developed in whole or in part with NHI funds must undergo tests and evaluations by persons other than the developer before it can be used." From all indications, the NHI officials were trying to stay on the good sides of both Cooley and DeBakey and still abide by the rules of the agency.

Cooley's reply to the impending investigation was that he had done more heart surgery than anyone in the world and was fully competent to determine what should be done for his patients. "I have," he said, "done equally bizarre things before and will again."

On Friday afternoon, April 11, a Baylor committee headed by Dr. Hebbel Hoff met in Dr. DeBakey's presidential office and opened hearings on the matter of the artificial heart.

The thirteen-man committee was composed of executive faculty and departmental chairmen selected by Dr. Hoff and Dr. DeBakey. Lucille McCutcheon took shorthand, while Jerry Maley recorded his summary impressions on tape. Testimonies of the witnesses were to be transcribed and then presented for signatures. After the first hour it was apparent to Mrs. McCutcheon and Mr. Maley that their system would not work: she could not record the testimonies fast enough; he became confused. Nonetheless, they tried to get everything down accurately.

Dr. Hoff opened the hearings by assuring everyone present that whatever transpired here was Baylor business and would consequently be held in strictest confidence. The main problem to be resolved was whether or not the artificial heart that Dr. Cooley used in Mr. Karp had been developed with federal funds. The committee would report their conclusions only to the Baylor Board of Trustees.

Dr. C. William Hall, who had flown up from San Antonio for the hearings, told the committee that Dr. Cooley had not participated in the artificial-heart experiments. He said the device implanted in Mr. Karp was identical to the one developed at Baylor under the NHI grant. The point was not raised that Hall had left Baylor on January 1, 1969, thirty days prior to the first Cooley-Liotta calf experiment, and so had no firsthand knowledge of the nature of the experiments or who had conducted them.

Dr. William O'Bannon, who built the control console for Cooley and Liotta, said that at the time he had thought he was simply "helping another investigator," that he had no idea Cooley was working independent of Dr. DeBakey. The console, he said, had not been designed for use in human implantations. That he had chosen to build the device in his garage, that he had tested it in the urodynamics lab at St. Luke's the night before the Karp operation, at which time he had seen the signed forms consenting to the operation, did not come up in O'Bannon's testimony. Nor did the fact that he was associated with Texas Medical Instruments, the commercial firm which stood to garner profits from the manufacture of power sources for artificial hearts.

Dr. Liotta testified that he and Dr. Cooley had developed the Karp artificial heart between January and April with private funds. Liotta said that the results of the calf experiments to which Hoff kept referring were based on Dr. DeBakey's personal interpretation of the notes which had been confiscated from Liotta's lab. DeBakey's conclusions, Liotta said, were inaccurate. When Ted Bowen, public-relations director for Methodist Hospital, interjected a question concerning the publicity surrounding the Karp operation, Liotta countered by recalling the left ventricular by-pass operation Dr. DeBakey had performed on Mr. DeRudder and the attendant "circus of news coverage." The matter was dropped.

Polk Smith, Arnold Friedman, and other technicians in the Baylor laboratory then gave their testimony. They were questioned about the procedures that had been followed in the winter and spring of 1969, who had given them instructions, and what had been said to them pertaining to the eventual use of the artificial heart on which they were working. All agreed that the heart had been built in the Baylor lab. It was during a lab assistant's testimony that Jerry Maley became concerned about the objectivity of the proceedings.

Maley: "These lab people worked for me. I knew who they liked and disliked, and one who testified hated Dr. Liotta. She thought he was unreasonable and made her work too hard. She had asked to be transferred several times. Her testimony was obviously colored by her dislike for him. The truth was, she had no expertise or authority to be giving testimony that reflected upon someone's professional career. That's what galled the hell out of me: that the committee would listen to these people who had no background from which to interpret the technical aspects of what had gone on in the lab. I concluded then and there that this committee was being used as a vehicle through which to ruin Dr. Cooley."

Maley then testified. He said that Dr. Cooley, as a full professor, had every right to use the lab in any way he wished, so long as the expenses for his personal experiments were billed directly to him. Regardless of the circumstances, Maley said, it was not for him or for any of the laboratory personnel to question what Cooley or Liotta did in the laboratory. Despite accusations otherwise, Maley did not feel that he had been disloyal to Baylor by allowing Dr. Cooley to avail himself of his privileges as a full professor.

Saturday, Dr. Cooley appeared before the Hoff committee. He said that he and Dr. Liotta had developed the artificial heart with private funds and had used it as an emergency measure. Unable to record Cooley's testimony verbatim, the following Monday Mrs. McCutcheon asked Mr. Maley if she could integrate his summary of Cooley's testimony into her own notes. He agreed. When the document was presented to Dr. Cooley, he refused to sign it on the grounds that it was grossly inaccurate. On April 17, Dr. Cooley wrote Dr. Hoff requesting another hearing in the presence of a trained court recorder. Hoff replied that Cooley's testimony had indeed not been accurately recorded, and in lieu of calling a second hearing sent a list of questions which Cooley answered in accordance with his testimony and returned. Since only four of the witnesses signed the transcriptions of their statements, there was no official report from the committee. Dr. Hoff made a verbal report to Dr. DeBakey and gave him the unofficial testimonies.

The April 18 issue of *Time* magazine included an article in which it was stated that the calf tests prior to the implantation of the artificial heart had been unsuccessful, indicating that the heart was not ready for use in humans. This article was based on Dr. DeBakey's interpretation of the Cooley-Liotta experiments, copies of which were sent to a number of magazines and newspapers and to officials of the National Heart Institute. On April 18, Dr. DeBakey called Dr. Liotta to his office. Dr. De-Bakey said he was disappointed that Liotta had not developed an artificial heart for him. He said he was going to reorganize the laboratory for total heart replacement according to Liotta's requests in the unanswered memos written in the fall of 1968. Liotta said he was considering leaving the Baylor program and going to work for Dr. Cooley and the Texas Heart Institute. Dr. DeBakey told Dr. Liotta to stay with him. Liotta said he had not yet decided. This was the first in a series of meetings where Liotta, besides dealing with his own problems, served as an unofficial liaison between Cooley and DeBakey.

In January 1969, Dr. Liotta had sent Dr. Vincent Gott at Johns Hopkins an abstract of a paper he wished to present to the spring meeting of the American Society of Artificial Internal Organs. Dr. Gott was to chair the meeting. The paper, which was later published in the *American Journal of Pathology*, dealt with a group of calves whose hearts had gone into fibrillation during testing of the left ventricular by-pass. On April 22, the day he was to fly to the meeting in Atlantic City, Liotta received a call from Dr. DeBakey. It was six o'clock in the morning.

DeBakey said he wanted to see Liotta before he left for the meeting. When Liotta arrived, DeBakey asked if he planned to present the artificial-heart calf experiments at the Artificial Internal Organ meeting. Liotta said no, and explained that his paper was on an entirely different series. He and Dr. Cooley had not yet begun the artificial-heart experiments when the abstract was sent to Dr. Gott. Besides, Dr. DeBakey still had Liotta's notes on the artificial-heart experiments. Liotta then told Dr. DeBakey that he and Dr. Cooley were presenting Karp as a clinical case. DeBakey asked Liotta not to persist in his association with Dr. Cooley. Liotta replied that he would consider the matter while he was in Atlantic City.

When Cooley and Liotta arrived in Atlantic City, they discovered that Dr. DeBakey had sent a telegram to Gott withdrawing Liotta's paper. As chairman of the Department of Surgery, this was Dr. DeBakey's prerogative. But the implication was that these left ventricular by-pass experiments were related to the Karp case and were not legally Liotta's to present.

Dr. Gott told Cooley and Liotta that neither he nor the society wished to become embroiled in the Baylor controversy. There was a great deal of confusion. Finally, the paper was withdrawn. However, Dr. Willem Kolff, the inventor of the artificial kidney and the man who brought Dr. Liotta to this country, arranged for an informal discussion session during which Dr. Cooley was invited to present the Karp case. He showed a film of the implantation and gave the results of the tests preceding and subsequent to the operation—no clotting in the device or in Mr. Karp's system, little blood trauma, no proof of irreversible kidney damage. Death resulted from pneumonia. Cooley and Liotta received a standing ovation.

Another question before the Baylor committee was Cooley's motivation for using the artificial heart. If it was a calculated experiment, then there was a case against Cooley, for he had not obtained the proper permissions. If it was, as Cooley maintained, a desperate effort to sustain a man's life until a human donor could be found, then Cooley was technically within his rights and obligations as a surgeon.

Although he said nothing to the press, Cooley was becoming increasingly exasperated with the campaign he felt was being launched against him. At one point he sent a note to L. F. McCollum, chairman of the Baylor Board of Trustees, suggesting that if he did not take steps to quiet Dr. DeBakey it might be necessary to bring attention to the DeRudder case once again. Indeed, there were similarities between the DeRudder case in which Dr. DeBakey used the left ventricular by-pass and the Karp case.

Following his return from Atlantic City, Dr. Liotta was once again summoned to Dr. DeBakey's office. DeBakey reminded him of the possible consequences if he continued to work with Dr. Cooley. Liotta balked, pridefully, and went to Cooley and told him of the conversation with DeBakey. Liotta felt DeBakey wanted to retain him in order to bolster his case against Cooley. Though he was not without vindictiveness, Cooley wanted to continue working with Liotta in order to prove the validity of the Karp case.

Cooley agreed that Liotta should immediately write a letter of resignation. Liotta wrote the letter and showed it to Cooley, who thought it was too strong. He advised Liotta to resign his full-time status and retain his clinical association with Baylor. Liotta wrote a second letter and sent it to DeBakey. There was no reply.

Cooley and Liotta had three more artificial hearts ready and two additional power consoles on order from Texas Medical Instruments. Cutter Laboratories in California had provided them with eight technicians who could construct a custom device within twenty-four hours. They waited—they were eager to follow up the first implant—but no potential recipient appeared. It was the first hint that the controversy might have adversely affected Dr. Cooley's referrals.

On May 1, Dr. Ted Cooper at the National Heart Institute received a letter from L. F. McCollum. Because the report of the Baylor committee was unacceptable as an official document, McCollum attempted to avoid the question by stating that the results of the Baylor investigation were to remain confidential. Cooper, however, knew that the press had received Xeroxed sheets that were purportedly the official minutes of the hearings.

The day that he received the letter from Mr. McCollum, Cooper replied that he was not satisfied. He wanted to know the origin of the heart, how well it had functioned, and whether federal guidelines had been violated.

Meanwhile, it came to light that there was a bill in the Texas State legislature proposing to give Baylor College of Medicine $5.5 million in annual aid. According to *Medical World News* of May 9, 1969, a magazine on which Dr. DeBakey served as an advisory editor, "Opponents who want the University of Texas to establish its own branch in the Medical Center now have additional ammunition." This was the first of several articles which depicted the Karp operation as the sole obstacle to Baylor's receiving financial backing from various sources; a similar rationale was behind Dr. DeBakey's insistence that the National Heart Institute demand a Baylor investigation.

In fact, the board of trustees of the University of Texas was not altogether displeased with the impending split between Cooley and DeBakey; they had finally gained a foothold in the Texas Medical Center. If Cooley was to leave Baylor over the artificial-heart controversy, he would be legally approachable to join the faculty of the forthcoming University of Texas Medical School. A financial arrangement in which Cooley would be exempt from the standard income-sharing plan at Texas had already been informally considered.

On May 15, L. F. McCollum's first and second letters to Dr. Ted Cooper were made public by the National Heart Institute. In the second letter McCollum stated that Cooley and Liotta's use of the artificial heart had been a violation of Baylor and federal guidelines, and the Karp operation was termed an experiment, rather than an emergency effort to prolong the patient's life. "The device was developed at Baylor under a federal grant, not as Cooley has said, with private funds . . . Baylor will insure in the future that NHI and federal guidelines on human experimentation will be followed."

Cooper's reply to McCollum was: "The NHI believes that this action taken by Baylor in this matter is evidence of its ability to enforce the NHI system of guidelines governing clinical research which relies heavily on the goodwill and integrity of the recipient institution." Cooper had assumed that McCollum's statements were based on an official report of the investigating committee, but due to the inaccurate recording of the hearings, there was no official report. Once again, the evidence most incriminating to Cooley and Liotta was Dr. DeBakey's interpretation of the calf experiments; copies of the preliminary manuscript, which was later to appear in *The Baylor Cardiovascular Bulletin*, had been circulated among the Baylor committee members.

Then toward the latter part of May another mass mailing went out from Baylor to newspapers, magazines, and a number of influential surgeons around the country. The document was a scissor-and-paste Xeroxed copy of what was purportedly "the notarized statement of the people who appeared before the Baylor faculty committee on the matter of the artificial heart." The introduction to this sixteen-page "report" depicted Dr. DeBakey as the victim of "Dr. Cooley's theft of the artificial heart." The report was unsigned. Several surgeons and publications were suspicious of its accuracy and forwarded their copies to Dr. Cooley.

Cooley still refused to discuss the matter with the press more than to say that he was satisfied that he had done the right thing. Instead, in an effort to prove his point, he accepted invitations to present the Karp case to medical meetings and conventions around the country.

From the 1968 Christmas meeting with Dr. Liotta when they began to discuss the development of an artificial heart, Cooley had anticipated problems. But he had assumed whatever disagreements might arise would be treated as Baylor business and would be settled within the processes of the college. While Cooley admired and perhaps envied DeBakey's political acumen and power within the profession, he had not imagined that the situation would literally become a federal case. Cooley was not a part of the federal grant to Baylor and consequently was not obliged to follow the attendant guidelines. But apparently Dr. DeBakey's approach had been to prove to the Baylor committee's satisfaction that Cooley had stolen the artificial heart and implanted it before the device had been proved safe, an accusation that was not offset by Cooley's somewhat cavalier reaction. Cooley then appeared to have jeopardized multimillion-dollar grants to the college from the federal government and the Texas State legislature.

In effect, Dr. DeBakey precipitated an investigation of himself; as director of the grant, he was responsible for seeing that the National Heart Institute guidelines were adhered to, that funds were not misappropriated. As the focus of guilt shifted to Cooley, DeBakey was absolved of any possible negligence in the administration of the grant. The NHI could do nothing to Cooley, but Baylor could. As could others: the Harris County Medical Society, the American College of Surgeons, and the Fountain subcommittee for the investigation of federal expenditures were organizing investigations as a result of the adverse publicity that surrounded the Baylor faculty hearings. Despite the fact that Cooley's many friends in the medical profession admired and respected him, others, whether jealous of the traditionally tight-lipped mystique of the profession or envious of Cooley's competence and accomplishments, felt that a reprimand was long overdue. His rush to the heart transplants, his continuing squabble with DeBakey, and now the artificial heart. That Cooley was young and handsome with the highest gross income of any surgeon in the world did not help allay the deep, secret image of him that some of his colleagues harbored. Nor did the fact that on occasion Dr. Christiaan Barnard had referred to Cooley as "the finest surgeon in the world."

Letters—critical, laudatory, and insane—came to Cooley from around the world. The initial reaction of most surgeons and physicians was a shrug in recognition of another spat between Cooley and DeBakey. But as the publicity continued, the gravity and proportions of the artificial-heart question became apparent. Either Cooley was a disrespectful opportunist, or he finally had gotten fed up with trying to work under DeBakey's thumb. The only point of agreement among those nearest the situation was that Dr. DeBakey's pride had been hurt.

If, as he later said, Cooley had based his decision to follow through with the Karp operation on Dr. DeBakey's belief that progress must not be impeded by a vain desire to avoid making enemies, he also emulated Dr. DeBakey's press relations following the DeRudder operation. After the implantation of the artificial heart, Cooley met with reporters. By way of justifying the procedure, he said only that the operation had been a desperate effort to salvage a patient; as soon as a human donor was found, he returned to stock replies altogether. But the constant rush of news releases from Baylor, both authorized and unauthorized, left Cooley in a difficult position: there was no way to tell his side of the story and, at the same time, maintain his professional dignity. He would not admit that there was a personal disagreement between himself and Dr. DeBakey.

Cooley's private reaction was a different matter. While at the outset he had been convinced that he was doing the right thing, the Baylor campaign and the incessant accusations of the press caused Cooley to wonder. His associates at St. Luke's began to notice a subtle but definite defensiveness in his otherwise candid and direct demeanor. Prior to the controversy tarnishing his halo, few of Cooley's surgical personnel, for fear of appearing blatantly envious, would risk criticizing him, but now a measure of resentment was evident. Some thought he was getting "too cocky." Others said he was guilty of using both Liotta and De-Bakey to his own ends. In reference to those on Cooley's service who had taken the opportunity to voice their dissent, a Baylor heart-lung machine technician said, "Regardless of what they say, Cooley's surgery is not a team effort, and they know it. Take away Dr. Cooley and you have a headless monster. It's only proper that he should get credit for what's done here. This would be less true at Methodist, where several heart surgeons do the operating and the research. And as for the artificial-heart affair, it bothered him. Dr. Cooley—his protestations to the contrary—has always been quick to admit a mistake. I don't know what he does or doesn't believe in, but Christian admission is part of his manner. The artificial heart? Who knows? No one, including him and Dr. DeBakey."

The May 16 issue of the *Medical World News* reported that, despite the conclusions offered by Mr. McCollum to Dr. Cooper, the Baylor committee had been split over the extent of federal funds involved in the development of the artificial heart and in the interpretation of the test-animal data. Dr. Cooper was reported as having said, "I'm not investigating Denton Cooley. I'm not interested in any personal controversies, only in grants management. I regret the notion that we are making clinical decisions from a desk in Washington. Clinical decisions have to be made at the bedside. I don't want to get involved in them." But, inadvertently or not, Dr. Cooper was involved.

On May 17, an *ad hoc* committee of the Baylor Board of
Trustees met to review the findings of the Baylor faculty committee. The Baylor board members were chosen by Mr. McCollum and Dr. DeBakey. At the suggestion of Dr. DeBakey, Dr.
Hoff proposed that each faculty member be required to sign a
statement swearing to abide by the guidelines of Baylor and the
NHI. The recommendation was accepted by the board. A letter
anticipating the acceptance of this proposal had already been
sent to Dr. Cooper and a news release was in preparation.

Two days later, Mr. McCollum issued a statement on the new
Baylor guideline policy. The release was written by Ben Kaplan, a Houston public-relations man, and was delivered by
messenger to the local news media. When the releases arrived,
Mr. McCollum had left for London and Mr. Kaplan was unable
to answer questions regarding its content.

In summary, Mr. McCollum acknowledged Dr. Cooper's fa-
vorable response to the report of the Baylor faculty committee,
stating that current and forthcoming federal grants might have
been jeopardized had Baylor been held responsible for the vio-
lations of federal guidelines which Cooley and Liotta had failed
to abide by. The logic of McCollum's statement was familiar.
"Dr. Cooper has vindicated the current administration of the
College. The Board of Trustees has asked me to express its
gratification for Dr. Cooper's statement and wishes to express
complete confidence in Dr. DeBakey. The violation was that
Denton A. Cooley and Domingo S. Liotta implanted the device
without knowledge or approval of Dr. DeBakey, who was desig-
nated by the NHI to be in charge of the program, or without
the knowledge or approval of the college's own Committee on
Research Involving Human Beings."

The newly required faculty guidelines agreement called for
the signatures of the experimenter and his departmental chairman.

Cooley felt that the guideline requirement was an attempt on

the part of Dr. DeBakey to shackle his research and prohibit
him from any further use of the artificial heart. That a proposal
for an experimental procedure necessitated the signatures of
the department chairman gave Dr. DeBakey a virtual veto
power over Cooley. The situation was identical to that which
had brought Dr. Liotta's research to a halt and had prompted
him to collaborate with Dr. Cooley on the artificial heart in the
first place.

Cooley's official reply to Mr. McCollum's statement was: "I
must study the guidelines to determine whether they permit
me to serve my patients in their best interests." Cooley added
that in the meantime he would use the artificial heart if it was
necessary to save a person's life. Then he made a speech concerned with how the rigidity of federal and institutional controls was stifling the progress of medicine.

May 20 in a speech before a group of Brooklyn physicians, Dr.
DeBakey, ignoring the Karp operation, called upon the medical
profession to find a mechanical replacement for the human
heart. To deny that an implantation *had* been performed
seemed oddly unrealistic. But the implantation of the first artificial heart was to have been the crowning achievement of Dr.
DeBakey's career—the accomplishment which his friends believed he hoped would bring him the Nobel Prize. Many researchers in the country working on an artificial heart under a
NHI grant felt that Dr. DeBakey would be awarded the honor
to implant the first device Washington deemed ready for human trial. To hedge his bet, Dr. DeBakey was surgical and
testing director of the two most promising privately funded
artificial-heart programs in the country: Sanders Nuclear Corporation and Cambridge Nuclear Corporation. He had reason
to deny that the Karp implantation had been successful, a question which in fact had not yet been settled.

When the reporters in Brooklyn asked about Dr. Cooley's
position, Dr. DeBakey said he had "no information" regarding

ETHICAL AND LEGAL COMPLICATIONS

Cooley's possible exit from Baylor, and added that Cooley had never worked in the school's artificial-heart program. The reporters assumed that there had been a viable artificial-heart program at Baylor. Dr. DeBakey said that the Karp operation had been performed in secret and left the reporters to form their own conclusions.

On May 22, the first of three scathing articles on Dr. Cooley appeared in the Washington *Star*.

June 7, the day Dr. Liotta was to fly to Montreal for the International Transplant Gala, Dr. DeBakey called him to his office once again. DeBakey asked Liotta to read a paper that he was going to publish with Liotta as the co-author. Liotta read the paper. It was Dr. DeBakey's interpretation of the confiscated Cooley-Liotta laboratory notes. Liotta said that the paper was inaccurate, that he would not be a co-author unless he could make some changes and add Dr. Cooley's name. He asked to take the paper with him to Montreal; he would rewrite it on the plane. Dr. DeBakey refused and said that Liotta should make up his mind here and now. But under no circumstances would he allow Dr. Cooley's name to appear on the paper. "In that case," Liotta said, "I will not be a party to it." And he left. The paper later appeared in the Baylor *Cardiovascular Bulletin* with an acknowledgment to Dr. Liotta for his "assistance in the artificial-heart experiments."

Harris County Medical Society, a local organization composed primarily of general practitioners, included a large anti-Cooley faction. Since December 1968, they had been attempting to get Cooley before their executive board to answer charges relating to the publicity surrounding the heart transplants he had performed. The more he avoided them, the more charges were brought against him. Then at the June 12 meeting of the organization, Dr. Irving Page, editor of *Modern Medicine* magazine, and Dr. Dwight Wilber, president of the American Medical Association, spoke to a general meeting of the organization. Page made a direct attack on the transplant publicity, declaring it was "advertising and clearly unethical." (Earlier in the *Saturday Review*, Page had published a bitterly severe editorial on the subject. This had brought a response from Cooley chastising Page for his short-sightedness, then excusing him because of his advanced age. In the editorial, Page neglected to mention that the transplant progress reports in medical journals had been so late and incomplete that Dr. Ted Cooper, when compiling data for the NHI, had relied primarily on the clipping service from the popular press.)

Dr. Wilber said little; the AMA had twice commended Cooley and St. Luke's for the manner in which they had handled the press during transplants. Still, the upshot of the meeting was to stir the Harris County Medical Society against Cooley. A letter demanding his presence at a hearing conducted by the discipline committee went out the following day.

The June 13 issue of *Medical World News* reported that the American College of Surgeons (whose investigations were traditionally super-secret) and the Fountain subcommittee were "digging into the affair." The Fountain committee, the article suggested, "may also want to explore the possible use of NHI funds in the development of the artificial heart." The decisions of the ACS and the Fountain committee to investigate Cooley were based on the unofficial Baylor report.

An auditor from the Fountain subcommittee, William Thurmond of Dallas, had been at Baylor prior to the Karp operation investigating Dr. Larry Lamb's charges against Dr. DeBakey.

Jerry Maley, executive assistant to Dr. DeBakey: "There were a lot of things that we had no reason to be proud of. I worked with Thurmond for a while and gave him whatever he asked for. Despite what was reported in *Medical World News*, the artificial-heart matter was coincidental to the Fountain investigation."

There was more in the *Medical World News* article. On the

morning of June 20, a reporter from the Houston *Chronicle* phoned Dr. Liotta and asked him if he had any comment to make regarding his dismissal from Baylor. Liotta was shocked; he hadn't heard about it. Dr. DeBakey had chosen the *Medical World News* through which to inform Dr. Liotta that he had been fired.

The Fountain subcommittee auditor was still going over the Baylor grant records on July 1 when Dr. Larry Lamb was paid a year's salary and left town. Following the arrangement with Lamb, Jerry Maley, who had been with Baylor for seven years, handed in his resignation.

Over the previous five weeks, Cooley had made numerous unsuccessful attempts to contact Dr. DeBakey. He sought the advice of his hospital board and, hoping to arrange an interview with Dr. DeBakey, he met with members of the Baylor board. All to no avail. Dr. DeBakey remained obdurate. The breach was to widen. On the day Lamb left town and Maley quit, Dr. Cooley wrote a letter to Dr. DeBakey requesting that he be dropped from full-time to clinical status. That night Cooley attended a hospital party with Mr. Leopold Meyer, chairman of the St. Luke's board. It was the first time anyone on his service had seen Cooley maudlin and unsmiling.

This partial resignation was intended as a threat as to what might happen if an amicable arrangement could not be worked out. But Dr. DeBakey did not respond. Hoping to press him into replying, Cooley wrote a letter to DeBakey requesting that he return the thousand dollars' worth of Wada valves that were in the artificial heart that he had confiscated. Again, no answer.

During a two-day marathon of meetings at the American Medical Association convention in New York, Cooley showed the Karp film to a disappointingly small audience, was interviewed on CBS, and had a long luncheon with Mr. McCollum at "21." Wherever he went he carried in his pocket a ventricle from the latest model of the artificial heart. During the convention, Cooley learned from friends that the American College of Surgeons planned to investigate him.

After the convention, Cooley went to Spain to receive the Order of the Grand Cross from General Francisco Franco. But his main purpose for going was to begin formal negotiations regarding an exchange program between the Texas Heart Institute and the Federal University of Madrid, a matter he had not seriously considered until he was convinced that no United States government money would soon be made available to him.

Dr. Liotta and his brother, Salvador, chief of cardiology at Madrid, had initiated a program in which the Texas Heart Institute would train Spanish heart surgeons and technicians, and in exchange the Spanish government would make research facilities available to Cooley and Liotta and would provide the Texas Heart Institute with a quarter of a million dollars. Madrid University Hospital would also serve as a clearing house for European referrals.

The irony was that the finest heart surgeon in the richest country in the world had found it necessary to go elsewhere for financial support.

On August 3, shortly after returning to the United States, Cooley was called to Chicago to appear before the Central Judiciary Committee of the American College of Surgeons. The specific allegations that the committee wanted answered were: (1) "That you intentionally made secret arrangements to obtain a substantial duplicate of the artificial heart which was being developed under the National Institutes of Health grant for clinical use at a time when those responsible for its development were convinced that it was not ready for clinical use." (2) "That your use of the artificial heart was deliberately planned prior to the operation on Mr. Karp, April 4, 1969." (3) "That you actively participated in immediate and extensive publicity given to the circumstances of this patient's care and the implantation of the artificial device."

The Board of Regents of the American College of Surgeons had received correspondence from its membership making these allegations. Upon review, the board had recommended an investigation.

To compound the subtler indictments against Cooley, on August 5 it was announced that he had topped all U. S. physicians in Medicare payments—$94,000. This caused more resentment in the medical community and precipitated a rash of letters from the public condemning him as a "blood-sucker" and a charlatan. (Oddly enough, a letter of commendation from President Nixon arrived the same day as the most denunciating letter from the public.)

The American College of Surgeons was undecided about the artificial-heart affair. The Baylor Board of Trustees had been asked to consider Cooley's dismissal, but they were not convinced that such a drastic step was necessary. On orders from Washington, Mr. Thurmond, the Fountain subcommittee auditor, returned to Dallas. In general, the furor seemed to be subsiding.

Then, on August 17, the Washington *Star* published another, more extensive article by Judith Randall suggesting that Cooley and Liotta were guilty of every accusation that had been brought against them. As for sources, Miss Randall wrote that she had "notarized statements to the Baylor committee by the people who built the artificial heart." Cooley believed her information was derived from the unsigned sixteen-page "report" and from Dr. DeBakey's interpretation of the laboratory notes. Miss Randall had visited Baylor and had attempted to interview several faculty members, though not Dr. Cooley. Since there was a rule at Baylor against granting interviews to unauthorized persons, one faculty member called the college public-relations office and asked if Miss Randall had clearance. It was then discovered that while no written permission existed, a series of selected interviews had been set up for her. In an effort to secure a collaborative statement, on August 8 Miss Randall sent Mrs. Karp copies of her two previous articles condemning Cooley and Liotta. Mrs. Karp refused to respond.

Two days after the Washington *Star* article, Dr. Cooley received a phone call from Dr. John Talbot, editor of *The Journal of the American Medical Association,* informing him that due to "unusual circumstances" his paper on the Karp case was not acceptable for publication. It would have been the most proper defense against the anti-Cooley crusade.

On August 20, Dr. Cooley and his family left for a ten-day vacation in Europe. They were greeted at the Rome airport by a large group of Italians whom Cooley had operated on. Aware of the situation in the United States, Mrs. Alessandra Profili, a former patient who had flown to and from Houston in a chartered 707, had arranged the reception.

After operating for two days in Rome, Cooley was invited to a private audience with Pope Paul. The Pope said he favored the artificial heart above human heart transplants, the problem being an acceptable definition of death. Cooley asked if he might be allowed to state his position on the matter. After deliberating with his interpreter, the Pope said yes, though he reserved the right not to reply. Cooley then gave his definition of death and compared it with the Roman Catholic criteria concerning the beginnings of life. He advocated transplants and the artificial heart equally. The Pope smiled but said nothing.

At a cocktail party later that evening, King Constantine presumed to advise Cooley how to handle the artificial-heart affair. In reply Cooley pointed out the errors which had brought Constantine to exile and suggested a method whereby he might regain his country. The family spent the rest of their vacation as guests of Bing and Katherine Crosby on Ischia and returned to Houston on August 30.

The Washington *Star* article had stirred up new interest in the controversy. What had changed, had changed for the worse. Convinced that no reconciliation was forthcoming, Dr. Cooley sent a letter of resignation to Dr. DeBakey. No one at Baylor had thought it would go this far.

By nature and training, Cooley was a team man—he believed in organization. Personal differences notwithstanding, Dr. De-Bakey was the chief, the senior man, a fact that Cooley was unable to dismiss even by leaving. Although he had cherished his association with Baylor, the practical alteration in Cooley's position was slight. Years earlier he had moved his surgery from Methodist, and then the furor aroused by the transplants had pushed him toward further independence. Cooley trained Baylor residents, the hiring and firing of his pump technicians and his billing was done through the college, otherwise his support came from St. Luke's–Texas Children's and the Texas Heart Institute. The main loss would be to Baylor College of Medicine.

The point of Dr. Cooley's financial contribution to the college was not included in a Baylor committee report which was eventually presented to the board of trustees. Baylor had just begun an endowment drive to raise $30 million, the income from which would be used for faculty salaries. At the meeting where Cooley's resignation was being considered, a member of the board asked the treasurer about the extent of Dr. Cooley's financial contribution. It ranged from between $500,000 and $750,000 annually and amounted to over one-sixth of the income from the $30 million they hoped to raise. The figures were startling. But the board, following the recommendation of the Baylor committee, decided to accept Cooley's resignation.

Dr. DeBakey then contacted Newell France, chief administrator of St. Luke's, and informed him that since Cooley was no longer a member of the Baylor faculty he could not, according to the Baylor associated hospitals agreement, remain at St. Luke's. France reminded Dr. DeBakey that Cooley was their chief of cardiovascular surgery, that the hospital board would consider disassociating from Baylor before they would fire Dr. Cooley. Cooley then learned that he never actually had been chief of cardiovascular surgery—Dr. DeBakey had not signed the appointment. Cooley's titular status was subsequently reduced to surgical consultant.

Soon after the Karp operation, Francis Flynn, publisher of the New York *Daily News*, arrived at Methodist Hospital for a checkup. Five years earlier, Dr. DeBakey had performed a vascular operation on him. The *News* had published several articles on Dr. DeBakey, and Mr. Flynn was a regular, five-figure contributor to the Dr. Michael E. DeBakey Foundation. One evening during rounds, Dr. DeBakey discussed the artificial-heart controversy with Mr. Flynn. A few weeks later, John Quinn, a reporter on the *News*, arrived in Houston.

On September 6, 1969, six days after Cooley's resignation, the first in a series of four artificial-heart articles by Quinn appeared in the *Daily News*. His source, Quinn wrote, was "the testimony taken by the Baylor College of Medicine." According to Quinn, "the government demanded the investigation"; "Dr. Cooley never tested the plastic heart himself"; "DeBakey was the most formidible witness in the hearing." Echoing the Washington *Star* article, Quinn wrote, "Despite investigative findings, Cooley and Liotta have still not been disciplined professionally . . . why has nothing been done?" Quinn questioned Liotta's research ability—"Some insiders argue that most of the creative ideas were supplied by others"—and erroneously quoted Liotta as saying that he and Cooley were "not prepared to go into clinical application." He also referred to the Karp operation (Mr. Karp was Jewish) as violating the rules laid down by the Nuremberg War Trials. Quinn concluded the series with an appeal for federal support for Dr. DeBakey and hinted that a Nobel Prize might be in the offing.

Meanwhile, at the request of National Educational Television, Mrs. Karp arrived in Houston to take part in a documentary, "The Heart Makers." Henry Reinhard, who had been a close adviser of Cooley's throughout this time, met her at the airport. He noticed that Mrs. Karp had lost weight and changed her hair style. From the airport to the Warwick Hotel, where a suite had been reserved for her, Mrs. Karp made comparisons between herself and the plight of Jacqueline Kennedy. She said she had reconsidered the matter of the NET program and had decided that she should receive some financial remuneration for her appearance. In the light of the publicity following her husband's operation, she was no longer convinced that she had done the right thing by signing the consent form. In fact, she said she could not recall reading, discussing, or signing the form. She insisted on speaking with Dr. Cooley before meeting David Prowett, the NET producer.

Dr. Cooley interrupted his operating schedule to speak with Mrs. Karp. She asked questions about her husband's misfortunes which Cooley could not answer and was not prepared to speculate on. She talked about her father, her childhood, and her own tragic life. Then Mrs. Karp asked if the artificial heart had really been properly tested, if Cooley had, as the papers said, stolen it. Cooley told her he felt he had done his best, as her husband wished. He advised her to evaluate her sources of information and decide what she was going to believe. Despite the reports in the press, Cooley said he was satisfied that the artificial heart had worked well. Mrs. Karp had no more specific questions to ask Dr. Cooley. Cooley called his wife and asked her to take Mrs. Karp to lunch at Brennen's restaurant. Then he returned to surgery.

After having dinner with Reinhard, David Prowett, and his assistant producer, Mrs. Karp was interviewed in her hotel suite. Dr. Cooley asked Reinhard to review the questions. She told Reinhard that she did not know what to say and asked his advice. He assured her that she did in fact discuss and sign the consent form for the artificial heart implant. In his estimation, Reinhard said it would be a breach of trust if she chose not to support Dr. Cooley, but the decision, as Cooley had advised, was entirely up to her.

Prowett drew a good interview from Mrs. Karp. Later she became upset that only a small portion of the interview appeared in the final film. In lieu of any remuneration beyond her expenses, she requested a print of the film.

On September 21, St. Luke's public-relations office released letters of good faith written by Mrs. Karp and Rabbi Nathan Whitkin. That same day Cooley performed his twenty-first transplant. The recipient was Henry Sims, the world's one hundred and forty-sixth and Cooley's last.

Toward the end of the month, two hundred and fifty anti-Cooley packets were mailed to surgeons and medical school administrators throughout the world. These packets included Xerox copies of the Judith Randall Washington *Star* articles, *The Cardiovascular Bulletin* piece on the calf tests, John Quinn's series from the New York *Daily News,* several articles from *Medical World News,* as well as a covering memo signed by Dr. Michael DeBakey. A second mailing the following month included the just-mentioned materials plus a transplant parody from the Harvard *Lampoon,* featuring "Dr. Desmond Coma." One of the packets was sent to Mr. Karp's son.

On October 2, Dr. Cooley appeared before the Disciplinary Committee of the Harris County Medical Society. The charges against him were (1) using his name in conjunction with a private patient; (2) soliciting patients during the heart transplants; and (3) promoting adulation by making unusual claims.

Cooley was bored by the subject and the proceedings. Regarding the first charge, he said that he had no control over the news media. The second charge was, he said, absurd: "Donors with dead brains are not patients. There might be something in the undertaker's code of ethics that prohibits soliciting dead people, but doctors, so far as I know, are not so restricted." As for promoting adulation, Cooley again said that he could not control the press and had no desire to edit their copy.

Dr. Arnold, chairman of the Harris County committee, recommended that Dr. Cooley plead guilty to the first charge and the other two would be dropped. After being assured that the matter would be held in strictest confidence, Cooley agreed. On Tuesday, October 7, the chiefs of staff of all the Houston hospitals were informed that Dr. Cooley had been formally censured by the Harris County Medical Society. The news was picked up by the wire services, which combined it with a second story: the Siegler Foundation of New York had that day named Cooley as the recipient of their humanitarian award.

The American College of Surgeons invited Cooley to take part in a press conference to publicize their October 14 meeting in San Francisco; his case with them was still pending. He agreed. Christiaan Barnard and Norman Shumway were on the program with Cooley. Later in the day he presented the Karp case, Barnard did a follow-up on Blaiberg, and Shumway discussed the past and future of transplants. Unbeknown to Cooley, the day before he arrived in San Francisco the Board of Governors of the ACS met and voted to censure him. "It's odd," he said, "the right hand of the college apparently didn't know what the left hand was doing. To me it demonstrated the frailty of humans. On an individual basis they are often jealous and vindictive; on an institutional level, they need me. Sometimes they are not content for the spotlight to simply fade from a man; they want to turn on the green light and make him look sick."

Instead of making a formal appeal, Cooley wrote the ACS that he thought their decision was unduly harsh. Rollin Hanlon was president of the ACS. William Longmire was chairman of the Board of Regents. Both had been residents and friends of Cooley's at Johns Hopkins. The probation would take effect in June 1970.

Specifically, the Board of Regents, on the recommendation of the Central Judiciary Committee, decided to put Cooley on probation for one year. He would not be allowed to present papers before the congress of the college or take part in any administrative activities, such as the Cardiovascular Committee. Once again he was assured that the action of the college against him would be held in strictest confidence. Cooley had the recourse of an appeal.

In November, Cooley was informed that the heart-lung technicians of Baylor would no longer be available to him. He was given one week to make other arrangements. This was a particularly serious turn of events, for without heart-lung machines his surgery would come to a halt.

Cooley offered the two top technicians raises if they would remain with him, but his stock was down and hospital rumor had it that his position at St. Luke's was shaky. Both technicians chose the relative security of Baylor, though one, Euford Martin, admitted that the slower pace at Methodist had influenced his decision. Their exit was a disappointment to Cooley and a blow to his ego.

The following Friday, Dr. Cooley's top scrub nurse, Barbara Licty, was instructed in the operation of the heart-lung machine. Substituting water for a blood or dextrose prime, she practiced over the weekend and on Monday assisted in five open-heart operations.

Part Five

I don't like divorces and I don't like professional divorces. They are distasteful and they do nothing but confuse the outsider. I would rather see men work together in what appears to be a harmonious atmosphere even though conflicts exist. Certain matters are family matters and should be confined to the home.

DENTON COOLEY, M.D.

Chapter 14

Conclusions

IT was a hot, humid afternoon late in the summer of 1970, and I was driving through *The Last Picture Show* country southwest of Houston on my way to meet Dr. Cooley at his Brazos River ranch. After seven months of catch-as-catch-can interviews in the operating room, in the gallery office between operations, in cars and airplanes and restaurants and walking down Fifth Avenue, this would be our last meeting. It was the proper time for conclusions, and I had arrived at several.

Over the past year and a half, I had interviewed scores of Dr. Cooley's colleagues, former colleagues, friends, and enemies in this country and in Europe. Their collective observations, combined with my own, convinced me that I knew more about Dr. Cooley and understood him better than anyone else. This is not to say that I *thoroughly* understood him, because in many ways he remained an enigma.

Cooley's essential appeal was one of physical and charismatic attractiveness—indeed, of complex sexuality. Norman Mailer expressed this reaction in his own manner. Mailer, whom Cooley referred to as "the brain surgeon from Brooklyn Heights," was at NASA researching his moon book when I wangled him an invitation to come to the hospital and meet Cooley and watch him operate. After an hour or so of touring the surgical suite, Cooley left us at the elevator. Mailer's remarks were, in sequence and verbatim: "Jesus, he's a handsome guy. If he hadn't been a surgeon, he could have been a movie star. I wonder if he's getting any."

With varying directness, everyone reacted the same way: the secretary in the Psychiatry Department who wasn't at ease until she could see Cooley's car in the Texas Children's parking lot. The close colleague who lambasted his cultural narrowness, and in the next breath, observing that they were both Leos and very much alike, lamented that he had never been admitted to Cooley's "inner circle." At a Baylor banquet, the pretty, tipsy woman who stood over him, awed and admiring, as he ate his steak. The tall arch-detractor from Pathology who fawned on him and fell over him at parties. The bitter-sweet, attractive medical reporter who had just registered her distaste for Cooley's "pretty boy" appearance when he happened by and said hello, and the smile on her flushed face gave her away. Student nurse Susan with the moist eyes and the candy stripes in the gallery. Indeed, my own wife, who on learning from him that I might be paralyzed from the waist down remarked that Cooley was the handsomest man she had ever seen.

Looks, intelligence, humanitarian accomplishment, and wealth were significant factors but, finally, did not provide the key to such frustrating magnetism. In time, the solution became apparent: despite the close colleague's lament, as far as I could discover there was no Cooley "inner circle." His work had reduced his old friends to acquaintances who dwelt on the past. His work had produced colleagues and associates. His work had provided him with fame and fortune and a justifiable aloofness that permitted him to be himself: a polite, charming man with a low boredom threshold who reserved the right to be unavail-

able. There was his work and his family; every other relationship and endeavor was secondary. He permitted no outsider to
get truly close to him, which within the scheme of human
vanity amplified his attractiveness. No matter how gentle the
rebuff, some admirers reacted with bewildered anger. Others
with jealousy and envy. And some few with wistful regrets that
success on a scale that Cooley had achieved so often begets
loneliness.

Again, after all the interviews and observations, after all the
statistics and soul-searching, in an effort to arrive at a respect-
able level of objectivity, I had concluded, insofar as it is possible
to make such a conclusion, that Cooley was the finest surgeon
in the world. And given the uncanny timing of his training—
that he took part in the most spectacular surgical innovations
in the history of the art—and the inevitability that medical
progress will in time make operations obsolete, it is possible that
the world will never produce another of his caliber.

A two-lane blacktop road straight into the vanishing point,
the flat, desolate countryside, and that big, boiling sky composed an appropriately safe and isolated scene in which to think
such grand thoughts.

I turned right on the gravel road across from a sulphur plant
in the middle of nowhere. A few listing frame houses, protected
from the sun by broad-leafed trees, were scattered across the
plains. The windmills in the feed yards resembled galvanized
roosters. A circular red clay drive led to the main house at Cool
Acres. When Cooley bought the property in the 1950s there
was a three-room shack on it. Then a patient, a construction
man, offered Cooley a deal. If he wanted a home on the place,
the man would provide an architect and build the house at cost.
The house I pulled up to: four bedrooms, two baths, air-condi-
tioned. A beautiful view of the river. After six months, when no
bill had arrived, Cooley called the contractor. On second
thought, the contractor had decided to give him the house.

The net on the basketball goal between the house and the pool was weathered and shredded; the backboard had once been painted Longhorn orange and white. The storage shed beside the pool housed a rusted, homemade go-cart with four flat tires, and the floor was littered with broken float toys, softballs and softball bats and gloves, unstrung badminton rackets, and the warped, dismembered elements of a croquet set.

We were sitting by the pool, Cooley in "somebody's" bathing trunks he had found in a drawer. He handed me an album of Polaroid snapshots. "We used to come out here a lot," he said. "And we used to have hospital parties out here. But the children began to grow up and acquire their own friends, develop their own interests. And I got too busy. The place should be used more."

The pictures were in sequence from the Cooley family in front of the original shack, through the stages in construction of the main house and the excavation for the pool. And hospital picnic shots of people with name tags and without suntans, drinking beer, blurred swinging at softballs, wearing funny hats and diving funny dives into the blue pool. There was a picture of a life-sized ceramic Mexican in the shadow of his sombrero, leaning asleep against the trunk of a tree; there was a sign on a string around his neck—MIKE. In the next shot Dr. DeBakey smiled reservedly, as though he was not above appreciating a good joke.

"You know something," Cooley said, "I have a vision of me years from now going to a family reunion and being the only one there named Cooley!"

I asked what he had been like as a kid.

"I don't know. As a teen-ager I was a rather shy person. Serious-minded, an achiever. I felt particularly insecure and awkward around girls. At fifteen, I was six-two and weighed in at one thirty-five; I used to pray that God would cut me down to five-ten. I had an oversized head, too, and a bad complexion.

I just didn't care for my looks, and consequently I didn't have a lot of self-assurance. I didn't go out much—basketball and working in the yard were my things. I think one of the reasons I didn't go out much is because my mother had convinced me that it wasn't necessary. I guess I was under her thumb, but I was a mature kid and I didn't want to cause my parents any additional trouble. In high school I didn't avail myself of the girls who could be won by my being an athlete.

"The University of Texas brought me out a lot. I had just turned seventeen when I entered, but I soon lost much of my shyness. I came to be recognized as a versatile fellow as my achievements increased—athletic ability helped immeasurably. You see, I deliberately wanted to improve my poise around girls. I soon found it convenient to go with one girl at a time, steady. That way, if I wanted companionship at nine o'clock at night, I just had to pick up the phone.

"I began to realize in high school that I was attractive to girls. In school publications, they would always say that I was a handsome man, but I still felt oversized. My brother, on the other hand, was shorter and had all this personality. But I was a good student and people respected me for that. They assumed I would get ahead because I was always at the top of the class, all the way through medical school.

"Anyway, I was still a little shy at Texas, but shortly after I entered medical school at Galveston I began to come around. I was known as something of a rake with the women there, a reputation which seemed to follow me when I transferred to Johns Hopkins. The people around Baltimore were more sophisticated than Texans, but I learned to respond properly in that atmosphere. Then, two years in the service was a help, and the time we spent in London. Through the years, I've gained more and more confidence in myself in that regard.

"Although I feel I belong to one of the so-called first families of Houston, we have always been middle-class working people.

My mother and father tried to teach us how to earn a living. I was working or looking for a job, even as a little boy. It's been something of a handicap as I've gotten older. Now I often wish I didn't have so much respect for earning power. There must be other things, but it's the strongest motivating force that I recognize. I wish I could believe that doing good is the ticket, but that's not the nature of our society, not yet. That's Utopia.

"Once, in the ninth grade, I goofed off. I lost my self-esteem, and I suddenly realized that I had nothing without it. I have a belief that in order to impart confidence and self-esteem to your children you should provide well for them. For example, give them a respectable-looking home; at least in our community this seems important. I feel that a girl who lives in a big white house like ours is, to a degree, protected. A boy with questionable intentions would hesitate to take on that sort of responsibility.

"There are so many things of this sort that contribute to a youngster's personal pride and self-respect. I want my daughters to have more advantages than I had coming along. I was a boy, and it didn't make that much difference then. But it did make some difference. I always had a bit of personal uneasiness about going into some big house out in River Oaks, you know, to a debutante party, knowing that I lived in a small bungalow in a less affluent section of town. These things are on a youngster's mind—I know that. Boys come to call on my daughters and, in general, they're top notch, though a few crumby ones have stopped by. I request, and sometimes I tell them, you get a boy who, regardless of his social standing and economic position, is an academic achiever and makes a good record, and he's welcome in my home—anytime. His personal habits may not be the best according to rumor, but if he's making good grades and stays in the upper part of his class, I believe that's as good an index as I want."

We walked up to the house and got some shells, some clay

pigeons, a skeet trap, and a rusty shotgun and took them out on the west lawn. The river was steep-banked, swift and muddy, like a mammoth, eroded ditch, and the reflected sky rippled in the wake of a small boat fighting the current way out there. Dr. Cooley, squinting in the sun without his glasses, was happy to win not too handily at singles and doubles. Despite his size, he seemed somehow too delicate to have acquired the faint UT brand on his chest as the initiation into a college leadership society, and in the same way wrong for the shotgun, too. But his form was perfect, and he was an excellent shot.

"One of the reasons I work the way I do, I want my daughters to have a strong sense of family pride, with me as the most stable member of the group. My wife says I'm permissive, but I have to keep up communications. Perhaps I'm not with them as much as I should be, but I feel it's the quality of the time you spend together, not the quantity. I want them to respect and love me and realize I would do anything for them. I would support and defend them because I am an accomplice in their lives. They have benefited from my recognition, now they must realize that they have to achieve something on their own. Naturally I'd like for them to go into medicine, but unfortunately the medical world isn't ready to take orders from women. I don't know. Being surrounded by women has changed my life . . . I can't direct them like I could direct a boy. They have different motivations.

"You realize there's such a thing as a work addict. I have worked all my life and want to continue. When things slow down at the hospital, I get unhappy, morose. I try to catch up on my articles and paperwork, but it's not the same thing. I like to see how much more I can do than the next fellow. And the next fellow happens to be Dr. DeBakey.

"Dr. DeBakey works long, long hours, but he apparently feels no need for diversification. His image is a man who constantly hustles. Mine is one of a sort of playboy who can also operate.

Still, nothing interests me as much as surgery because nothing else is so challenging and rewarding. Night before last I was thinking, the happiest I've been in a good while was after I operated on that kid from the Virgin Islands. They brought him over that distance to me—chartered a plane. His doctor thought I was the one man in the world. It was an enormous satisfaction. It happens a lot, but it's always great, I'm always thrilled. I didn't get where I am by fondling my credentials. I'm not a baseball player trying to keep my average up. I don't keep trying to hit home runs in order to look good in the record book. When I don't do my best and take chances, people die. I play the game full tilt all the time."

I asked Dr. Cooley what he would do if the bottom fell out of his world. He did not seem to understand the question. I elaborated: what would he do if everything went wrong at once, if it all turned to ashes at this very moment. He thought for a while. "Well, if it was a legal matter," he said, "I think I would call—" I told him what I meant was an overwhelming disintegration of everything that mattered in his life. He hesitated. "If it was a medical matter, something at the hospital or sickness in my family. . . ."

After a while he discussed religion.

"I see that more often dramatized in the family room at the hospital. Sometimes there are people who don't thank you for saving a relative, or they give you an, 'Oh, fine.' This is particularly true with poor, ignorant people. It bothers me, but you must feel compassion for them. Never let them think you're mad at them—that's not fair. But doctors are human, even though they try to act like they're not.

"One priest impressed me in particular. The patient had died. I was trying to console the family, but they kept shouting and raving hysterically. The priest finally intervened and said they were embarrassing him after all his work with their faith. They persisted, and he slapped one of the women. I thought he was right. That's what religion is all about: it's for people who need a sanctuary and protection from life's more unbearable events.

"I find myself feeling slightly hypocritical when I ask them how much faith they have and then tell them, 'Now is the time to use it. You're in distress and it's raining. Call on your faith in God.' Religion has its usefulness for some.

"I like to think I can handle things. There have been close calls—like the automobile accident when Louise was pregnant and was cut up so badly—but my life, as far as I can tell, has been devoid of tragedy. When and if I meet a personal tragedy, I might well react like everyone else. But my life is very busy. My operating schedule would help me. For example, all problems and controversy over the artificial heart and the Karp operation —my schedule helped me get through. I don't have time to brood. I'm too busy, too active.

"I've gotten used to life-and-death situations. In fact, I tend to classify people according to how they react to tragedy. When I die, I want Louise to show concern but not be overly demonstrative. If that's necessary, she should wait until she's in private. There would be no need to make the doctor suffer.

"I hope I live long enough to become tired of life—that's my only concern about my own death. My ancestors haven't died prematurely. I don't smoke—I must be careful not to overdrink. I hope I'll live to my eighties or older—if I am still coherent and still respected and not a burden. I would like to contribute up to the end. Life is a distance race, you know, you must save for the final kick, the gun lap.

"In a sense, I don't take care of myself—I admit that. But others contend that I abuse myself. I'm not sure. Look at me: For a man over fifty, I'm not overweight. I can do my work and still play. I exercise and I can do things that many younger men can't do. I'm not a faddist dieter—most weight problems are built-in metabolism. I want to look, act, and think young. I suppose that's vanity. But a man who lets his physique go has lost his pride somewhere. What good is your mind, your ideas, if they are not in a healthy body?

"About religion, when I was in Rome I went over to the hospital San Camillo to operate some with my friend Dr. Guido Kidikimo, who is head of cardiac surgery there. He said he had arranged for me to have an audience with the Pope. When I returned to the hotel, I found that my wife and daughters had been denied entrance to St. Peter's because of their miniskirts.

"The Pope was very cordial, smaller than my children, but he had a big handshake and a warm personality. He said he had followed my work very carefully and thought it was wonderful that I had been able to save so many lives. He thought what I had done that was revolutionary was for the good of mankind. I asked if he had any personal misgivings about the transplantation of the human heart. His only concern was whether the donor was alive or dead, and he was uncertain on that point. I told him I had worked to establish a definition of death that would be morally and ethically acceptable and, at the same time, not obviate the progress of medical science. Brain death —I explained it to him. He said he was willing to accept the idea, though with some reservations. He hoped the time would come when it would not be necessary to make these decisions in transplant programs.

"I asked for permission to question him, and he agreed. I told him that he seemed like most laymen in that he was so concerned with the life of the donor and was neglecting the life of the recipient. After all, removing the diseased heart from a patient is serious, too: there can be no recovery without the presence of a strong heart. He said yes, but this brings in the point of informed, willful consent. To which I replied, 'When a person signs a consent form he is agreeing to suicide. But the surgeon's responsibility may be even greater since he, when he removes the heart, is performing an act of homicide.' I explained that in order to exonerate himself, the surgeon must salvage that life by using a healthy, substitute heart. Therefore, before everyone can be satisfied as to the presence of life or death, the surgeon is impelled to make a decision.

"He said these matters were beyond the Church and should be decided by medical science. He thought that so long as the recipient had given his willful consent, that was sufficient. But he was still concerned about whether the donor was alive or dead. Then he said it would be helpful if we could develop a substitute other than a human heart. I told him I had read the Vatican laws and that some six or seven years ago they had made a pronouncement regarding the transplantation of natural organs and that they had urged the use of them when it was possible. The other alternative was to develop artificial organs, an artificial heart. He was familiar with the Karp operation and was very much in favor of it. He wanted to know my opinion regarding the eventual construction of a full-time artificial heart. I said it was inevitable within the next few decades, that it was the ultimate goal.

"I explained that our progress in transplants was philosophical as well as scientific. In a space of a few months we have come closer to defining the meaning of death than from the beginning of civilization. The beginning and the end of life. The Church has always been involved, particularly in the beginning of life. I asked him if life began at conception or after three months. He twinkled a bit but he didn't say anything. Now we are placing a direct focus on the end of life and are having just as much difficulty defining this to everyone's satisfaction.

"We had a very nice conversation, though I was a little uneasy about whether to say yes sir, which is my custom, or Your Holiness. He gave Louise and me medals and gave each of the children a recognition piece. He switched medals at the desk. The first had apparently been set out for Catholics. Ours were gold—I assume the other ones were less valuable."

We went down by the pool and talked some more. The sun was setting in deep pinks and purples over the river. There was a cool breeze, and the crickets began.

I asked him about his progress with the Texas Heart Institute.

"There's a slowdown at the moment. We're having some labor difficulties and we're in something of a recession. I suppose the bad publicity brought on by the Karp operation has something to do with it. But we'll recover, this will pass, I still have a few friends left! We were in the doldrums once before.

"In 1966, when my fund-raising was at a low level, I attended a cocktail party at Claude Williams's house—C. K. Williams, who lives just across the street from us. It was the usual type of cocktail party. Business was the last thing on my mind. Then out of the blue Bob Herring came up to me and asked if I had any projects deserving of support. I said, 'Bob, I've got deals ranging in ambition from ten to ten million dollars. Just tell me what price range you have in mind, and I'll let you know what part of the store to shop in.'

"That very day Bob had been appointed president of the Ray C. Fish Foundation—a fund which had been set up by a wealthy pipeline contractor who had actually died of coronary disease about four years earlier. He left sufficient funds in this foundation to do something rather meaningful. I knew that. I asked Bob how much money he thought there was. He estimated the assets at fifteen million dollars. This was not something to discuss at a cocktail party, so I suggested calling on Bob the next morning; he lived two doors down from me.

"Saturday morning I went by with my plans for the Texas Heart Institute, showed them to Bob Herring, and he immediately concluded that we should be the beneficiary of the Ray C. Fish Foundation. He asked me how much my plans were going to cost. I told him the THI share of the three-institution complex would be around ten million dollars, but I would prefer that the Fish Foundation give half rather than all of it. I wanted it to be a community project. He assumed that I wanted him to give me five million then and there. I said no, I didn't want the cash, and asked him how much he thought this fifteen million asset would guarantee in terms of income. He estimated five hundred thousand a year. So I recommended that the foundation pledge half a million a year for ten years. At the end of that time we would still have the corpus of the foundation intact, which by then may have doubled in value. A pledge would permit me to go ahead and organize my approach in such a way to get more people interested.

"Bob took my proposal to his board and, not without some problems, got their approval. Now three members of the Ray C. Fish Foundation board are on the board of the Texas Heart Institute. This got us started.

"I approached Mr. Benjamin Clayton a second time—the gentleman who had not been interested in brick and mortar when I first went to him. After Mr. Clayton was assured that his name would not appear on any of the contracts or commemorative plaques, he gave me a substantial donation, much more than I had asked for. Soon after that, the executors of Mr. Will Clayton's estate—he was Ben Clayton's brother—made a large donation. The value of the idea began to catch on and several donations of two hundred and fifty thousand dollars came in from friends and former patients. One incident was particularly interesting.

"Mr. Harry Blum, chairman of the board of Jim Beam Distillery, was flown down to me from Chicago one Saturday afternoon. He had a ruptured abdominal aneurysm and had about bled out. I put a graft in him, and he came through all right.

"Ten days later Mr. Blum invited my wife and me to stop by his suite at the Shamrock. After I examined him and confirmed his complete recovery, he buttoned up his shirt and said, 'That's the good news, now give me the bad news.' I told him he couldn't afford a fee large enough to repay me for what I had done. He said he had seen my plans for expansion of the hospitals and asked, point blank, 'How much?' I said I thought a million was a reasonable figure. He agreed and told me to have contract drawn up. I was aware, of course, that this was the moment to move, so I got out my pen and a piece of paper and drew up a contract then and there. He signed it, and he honored it. I had my ten million, string-free with the exception of Ben Clayton's gift. His money will build nine operating rooms and a diagnostic unit for cardiovascular work. On my death or retirement, this will be known as the Cooley Surgical and Diagnostic Suite.

"The original plans for the Texas Heart Institute called for an eighteen-story building, but I persuaded the board to build up as far as our foundation would permit. So now we're going to twenty-nine floors. If not the tallest, it will be one of the tallest hospitals in the world."

I asked if the Texas Heart Institute was being built entirely with private money.

"Yes. I prefer funding programs in this manner. You don't have to make extensive reports of your work. You don't have to prevaricate and say you're going to carry out a group of studies in order to pad up the applications. Federal money has always been sort of off limits to me because I had to go through the Department of Surgery at Baylor, and I was already working that saw about as hard as I could. We got precious little, if any, of those funds for my work. So I stuck with private philanthropy. Now, of course, I'm relieved that I did. Private money means flexibility and availability. No complications like those endless meetings and lengthy proposals. No waiting and committee bickering and all that. Federal funds and the like may be delayed for a year, and what about the sick people who are waiting? Most of my needs can be fulfilled with a telephone call, and the money is there on the spot.

"The Texas Heart Institute won't be privately funded forever

—I don't think it should be. I have no objection to federal money—it's just that I've never had access to any. I see no need in being less than frank about it: our work is the largest resource of clinical cardiovascular material in the world. I agree with the people at the National Institutes of Health: we should have their help.

"No question, at times we've profited greatly from the freedom of private backing. I've been able to do some things with good conscience that I wouldn't have been able to do otherwise. Like construct and implant the first artificial heart."

How did he feel about the censures and results of the various investigations now?

"That's all past, I hope. I must say I hadn't anticipated things would happen the way they did. I can't say that I'm repentant because I believe I was right in what I did.

"Frankly, I'm sick of the whole business. I'm appalled at how people waste their time. The committee at Baylor, for example, sitting there for hours at a time, chiefs and department chairmen, people who should have been working, doing creative things, and taking care of important business. To me it was absurd: get everybody involved with inconsequential pursuits so the chief can do the important things. I don't believe in tying up my people. I want to stimulate them to accomplish things on their own. Their time is valuable, just as mine is.

"The artificial heart will stimulate people to move more quickly toward what's important. It already has. It's stimulated Baylor—the biggest enema they've had in a long time. We've moved the people in Washington ahead five or ten years in the artificial-heart field. And we've boosted ourselves: we're now working on refinement and development of the artificial heart with Cutter Laboratories, the University of Utah, the University of Texas, and the Spanish government.

"The federal government might have learned something from the operational methods of free enterprise. We were able to move ahead when the federally funded programs weren't. People in the profession are concerned, particularly the practicing physicians. The medical profession is divided between practicing physicians and salaried physicians. The salaried physicians don't care much about federal involvement in medical affairs, you know; they're not personally concerned because the matter doesn't really affect their pocketbooks—a tender spot to most men. But the practicing physicians don't want to be stymied and directed by someone in Washington.

"I'm still pretty much a free agent. There's a lot left to do and I'm eager. I was always impressed with some advice by Professor William Firior at Johns Hopkins. He said what you need is a burning curiosity. Don't accept anything as fact. Keep asking why? If? How? Don't accept the so-called established surgical principles. They are often based on faulty impressions.

"I have assumed a rather disrespectful attitude toward many concepts and have been willing to challenge them. This has paid off. Look at a problem: this is a mechanical difficulty that won't be remedied by altering the patient's metabolism. Take it out. When I came to Baylor, the only treatment for an amoebic abscess of the liver was to aspirate it with a needle, a method that had been devised prior to modern antibiotics. My idea was to drain the pus out, collapse the cavity, and that would be the end of it. It was. That's the accepted method today. I always thought the heart transplant programs suffered from the fact that no prominent personality had had one. I thought the ideal situation would have been to put Bobby Kennedy's heart in Dwight Eisenhower—then you would have something.

"Bobby Kennedy was an ideal donor; his heart functioned eighteen hours after he was dead—that's plenty of time to set up. Eisenhower was certainly deserving of some form of plastic procedure. In fact, reporters kept asking me if I would consider transplanting a heart into Eisenhower. I told them this was embarrassing to me because I didn't want to put General Eisen-

hower or his family in an awkward position. I said I would not
refuse to operate on him on the basis of his age alone, that if he
and his family were anxious to try this, and his cardiologist was
willing to participate, I wouldn't turn them down. I left it that
way—a sort of double negative.

"Then I read that a transplant was not out of the question for
Eisenhower. We were preparing to fly to Acapulco with the
children at the time. It seemed almost possible to me that the
General, as a courageous soldier, might want to participate and
set a real example to heart patients everywhere. He had recovered from a serious heart attack and served two terms as President. Whereas twenty years ago a man would have taken to his
rocking chair and stayed there till death do us part. Eisenhower
dramatized the modern approach to heart patients.

"Anyway, I thought he might want to continue setting this
sort of example as a transplant recipient. I very quietly called
Bob Hall, Eisenhower's cardiologist, whom I knew rather casu-
ally at that time. I told him what I had read and said I wanted
to talk with him because I was leaving town. I said if there was
any thought of submitting the General to a transplant, I would
stay home and stand by. Hall said neither the General nor his
family—particularly his family—really wanted to consider a
heart transplant. I said, 'Well, fine, I'll stifle anything from this
end.' As it turned out I had been in Acapulco thirty minutes
when I was called back to Houston to perform two transplants.
A few months later Dr. Robert Hall joined the Texas Heart
Institute as medical director.

How did he feel now about Dr. DeBakey?

"There is an inevitable conflict when two men of great eagerness are put together. Fundamentally, Dr. DeBakey and I are
both ambitious, industrious people who aren't easily satisfied. If
I win some little award or badge, I don't rest on it—these things
don't represent my ultimate goal in life. I go on to the next
challenge. Dr. DeBakey is the same way. My goal is not to reach

a comfortable retirement—that's going to be a critical time and I don't relish it. I want to continue being useful and creative. Dr. DeBakey is in his sixties and he's still creating. But he's also devoting himself to administrative matters. He wants to do it all himself, and while I recognize his competence, I don't think he can spread himself that thin.

"Dr. DeBakey is the senior man. In his eyes, regardless of what I accomplish, I will always be the junior man. We will never be able to share equal status. He would find that intolerable. It would be like someone declaring that Grady Hallman, my associate, was equal in ability to me. That would be difficult for me to accept, although, unlike Dr. DeBakey, I'm not a power-structure man. From my point of view, power is not an accomplishment in itself.

"People who know little about the matter assume that Dr. DeBakey and I are equally able in all areas, which might not be true. Princess Lillian of Belgium came to Houston once and awarded Dr. DeBakey a medal. She had assumed that he was doing all the infant heart surgery in the department. When she learned that it was my work instead of his, she sent for me to come to Brussels. Dr. DeBakey is a fine administrator, no argument about that, a good organizer and a man of good judgment. But I like to think that my personality is better suited to conduct a surgical program and maintain a massive operating schedule. You need coolness for this. You must make your residents and fellows feel that they are an integral part of the program, members of the team. I believe in sportsmanship in surgery. The surgical team. As captain of the team, the chief surgeon should have the confidence and support of his people. This is often not the case. If some of these tyrannical surgeons were captain of a rugger team, Lord help them if they ever got into a good scrub: their own men would kick their brains out.

"In a surgical program, you've got to be fair. You can't step on your men when they're down. This is particularly true when one of them makes a mistake that leads to serious complications. Just the other day one of my assistants made an error that would have gotten him fired from many places. On similar occasions, other young surgeons have been dressed down in the operating room: "You killed my patient!" A fellow has to have pretty thick skin at an early age to assimilate an accusation as serious as that. The burden is too heavy. I try to temper my remarks. If a patient dies at the hands of a young surgeon, you have to be very careful how you handle it. They're human, you see, and bound to err. If they were perfect, they wouldn't be on my service. They are there to learn. Unfortunately, everybody makes mistakes."

I asked if Dr. Cooley felt he was a better surgeon than Dr. DeBakey.

"I'll say this: a successful cardiovascular surgeon should be a man who, when asked to name the three best surgeons in the world, would have difficulty deciding on the other two. I've seen Dr. DeBakey operate and I consider him very able, but his personality is such that he occasionally gets rattled and loses his composure. Many surgeons are like this—to varying degrees, Dr. Blalock and Lord Brock were. I have a greater capacity for pressure. Say you're in one room and a tear occurs in a blood vessel, then you hear across the way that a patient you just did has arrested; due to the nature of the disease or the inner tensions of an assistant, something has gone wrong and his heart has stopped. Suddenly, your services are demanded in both rooms at the same time. You must maintain your cool. You can't get flustered and lose both of them. You've got to rally everybody and keep them calm, too. So you work on the bleeder and shout instructions to someone else to resuscitate the stopped heart.

"Pressure can make for grave errors. I learned to handle it as an athlete. You're shooting a freethrow after the final buzzer, and everyone in Madison Square Garden is watching you.

Before each heart transplant, I made a conscious effort to tense myself, to psych myself to a peak of readiness. I wanted my entire team to feel that no one in the world could handle the surgery better, that their chances of keeping the patient alive were not going to be jeopardized by any clumsiness on my part. No fuss, no talk, just get in there and get it done. 'Dr. Cooley did a beautiful job. Now we must carry on at the same level of excellence.' That's the way I want them to feel."

I asked if the people surrounding him were always as up as he was.

"Not always. They can afford to be more relaxed. They don't always take matters as seriously because it's my reputation on the line. Their reputations will be enhanced by my success, but they will not be hurt by my failure. I am the responsible person. I excluded Dr. Hallman and Dr. Bloodwell from the development of the artificial heart for one reason: I wanted them to benefit from whatever success we had and yet not be handicapped by our failures. I'm carrying the brunt of the repercussions from the artificial-heart implant. But of course I will receive the praise when it comes . . . if it comes.

"The time will come when we will see the artificial heart in wide usage. We will see a time when we won't let a young man die of heart disease, and young people are dying like this every day. What if *you* had a young man dying of a dilated heart? You say, 'Look, I think we can keep him alive.' They say, 'Well, do anything you can, Doctor.' So you go in there, put him on the pump-oxygenator, you take his heart out, and put an artificial heart in. He's alive. He wakes up. Are you going to give him that chance or are you going to let him drift on out?

"No one is immortal, of course. All we're trying to do is buy time. Aren't we? You can't fight off death forever. You know you're going to die, you just don't want to do it tomorrow. Everything I do in surgery is a temporizing measure. Time is precious. You want to enjoy life as you go along—get a good smell of the flowers, and die when you're tired and worn out. Fortunately, in the right kind of death everything sort of wears out at once. But it's a terrible defeat to a patient and to a surgeon when the heart dies while the brain is still good, while the arteries are still strong, and the organs are still functioning. Just because one organ is failing is no reason to sacrifice everything else. It doesn't make sense. And that's what I mean by prolonging life whenever and however you can. Even a week to me is meaningful—it's very important."

Epilogue

D R. Domingo Liotta left Houston for Spain, where he developed a laboratory for artificial-heart research and coordinated the exchange program between Dr. Cooley's group and the University of Madrid Hospital. He then returned to his native Argentina and was received as a national hero. He is there now, building a heart institute and working with Dr. Cooley and their colleagues in Spain.

On June 2, 1972, ten years after Dr. Cooley presented his initial proposal for a comprehensive cardiovascular hospital, the Texas Heart Institute was formally dedicated. Dr. Theodore Cooper, Head of the National Heart and Lung Institute—the man whose letter precipitated the Baylor investigation of the artificial heart Dr. Cooley implanted in Haskell Karp—spoke at the dedication dinner. Dr. Norman Shumway, who did the definitive research on heart transplantation, received the first Ray C. Fish Award. Dr. Don Wukash assumed the podium and announced the founding of the Denton A. Cooley Cardiovascular Surgical Foundation—an organization composed of the heart surgeons who have trained under Dr. Cooley.

One month after the dedication of the Texas Heart Institute, United States District Judge John V. Singleton, after several days of hearing testimony from everyone involved in the operations performed on Haskell Karp, dismissed a $4.5 million malpractice suit Mr. Karp's widow had brought against Dr. Cooley and Dr. Liotta.

Friday, September 22, 1972, Dr. Cooley, in his scrub suit, was presented a plaque for having just performed his ten thousandth open-heart operation. Then he went back to surgery and finished the day's schedule.

There is a bronze bust of Dr. Cooley in the lobby of the Texas Heart Institute and a poem on the wall beside it.

> Isn't it strange
> That princes and kings,
> And clowns that caper
> In sawdust rings,
> And common people
> Like you and me
> Are builders for eternity?
>
> Each is given a bag of tools,
> A shapeless mass
> A book of rules;
> And each must make—
> Ere life has flown—
> A stumbling block
> Or a stepping stone.

Appendix

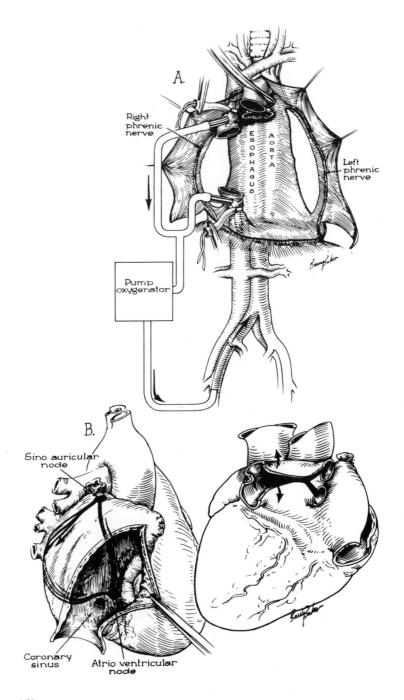

A

Right
phrenic
nerve

ESOPHAGUS

AORTA

Left
phrenic
nerve

Pump
oxygenator

B.

Sino auricular
node

Coronary
sinus

Atrio ventricular
node

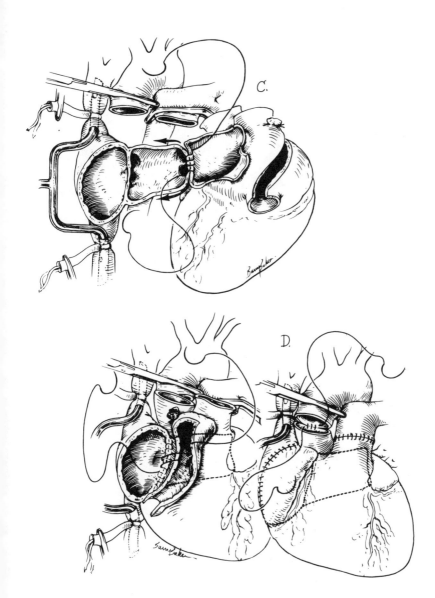

Cardiac transplantation sequence. A: The donor heart has been removed. B: The donor heart, continuing to beat on its own electrical impulses, is tailored for anastomosis (joining by suture). C: The left atria (upper chambers) of the donor and recipient hearts are joined. D: The right atria of the donor and recipient hearts are joined, and the pulmonary arteries and aortae are anastomosed.

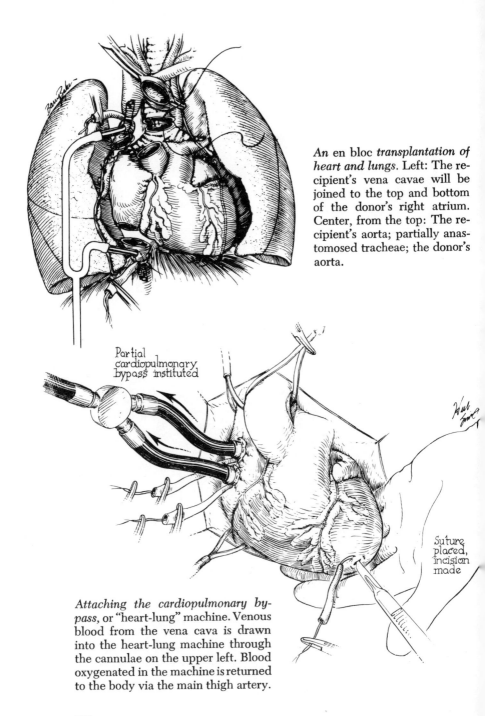

An en bloc *transplantation of heart and lungs.* Left: The recipient's vena cavae will be joined to the top and bottom of the donor's right atrium. Center, from the top: The recipient's aorta; partially anastomosed tracheae; the donor's aorta.

Partial
cardiopulmonary
bypass instituted

Suture
placed,
incision
made

Attaching the cardiopulmonary bypass, or "heart-lung" machine. Venous blood from the vena cava is drawn into the heart-lung machine through the cannulae on the upper left. Blood oxygenated in the machine is returned to the body via the main thigh artery.

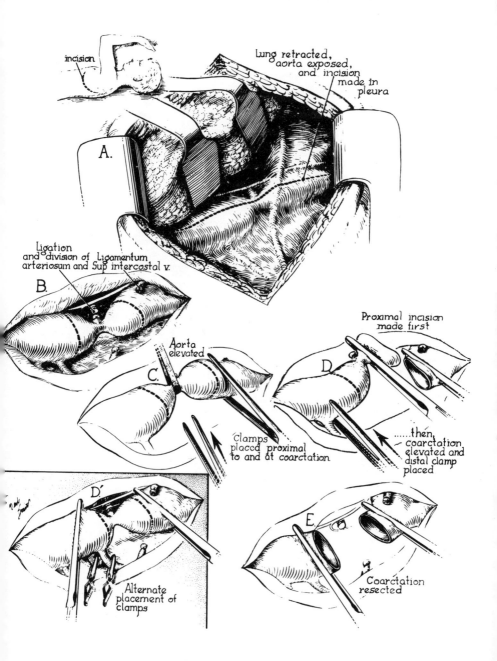

incision

Lung retracted, aorta exposed, and incision made in pleura

A.

Ligation and division of Ligamentum arteriosum and Sup. intercostal v.

B.

Aorta elevated

C.

Clamps placed proximal to and at coarctation

Proximal incision made first

D.

......then, coarctation elevated and distal clamp placed

D´.

Alternate placement of clamps

E.

Coarctation resected

Coarctation of the aorta—a congenital narrowing of the first artery out of the heart. A-E: Removing the constricted segment.

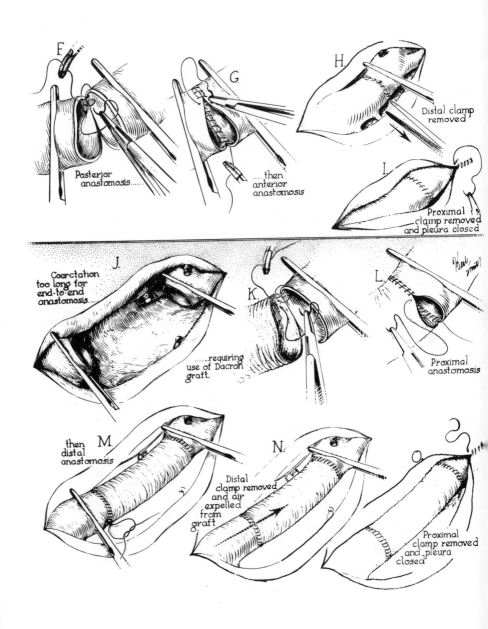

Coarctation of the aorta (cont.). F-I: End-to-end anastomosis. J-O: Using the Dacron graft.

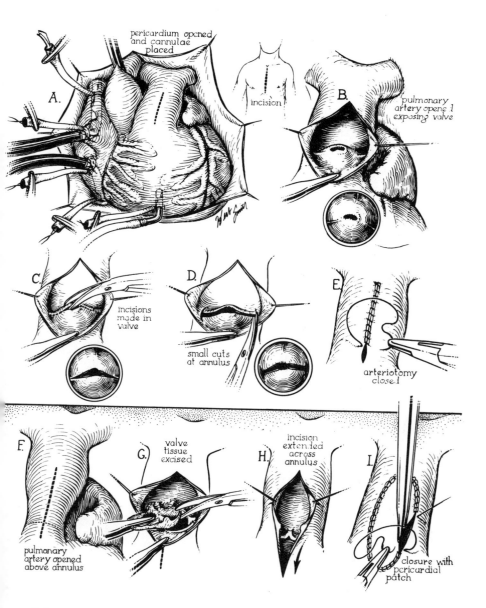

Pulmonary stenosis—a condition that occurs when the diameter of the pulmonary valve is constricted. B-D: Opening the pulmonary valve. F-I: Removing the pulmonary valve.

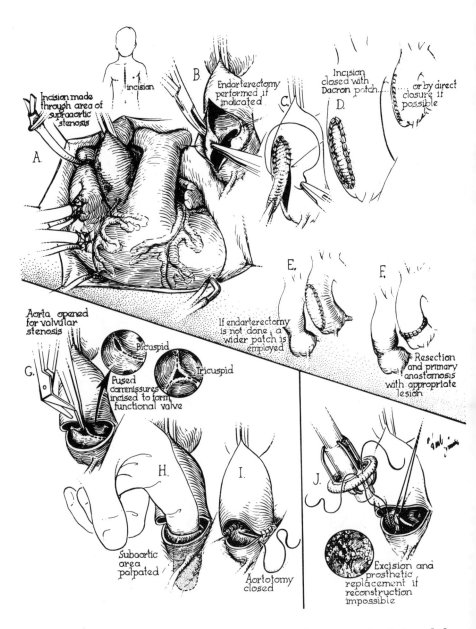

Aortic stenosis—a condition that occurs when the aortic valve is impeded by constriction. B-F: Various methods used to widen the constriction by increasing the diameter of the artery. G-I: Opening the fused leaves of the aortic valve. J: When stenosis is not correctable by any of the above methods, an artificial valve is implanted.

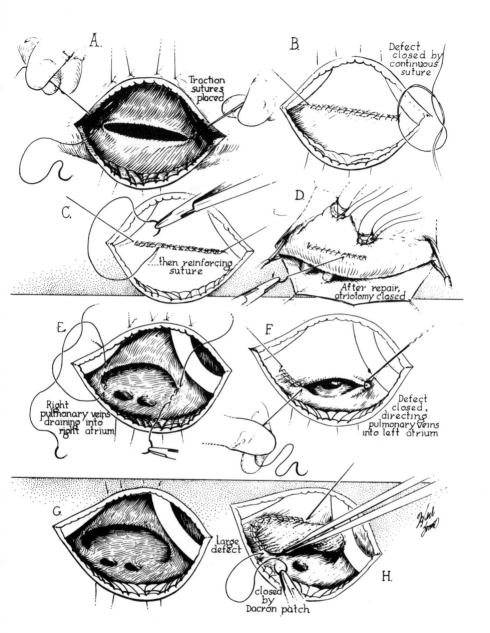

Atrial septal defect—a hole between the upper chambers of the heart. E-F: A two-pole overlapping suture technique used when some or all of the veins from the lungs drain into the right upper chamber. G-H: If the defect is too large to employ a primary closure, as in A-D and E-F, a Dacron patch is used.

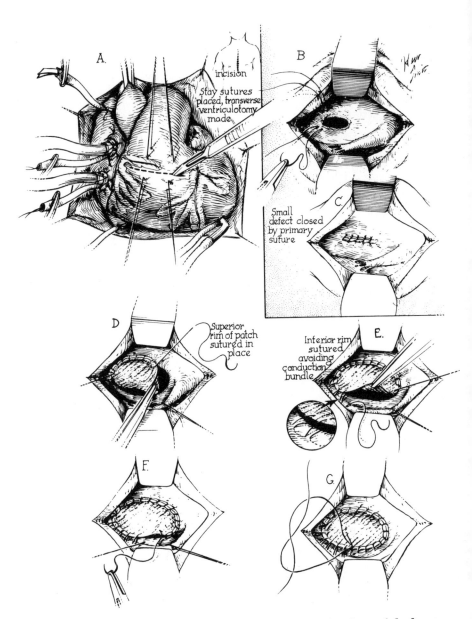

Ventricular septal defect—a hole between the lower chambers of the heart. B-C: Closing a small defect with sutures. D-G: Repairing a large defect with a Dacron patch. H-I (facing page): The pulmonary artery is often banded to reduce cardiac failure in infants (approximately two months). When the ventricular septal defect is later repaired (approximately four years), the band is removed and the constriction widened.

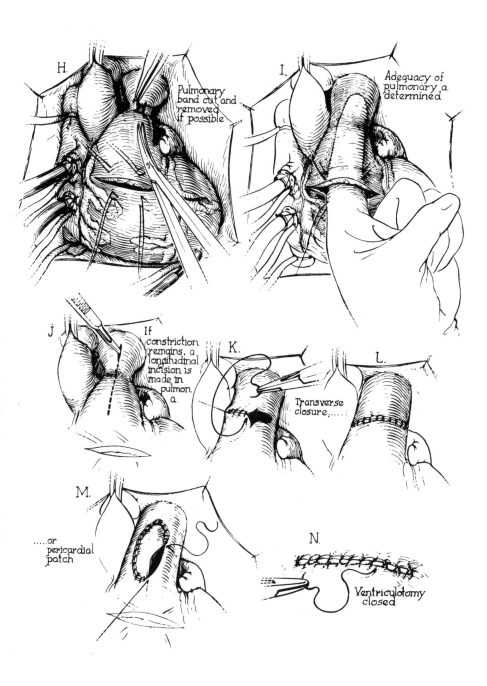

H. Pulmonary band cut and removed if possible

I. Adequacy of pulmonary a. determined

J. If constriction remains, a longitudinal incision is made in pulmon. a.

K.

L. Transverse closure.....

M. .....or pericardial patch

N. Ventriculotomy closed

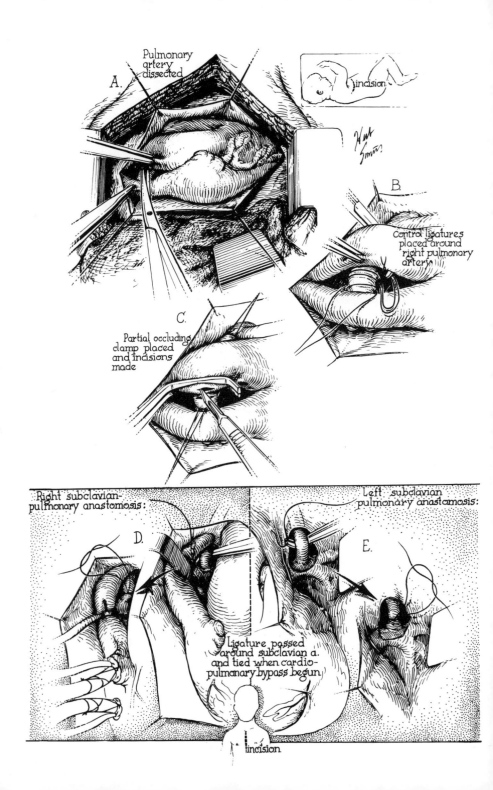

A. Pulmonary artery dissected

incision

B. Control ligatures placed around right pulmonary artery

C. Partial occluding clamp placed and incisions made

D. Right subclavian-pulmonary anastomosis:

E. Left subclavian pulmonary anastomosis:

Ligature passed around subclavian a. and tied when cardio-pulmonary bypass begun

incision

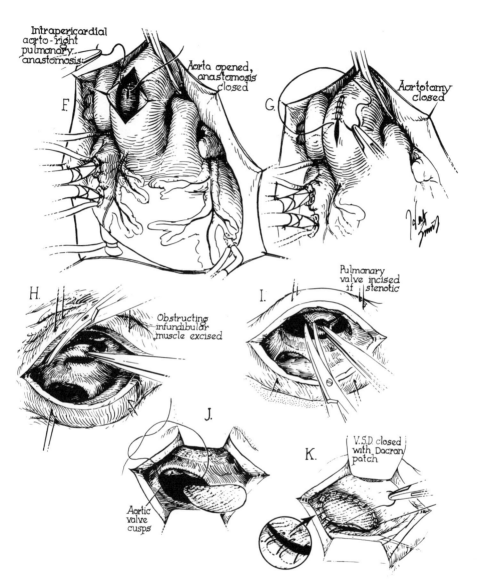

Tetralogy of Fallot—variations for the total correction of a complex, congenital cardiac deformity. A-C (facing page): Closing an earlier palliative joining of the aorta and the pulmonary artery. D-E: Closing an earlier palliative joining of the pulmonary and subclavian arteries. F-G: Closing an earlier palliative joining of right pulmonary and the aorta. The incision depends on what type of shunts were employed earlier. H: Excising obstructing muscle. I: Repairing the defective pulmonary valve. J-K: Repairing the ventricular septal defect with a Dacron patch.

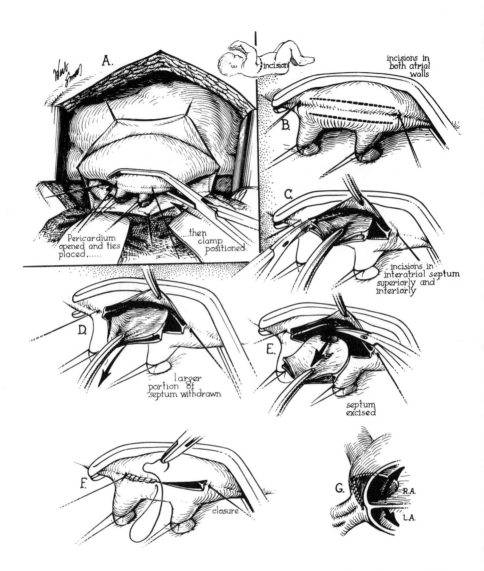

Complete transposition of the great vessels—a congenital condition in which the aorta and the pulmonary artery stem from the wrong ventricles, reducing the circulation of oxygenated blood. A-G *(stage one):* A palliative procedure performed on infants. Creation of an atrial septal defect (a hole between the upper chambers of the heart) to improve circulation of oxygenated blood and reduce pressure on the heart.

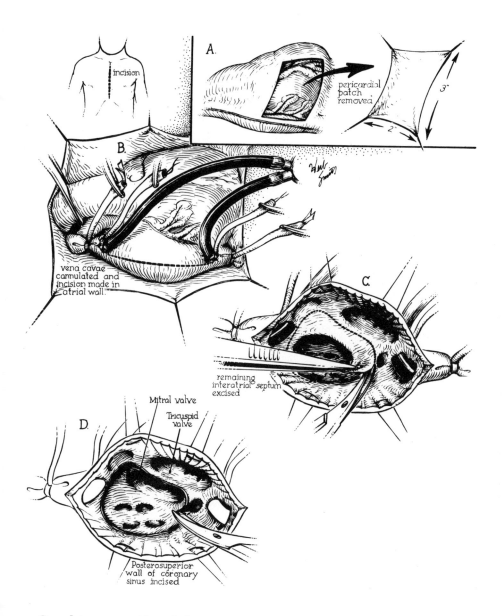

A.

incision

pericardial patch removed

3"

2"

B.

vena cavae cannulated and incision made in atrial wall.

C.

remaining interatrial septum excised

D.

Mitral valve

Tricuspid valve

Posterosuperior wall of coronary sinus incised

Complete transposition of the great vessels (cont.) C-D *(stage two):* The atrial septum (the partition between the upper chambers of the heart) is removed.

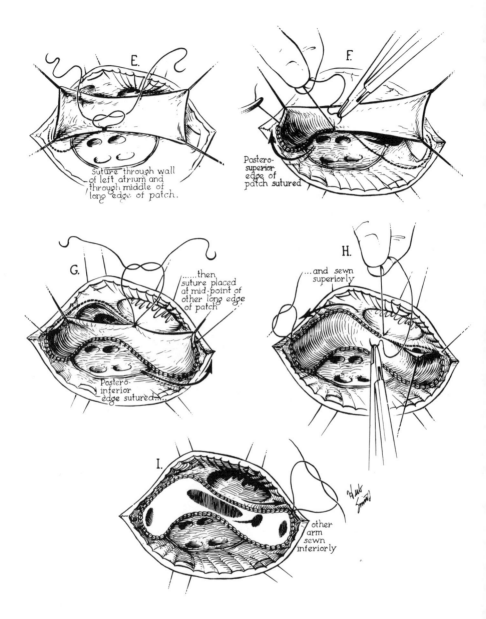

Complete transposition of the great vessels, stage two (cont.). E-I: A patch is tailored from the membranous sac that surrounds the heart and is sewn into the common atrial chamber in such a manner as to reverse the inflow of unoxygenated blood.

Index

Index

Schnur, Sidney, 133
Schumacher, Harry, 130 n.
Scrub nurse, 190
Seamans, Bill, 70
Seatting, 119
Sechas, 198
Security guards, 52, 59
Sen, P. K., 158
Senning, Ake, 155, 200
Shanbag, 205
Shumway, Norman, 152, 153, 156–157, 243, 268
Siegler Foundation, 243
Sims, Henry, 242
Singleton, John V., 269
Smith, Arnold, 85 n.
Smith, C. T., 52
Smith, Charlie, 51, 66, 69, 70, 71, 72, 73, 74
Smith, Polk, 221
Sommerville case, 133
South American tour, 136
Southwest Research Institute, 28
Souttar, Henry, 110
Sportsmanship in surgery, 264–265
Starr, Rother, and Howes, 148
Starr artificial heart valve, 143
Stenosis, aortic, 278
  mitral, 116
  pulmonary, 89, 277
Stephenson, Hugh, 3
Strong, 190, 199, 201, 202, 207
Stuckwish, James, 163, 164–165
Stuttgart, 100
Sugar-water prime, 10, 67
Surgeons, differences between researchers and, 158–159
  stereotype of, 129
Surgical team, 8–19, 103, 117–118, 120, 189–190, 264–265, 266
Sylvester, Ruth, 52

Talbot, John, 238
Taliani, Tomas, 25

Tanaka, 198, 212
Taub, Ben, 127 n.
Taussig, Helen, 88, 90–91, 103–104, 107, 117
Teamwork, surgical, 8–19, 103, 117–118, 120, 189–190, 264–265, 266
Tetralogy of Fallot, 89, 97, 104, 110, 192 n., 200
  repair of, 282–283
Texas, University of, 85 n., 126, 146–147, 184, 226
Texas Children's Hospital, 134, 144, 146, 149, 182–183, 184, 188
Texas Heart Institute, 30, 39, 50, 183, 190, 258–261, 269
  concept of, 147–149
  dedication of, 268
  exchange program between University of Madrid and, 236, 268
Texas Medical Center, 146–147, 182, 183, 226
Texas Medical Instruments, 32, 34–35, 47, 48, 221, 225
Texas Rangers, 85 n.
Thomas, Eddy, 108
Thomas, Everett, 25, 159–163, 165, 169, 213
Thomas, Mrs. Everett, 164
Thomas, Louise. See Cooley, Louise
Thomas, Vivien, 84, 88–89, 90
Thurmond, William, 234, 237
Tibideau, C. J., 132
Time, 223
Tokyo Hospital, 137–138
Top Hat Jet Service, 51, 66, 69
Transposition of great vessels, 284–286
Triple valve replacement, 160
Tubbs, Oswald, 118

Valvulotome, 110
Vanderbilt University Hospital, 84
Vascular x rays, 116
Ventricular aneurysm, 211

298   INDEX

Ventricular septal defect, repair of, 280–281, 283
Vucinic, Michi, 198, 199, 205

Wada, Juro, 198
Wada-Cutter valves, 36
Ward, Grant, 92–93, 128
Washington Star, 233, 237, 239
Washington University lecture, 177–180
Washkansky, Louis, 152, 154, 155–156
Wedge procedure, 11
White, Virginia May, 157
Whitkin, Nathan, 54, 78, 242

Wilber, Dwight, 233, 234
Williams, Claude K., 258
Windsor, Duke of, 150
Wobbe, Winifred, 70, 73
Woolridge, Bonnie Sue, 53, 55, 67, 161
Wortham, Gus, 181
Wukash, Don, 194, 198, 212, 213, 268

Yates, Duke, 153

Zimmerman, Jacob, 155
Zumbro Hotel, 1
Zwer, Joachim, 51, 58